THE

COURAGE

TO

STAND

ALONE

魏京生

Edited and Translated by

Kristina M. Torgeson

With Essays by

Andrew J. Nathan

Liu Qing

Sophia Woodman

THE

COURAGE

TO

STAND

ALONE

wei jingsheng

魏京生

Letters

from

Prison

and

Other

Writings

VIKING

VIKING
Published by the Penguin Group
Penguin Books USA Inc., 375 Hudson Street,
New York, New York, 10014, U.S.A.
Penguin Books Ltd, 27 Wrights Lane,
London W8 5TZ, England
Penguin Books Australia Ltd, Ringwood,
Victoria, Australia
Penguin Books Canada Ltd, 10 Alcorn Avenue,
Toronto, Ontario, Canada M4V 3B2
Penguin Books (N.Z.) Ltd, 182–190 Wairau Road,
Auckland 10, New Zealand

Penguin Books Ltd, Registered Offices:
Harmondsworth, Middlesex, England

First published in 1997 by Viking Penguin,
a division of Penguin Books USA Inc.

10 9 8 7 6 5 4 3 2 1

Calligraphy by Wu Ming

LIBRARY OF CONGRESS CATALOGING IN PUBLICATION DATA
Wei, Ching-sheng.
    The courage to stand alone : letters from prison and other writings / Wei Jingsheng ;
edited and translated by Kristina M. Torgeson.
      p.   cm.
    ISBN 0-670-87249-0
    1. Wei, Ching-sheng.   2. Political prisoners—China—Correspondence.   3. China—
Politics and government—1976–   I. Torgeson, Kristina M.   II. Title.
    DS779.29.W45A4   1997
    323'0951—dc21   96-50179

This book is printed on acid-free paper.

Printed in the United States of America
Set in Bodoni Book
Designed by Pei Koay

This book is dedicated to all those

who have suffered and sacrificed for

human rights and democracy

in China

僅將此書獻給
所有為中國人權民主
犧牲和受難的人

Acknowledgments

This book is in many ways a cooperative effort on the part of a large number of people who have worked tirelessly on behalf of Wei Jingsheng and the cause of human rights and democracy in China. Foremost are Robert Bernstein, Liu Qing, and Xiao Qiang, who have played the most crucial roles in initiating this project and bringing it to fruition. Wei Jingsheng's sister Shanshan Wei-Blank (née Wei Shanshan) has supported the book from its inception and offered invaluable help throughout. Instrumental also were the efforts of Robin Munro of Human Rights Watch/Asia and several of Wei's longtime friends from the Democracy Wall days, including Huang Rui, Marie Holzman, Li Shuang, and Emmanuel Bellefroid. In addition, a deep appreciation goes to those individuals in China who have aided in the preparation of this book, but whose names must, for now, be kept silent.

Expert assistance with translation and terminology questions was generously provided by Andrew J. Nathan, Guo Luoji, Yu Ping, Liu Yadong, and Joanne Mariner. Amy D. Dooling, Hart Fessenden, and Francesca Dal Lago offered invaluable editorial suggestions and advice, Steven Ciaschi helped to locate photographs, and Ta-Ling Lee and Miriam London graciously provided help with the translation of Wei's autobiographical essay. I am grateful also to John Ackerly and the International Campaign for Tibet for permission to reprint its translation of Wei's letter on the Tibet question, the U.S. Foreign Broadcast Information Service for use of translations of Wei's letters of September 5, 1990, and June 15, 1991, and James Seymour and the Society for the Protection of East Asians' Human Rights for permission to reprint its version of Wei's 1979 trial defense statement. Thanks also to Adrian Bradshaw and Trudie Styler for providing additional photographs.

An enormous debt of gratitude goes to the entire staff of Human Rights in China (HRIC), an independent human rights organization founded by Chinese students and scholars on March 29, 1989, the tenth anniversary of Wei Jingsheng's arrest. Liu Qing, Sophia Woodman, Wang Yu, and especially Xiao Qiang gave hours of their time answering questions, going over translations, and helping to procure materials and photographs. Mark Goellner and Beatrice Laroche also provided valuable assistance.

Special thanks go to Wendy Wolf, the book's editor at Viking Penguin, for seeing merit in this project and always showing great patience and understanding for its special circumstances. I am also very grateful to my parents, Kathryn and Dewayne Torgeson, who provided technical, editorial, and moral support.

Finally, there are countless other individuals and organizations whose work over the years to keep world attention focused on the plight of Wei Jingsheng and other prisoners of conscience in China should be acknowledged for the supporting roles they played in making this book possible. These include Amnesty International, Human Rights Watch/Asia (especially Sidney Jones, Robin Munro, Mike Jendrzejczyk, and Mickey Spiegel), International PEN, the Robert F. Kennedy Memorial Center for Human Rights, the Transnational Radical Party, as well as Bei Dao, Chen Maiping, Leila Conners, Fang Lizhi, Alan Gleitsman, Larry Guo, Mab Huang, Han Xiaorong, Hu Ping, Li Lu, Perry Link, Aryeh Neier and the Open Society Institute, Nancy Pelosi, Orville Schell, Frank Wolf, and Yan Jiaqi.

Wei Jingsheng, who was already in prison when this book was conceived in the spring of 1996, was not consulted and bears no responsibility for its publication. All royalties are being held for Wei until his release.

—Kristina M. Torgeson

Contents

Acknowledgments   *vii*

Foreword / *Andrew J. Nathan*   *xi*

Preface / *Liu Qing*   *xvii*

Editor's Note / *Kristina M. Torgeson*   *xxxi*

THE PRISON LETTERS   1

Appendices

  I. THE FIFTH MODERNIZATION: DEMOCRACY (DECEMBER 1978) *199*

  II. THE TRIAL OF WEI JINGSHENG (OCTOBER 1979)   *213*

  III. FROM MAOIST FANATIC TO POLITICAL DISSIDENT:
       AN AUTOBIOGRAPHICAL ESSAY (1979)   *227*

Wei Jingsheng's Lifelong Battle for Democracy /
    Sophia Woodman   *249*

Glossary   *273*

Contributors   *284*

Foreword

Andrew J. Nathan

Wei Jingsheng's prison writings show how much his career as a political prisoner has been a kind of performance art. His tragedy did not simply befall him; he created and shaped it. With no materials other than his body, his mind, and the span of his adult life, Wei has created a living tableau that overshadows the self-congratulatory propaganda of the Chinese government and throws a grim light on the self-interested confusion of those who chose to believe that propaganda. Although Wei is the victim, he has controlled his fate far more than his jailers. We can see between the lines of his letters how they are driven to distraction as he forces them to enact the true nature of their regime. The question is how long he can survive the rigors of their response.

One can almost sympathize with the authorities who pull the strings to which Wei's judges and jailors dance. What could be more outrageous? The prisoner says things that cannot be allowed to be said, but has the cheek in doing so to break no laws, to cite the Communist classics, to take the government's boasts about human rights at face value. He even presumes to recite words from the "Internationale." By such devices he forces the regime to behave in the same way as the recently departed and (by the current leaders) little lamented Mao Zedong, the dictator who persecuted Deng Xiaoping and whose system Deng claims to have reformed by establishing the courts and passing the laws that would prevent any honest prosecution of Wei.

In December 1978, Wei suddenly appears on the stage of Chinese history with his wall poster, "The Fifth Modernization," demanding democracy as a matter of right. We learn from his autobiography that this moment took long to prepare. Wei had lived through the Cultural Revolution and seen the reality of the society around him. That someone should have drawn the conclusions he did is not remarkable; more remarkable was that few Chinese in the early Deng years had the courage to say what they all knew.

Although Deng initially welcomes the democracy movement for its help in ousting his rivals from the leadership, Wei's audacity is impermissible. In 1979, Deng orders his arrest and conviction under the serviceable procedures of the court system that is being put into place. Wei's powerful statement of self-defense exposes how little difference there is between the new legal system and the old absence of a legal system. The prosecutors and judges search for a crime and find none, but they obey orders. They sentence Wei to fifteen years.

The outside world is outraged, but most Chinese at the time are wiser. They see Wei as the victim of his own naïveté. He failed to appreciate the unwritten limits to free speech and legal reform. He committed the greatest offense in a dictatorship: taking words at face value.

Wei now begins a course of physical and mental suffering that is only hinted at in the prison letters. His teeth fall out, his heart weakens, he develops high blood pressure, arthritis, headaches, and depression. Yet by refusing to die or to crack, he pressures his jailers more ruthlessly than they do him. He insists on writing to the leaders about the need for political reform, intractable in his belief in principle and intoxicated with the plain meanings of words. Wei is like "the foolish old man who moved the mountains," the fable Mao loved to quote to show how human effort could change nature. Wei, however, unlike the foolish old man, has been deprived by his government of the chance to have a wife and sons. He has to move mountains alone, and not by acting but by suffering.

Over the years, Wei becomes a cause célèbre in China's foreign policy. His case is taken up by Amnesty International, Human

Rights Watch/Asia, presidents, legislators, and citizens around the world. Deng may say, as he does in late December 1986, "We put Wei Jingsheng behind bars, didn't we? Did that damage China's reputation? We haven't released him, but China's image has not been tarnished; in fact our reputation improves day by day." Yet slowly international attention is paid, and the Chinese government finds its diplomacy inconvenienced. Worse, Wei becomes an issue in China. The atmosphere is changing.

Intellectuals and students are disillusioned with Deng's mixture of capitalism and dictatorship. In early 1989, Fang Lizhi sends an open letter to Deng Xiaoping calling for Wei's release. Over a hundred other prominent intellectuals write to the Standing Committee of the National People's Congress and the Central Committee of the Chinese Communist Party asking a pardon for Wei and other political prisoners. The government for the time being does nothing against them. This is one among many events that open into the panorama of spring 1989, when people show how little confidence they have in the government and the party reasserts its authority Mao's way, "through the barrel of a gun."

Foreign pressure intensifies. Wei becomes the best-known international symbol of human rights abuses in China. He is nominated for the Nobel Peace Prize. His imprisonment is a burden harder for the government to bear—they imagine—than his release. On September 14, 1993, he is freed on parole, days before the International Olympic Committee's decision on whether to award the 2000 Olympics to the city of Beijing. Yet Beijing is not chosen.

Wei is still as clever—or as stupid—as ever. He acts as if he were a free man who is allowed to think and write. He even takes advantage of the government's moment of weakness to get permission to publish some of his essays abroad. The clarity and common sense of the writings win new attention for the human rights cause. Wei speaks with fellow dissidents on the telephone, heedless of government taps. He meets with U.S. Assistant Secretary of State John Shattuck, impudently seconding the government's position that the United States should not cancel China's trade privileges. In short, he exercises his rights under the Chinese constitution. After fourteen years in prison, he still doesn't get it.

Wei is now so well known at home and abroad, so clear in his perceptions of Chinese reality, so consistent in his strategy of reason and moderation, that his presence offers a center around which the despairing democratic movement begins to regroup. Meeting with American publisher Robert Bernstein, Wei jots down a few ideas for activities the movement might undertake if funding were to become available. Monstrously, all are legal. Such a man is intolerable.

The government is trapped in the fabric of its own laws. It cannot shut Wei up, it cannot kill him, it has no excuse to arrest him. It goes Latin American: It disappears him. An awkward interlude ensues, stretching over a year. Government spokesmen claim to know nothing of his whereabouts. Suddenly a decision is reached. The courts will again perform their alchemy. The government's crimes will be legalized; Wei's acts will be criminalized. Another trial, another humiliation for the courts inflicted by Wei's stubborn refusal to commit crimes.

Today he sits in jail, an international symbol of what has not changed in the Chinese system in two decades, a living rebuttal to reams of human rights white papers and Chinese government UN statements. He survives, although we cannot know for how long, as the Chinese government knowingly allows its officials to mistreat him in violation of its obligations under the Convention Against Torture and Other Cruel, Inhuman, or Degrading Treatment or Punishment, which it has signed; and, for that matter, in violation of its own newly adopted, handsomely phrased Prison Law.

The Chinese leaders do not know how lucky they are. They should be grateful to have as their hardest opponent a man who shares the best values of Chinese socialism and nationalism, who is committed to peace and reason, who refrains from organizing opposition or breaking Chinese law.

In many ways, Wei Jingsheng is an ordinary man. In the eyes of his keepers this very simplicity is the fatal flaw they must teach him to correct. They are killing a man they should want to survive.

Readers of this book are lucky too. In the comfort of their armchairs they can be treated to the eloquent, logical insights Wei has drawn from years of confrontation with the Chinese system. There are times and places in history when the greatest intellectual contribution is to see straight. At such junctures, the greatest thinkers are those who speak simply and vividly. Wei is such a person. His contribution to Chinese intellectual history and to the universal history of the human rights idea is offered in accessible, passionate words and in examples constructed from the material of his own life. The price he pays so we can learn comes closer and closer to being total.

Preface

Liu Qing

The Chinese prison system is the iron curtain behind the iron curtain—very little news ever leaks out from inside it. In publishing letters written by my friend Wei Jingsheng during fourteen and a half years spent in Chinese prisons, this book is unprecedented. Wei is currently serving yet another heavy prison sentence and all news of him is concealed behind high walls and electric fences, making the letters he wrote during his first imprisonment from 1979 to 1993 all the more valuable and important. Addressed to family members, prison officials, and Chinese government leaders, these letters display Wei's vibrant personality and provide a clear picture of his political convictions and wisdom. Through them we meet a courageous hero of democracy who has spoken out boldly and bravely on behalf of his country and his people.

Wei Jingsheng and I met during the Democracy Wall Movement of 1978–79. This was the first open, purposeful, and organized democracy movement in China since the Communist government came to power in 1949. At its height, the Democracy Wall Movement encompassed several hundred unofficial journals and "mass organizations" around the country, over thirty of them in Beijing alone. Despite unrelenting persecution and attempts on the part of Deng Xiaoping to divide the movement, it remained firmly entrenched in society for nearly a year. Democracy Wall towered above the walls that had kept the Chinese people out of the arena of politics for so long. Left behind it were the former silence, fear, and submissiveness of the Chinese people; the Cultural Revolution, the Great Leap Forward, and countless other tragedies; as well as the corpses of the tens of thousands who had died wrongful deaths because of them. Before the wall, facing great pressure and the threat of a crackdown, dissenting voices arose steadfast in their resistance, as people awoke to the meaning of human rights and democracy. Wei stood out as a prominent figure among the many leaders who emerged during this epoch-making period. He was the first to point out that before China could realize Deng's call for "Four Modernizations" it had to achieve what he called the "fifth modernization," democracy. He was also the first to see that Deng Xiaoping, who had just been swept back into power with the people's support, was continuing to practice dictatorship.

In late 1978, the power struggle between Deng Xiaoping and Hua Guofeng, the chairman of the Communist Party at the time, had reached a tense stalemate just as Democracy Wall arose to tip the political scales in favor of Deng. But instead of thanks, Deng reacted by throwing group after group of Democracy Wall activists into jail; the master architect appeared to be cleaning up the bricks and tiles broken on his route to power. Never once did he imagine that something he discarded so casually might later explode like a bomb with reverberations felt around the world. Wei Jingsheng was his nemesis, and shamed into anger, Deng Xiaoping brutally crushed first Wei and then the Democracy Wall Movement, completely forgetting how Democracy Wall had just come to his aid.

When Wei was tried in 1979, only a handful of select members of the Chinese government were allowed into the courtroom. A few friends from Democracy Wall and I were, however, able to obtain a live recording of the trial proceedings. We made public a transcript of the tape so that people could see that the "crimes" Wei was convicted of were nothing more than voicing criticisms of Deng Xiaoping and telling a reporter the name of a military general commonly known to be leading the Chinese forces in Vietnam. The release of the trial transcript led to my own arrest, and this, coupled with publishing articles, leading demonstrations, and taking part in other activities, resulted in my being imprisoned for the next ten years.

By the time Wei was tried a second time in 1995, the Chinese government had learned its lesson. No outsiders were allowed to get anywhere near the courtroom or to get any details of the so-called "open trial." But once again, my friends and I managed to obtain and publicize details of the trial and the international community was shocked to learn that the Chinese government had turned Wei's philanthropic, cultural, and economic activities, and even his correspondence with me, into "counterrevolutionary" criminal offenses aimed at overthrowing the government. Shocked by such a sham of a trial, the Chinese people and the international community could say little more than "This is true madness!" Actually, the country's leaders hidden away behind the walls of Zhongnanhai were in full control of their senses and very clear about what they were doing. If we crush Wei Jingsheng, they thought, not only do we persecute and settle our score with him, but more importantly, by silencing the most prominent symbol and outspoken champion of democracy in China, we force the entire Chinese democracy movement into submission.

Yet never once during more than fourteen years of imprisonment did Wei Jingsheng cower in fear or falter in his courage; never once did he place blame on others or voice regrets. Illness, solitary confinement, persecution by guards and other prisoners, the odious threat of "reform," and the enticing allure of a shortened sentence or improved treatment—all methods that had weakened imprisoned emperors and war criminals before him—had no effect on Wei. Yet what's more startling is that in spite of his perilous situation, Wei never abandons his sense of responsibility toward history and the Chinese people. In his letters to Deng Xiaoping and the other Communist Party leaders who were responsible for the harsh sentence imposed upon him, Wei's sense of duty surfaces again and again. It is what most occupied his thoughts during the many months and years of his imprisonment.

Wei Jingsheng's letters contain little of the traditional blind devotion and self-denigration of memorials sent to emperors by officials in ancient China; they are, instead, a unique form of writing shaped by Wei's own personality and ideas. Even when addressing those who held the power of life and death over him, Wei never stopped himself from hurling ridicule or offering impassioned criticism. The harsh reality of prison life failed to weaken Wei's proud sense of personal integrity, and he continued demanding that the government abide by the law and rectify its mistakes. This is the character and personality of the Wei Jingsheng I know. To him, a prison is nothing more than four high walls—he will always remain true to himself in spite of constant mental and physical persecution.

The foremost goal of a Chinese prison is to reform a prisoner. His spirit is broken so that it can be remolded as the authorities see fit. This process always begins with painful physical persecution and often torture. To maintain one's sense of self, as well as one's intellect and courage, within a prison that specializes in remolding that self requires one to be a true idealist. It also takes a moral character that feeds on visions and ideals, and shrugs off the enticements and threats dangled before it. Wei Jingsheng is precisely such an idealist. When the prison tried to stifle his thinking and even prohibited him from discussing politics in his letters, Wei turned his energies to scientific inquiry and invention or to raising rabbits. Whether contemplating social and political development, or pondering science and inventions, or exploring possible futures for the arid lands surrounding his labor camp, Wei never failed to uphold the ideal he established for himself as a boy: Make a contribution to society and the people.

This might sound like a Communist Party cliché about "selfless devotion," but Wei Jingsheng speaks from a completely different plane. In one of his letters, he urges his brother and sisters not to heed propaganda in the newspaper calling for "self-sacrifice," exhorting them instead to sacrifice themselves for their own "interests, convictions, and aspirations." "Selflessness" in Party terms, he infers, means little more than submitting to the needs and interests of the Party—a basic distinction that many people in China have failed to understand and therefore have sacrificed everything, including their common best interests, for. By casting aside the needs and interests of the Party and adhering instead to his own values and principles, Wei Jingsheng, by virtue of his own strong sense of self, defeated prison and the pressure it exerted upon him to "reform" in the name of the Party.

Because he is an optimist, a lover of life, and a person of many interests, Wei Jingsheng's personality stands out in strong contrast to the dark, imposing atmosphere of the prison. In a number of letters to his brother and sisters, Wei enthusiastically asks them to send music tapes. Even under heavy guard during a long rail journey to a labor camp in remote Qinghai province, Wei managed to enjoy the music being broadcast on the train. In other letters to his family, Wei writes unrestrainedly on a wide range of art and literary topics. Despite years of strict isolation, constant physical and mental persecution and deprivation, and the ever-looming specter of death, Wei is still overflowing with life and vitality. He remains fiercely determined to defeat the threats of physical and spiritual collapse.

Whether criticizing the government or discussing family matters, drafting notes to ordinary prison guards or to powerful government leaders like Deng Xiaoping, Wei Jingsheng never minces words. His frankness and honesty pour from every line. In an experienced politician, such a posture might appear too forthright, but in a dissident speaking out alone against a totalitarian society, such an attitude and personality are essential. Without them, he would be unable to shake a slumbering nation awake or lash out at a society long scared into silence.

Wei Jingsheng and I grew to be friends during the Democracy Wall Movement as members of the Joint Council, an organization that led and coordinated relations between the growing number of unofficial popular journals and grassroots groups affiliated with Democracy Wall. I was convener of the council and Wei Jingsheng was the representative from his magazine *Exploration*. As our opinions on the best methods for attaining human rights and democracy in China often differed, we sometimes found ourselves locked in heated debate. Fourteen years later, during our first phone conversation after Wei's release from prison in 1993, we joked about our old disagreements as if they were all things of the past. But it wasn't long before we took up our debate again and continued it over the phone and in letters. I don't always agree with all of Wei's views on practical strategies, and both of us have staunchly upheld our individual opinions, but what is more important and revealing about our arguments is that they are always undertaken with the intention of clarifying our ideas and correcting our mistakes. In this way, Wei possesses the traits a true champion of democracy should: tolerance and a willingness to cooperate and to accept defeat.

Wei Jingsheng is a natural-born hero; the desire and impulse to accomplish great things burn in his veins. He once said to me that there were plenty of other people who knew more and could write more eloquently than he, but those people were always searching or waiting for opportunity rather than finding their own courage to accomplish things. History, he said, is created by those brave enough to propel it forward. When, in the spring of 1979, Deng Xiaoping launched a crackdown on the Democracy Wall Movement and rumor had it that the leaders of *Exploration* magazine were to be targeted, Wei kept his composure and told the other members of *Exploration* that he would assume full responsibility for the groups' activities. Later, when fellow *Exploration* editor Yang Guang submitted testimony against Wei during his trial, Wei stuck to his promise and accepted the responsibility and the fifteen-year sentence.

During the tense period before his arrest, Wei sought me out every day to discuss how the Joint Council should continue to perform its duties and aid others, to tell me who should be the alternate representative for *Exploration*, and to arrange other matters in the event of his arrest. In the days leading up to his arrest, Wei was like a hunted animal surrounded by menacing figures, yet he remained calm and kept a hopeful smile on his face. Late on the night before Wei's arrest, I was walking him to his bus stop when two small, slow-moving cars appeared on either side of us, squeezing us closely together. But Wei Jingsheng was still able to laugh it off, saying, "You see, I'm not being overly suspicious, am I?" And with that, he got on a bus and went off into the endless darkness.

There were, of course, moments when even Wei Jingsheng had his uncertainties. Faced with arrest in 1979, he considered going into hiding, but his courage and sense of responsibility prevailed upon him to wait for the police to arrest him. Later, tormented by illness and appalling prison conditions, he hoped that through negotiation he might improve his situation or even gain release. He wrote letters to many high-level officials, including Deng Xiaoping, the person he suspected of being the direct cause of his persecution, and even promised that he would never again get involved in politics. But in all these pleas, there was always a line he would not cross. He would never do anything that ran counter to his own conscience or dignity. In one letter, he writes, "I will never again consider abandoning my principles to strike a bargain." This is a true hero. Those heroes who are never selfish or fearful, have unparalleled resolve and boundless honor, are just figments of the imagination. After my own prolonged stay in jail, I know that in prison a real hero is the person who can triumph over himself, who can conquer his doubts and his fears, and who never trades his conscience or self-respect for some meager improvement in conditions or an early release. Wei Jingsheng's determination and courage grows out of such an innate sense of integrity and dignity.

A wealth of benevolence and sympathy—this is another source of Wei Jingsheng's courage. During the Democracy Wall Movement, at Wei's invitation, many people who had come to Beijing to lodge complaints with the government stayed at his home. He helped them out with food and money as well. In 1993, after his release on parole, Wei began actively seeking out donations in China and abroad to help the orphans and helpless families of victims of the 1989 Beijing Massacre and other dissidents facing extreme hardships. In one emotional phone call, he told me that he and others had gathered together some fine handicrafts made by prisoners of conscience from the 1989 democracy movement. He asked me whether I might organize an exhibition in order to sell these items abroad because, he said, "Those who've been released as well as those still in prison are all suffering; there are even some who don't have enough for food or medicine." Wei himself had yet to obtain a residence permit or other personal documents from the police, but he was already busy helping others.

During the half a year Wei Jingsheng was out of prison, we were, unfortunately, never able to meet, although we talked over the phone often. I was only able to catch a few brief glimpses of him in televised videotapes made by the government expressly for the international community. The change in Wei's appearance since the Democracy Wall days was enormous. At the time, he had been young and in his prime, high-spirited and full of life—the very picture of a handsome young fellow. But the Wei Jingsheng I saw on the television screen displayed none of his formerly cheerful demeanor, and he looked like the middle-aged man he now was. I know how long and difficult fourteen and a half years in prison is, but in my heart I still can't help sighing when I realize that even heroes grow old.

But Wei's steadfast belief in human rights and democracy remains unchanged. Immediately following his release and still under police guard, Wei told relatives that he planned to continue his involvement in politics in order to promote human rights and democracy in China. At the time, China was still recovering from the reign of terror that had followed the 1989 Beijing Massacre and a new social impetus toward achieving human rights and democracy was just beginning to take shape and gain momentum. Wei's immediate and enthusiastic reinvolvement in the democracy movement coupled with the example of moral strength and courage he still showed after fourteen and a half years of life behind bars was a great inspiration to the newly revitalized movement. Wei Jingsheng's spirit and resiliency, shaped as they were by years of hardship, were just what people who had been so demoralized needed to see.

I feel that the qualities Wei displayed after his release in 1993 were positive indications that a once hot-blooded fighter for democracy had developed into a mature political dissident. This is precisely the kind of person I believe will be most valuable in helping China make the complex transformation from dictatorship to democracy. Democracy in China cannot be established overnight. It must surmount a long tradition of autocratic rule and the lack of a well-developed social understanding of the practices of human rights and democracy. Yet we cannot simply wait for human rights and democracy in China to happen—there has never been a dictatorial government that has voluntarily given these rights to its people. Therefore, society must act on its own initiative to force the government to change and improve. By doing so, society will also gain firsthand knowledge of human rights and democracy in practice. Only with the guidance of mature political dissidents like Wei Jingsheng is there hope for the cause of human rights and democracy in China.

Wei Jingsheng's letters describe a number of aspects of prison life in China that will be unfamiliar to most readers. Although Wei and I were held in different prisons, many things are common to all Chinese prisons.

Wei Jingsheng's letters are addressed to three groups of people: his brother and two sisters, the prison authorities and judicial organs, and policy-making officials in the Communist Party. People might wonder why he writes so often to these people. Why didn't he write to his father, his girlfriend, or other close friends? This is most likely because the prison prohibited it, or because in the case of his father, a former Communist Party official, Wei did not want to give him trouble by writing to him directly. Prison regulations allow prisoners to write letters only to their immediate relatives and their content is limited to discussion of the progress and intent of their reform, and their health and personal needs. You cannot write to anyone involved in or related to your case, nor can you raise their names in your letters to others. The content of letters written by prisoners of conscience like Wei and myself is not only strictly controlled, but the inspection process is special as well. My letters, for example, passed first through an inspection in the prison, were then handed over to the district Public Security Office for inspection and then on to the provincial Public Security Bureau, and were possibly checked again at an even higher level before being delivered.

Any reference in one's letters to persecution suffered in prison such as torture or corporal punishment is strictly forbidden. It would have been impossible for Wei to write about such matters. I asked him about this during a telephone conversation following his release and he replied that if what I meant by corporal punishment was the intentional infliction of physical pain, then yes, he had suffered quite a bit of torture. He didn't feel at ease discussing it over the phone, so there is little likelihood that he would describe such matters in letters, though there is little doubt that he was physically punished.

There are several reasons Wei Jingsheng wrote so many letters to Deng Xiaoping and other senior leaders in the central government. First of all, the "crimes" of prisoners of conscience like Wei and myself were determined by the upper echelons of the Communist Party leadership. Therefore, if you wanted to appeal your verdict or improve your conditions, you had to address your request to senior Party leaders. Second, there are certain times when the prison authorities might actually propose that you write to these leaders. I was often told this, but I only wrote one twenty-thousand-word letter to Deng Xiaoping, Hu Yaobang, and other leaders following an unsuccessful suicide attempt in 1986. I doubt that the letter ever made it into Deng Xiaoping's hands, but I assume the authorities suggested I write it in order to gauge my current thinking so they could determine how best to deal with me. This is the reason I chose not to write many such letters. I felt that if I wrote the truth it would only lead to trouble, and I refused to write lies.

Why, then, did Wei choose to write such letters? I believe the reasons are complex. The hope that his opinions and his dissatisfaction with the present corrupt state of affairs in China might one day be useful to society and history was clearly foremost in Wei's mind, even if he did realize just how uncertain fulfillment of this hope was. In addition, living in isolation year after year, many exceptional thoughts come to one's mind and Wei certainly used these letters as a way to organize and record his ideas. They were also, as he wrote to his brother and sisters, "a way for me to relieve my boredom." The language in Wei's letters to government leaders is often sharp and his tone derisive, and I feel that at times he used his letters to vent some of his anger.

In a number of his letters, Wei refers to undertaking several long-term hunger strikes, but it is unclear how the prison responded to his actions. From my own personal experience I know that carrying out a hunger strike inside a Chinese prison is no small matter. On the sixth evening of a hunger strike I undertook at Weinan Number Two Prison in Shaanxi province, the prison police ordered a dozen or so other prisoners to use handcuffs and rope to tie me to a special metal chair. Some of the prisoners lifted my legs in the air while kneading and pressing down on my stomach, saying that it was to keep me from using *qigong* breathing techniques to resist a feeding tube. Another prisoner squeezed my throat tight and pinched my nose shut so that I was forced to open my mouth in order to gasp for breath. A prison doctor then stuck a metal brace into my mouth, twisting it open so wide that the skin on the corners of my mouth ripped open. He then clamped a pair of metal pliers onto my tongue, pulling it way out of my mouth before sliding a length of tubing into my esophagus. After he had funneled a salty broth through the tube and into my stomach, the floor was covered with pools of blood and broth and my mouth was a numb and swollen mound of raw flesh. One of the prison guards even laughed at me and said, "We can take care of things if you don't eat, but we can't guarantee your comfort. . . . That's what we call 'revolutionary humanism'!"

In the letters Wei Jingsheng wrote to prison authorities and organs of the judiciary, he often complains of harassment and persecution on the part of other prisoners. These "trusties" are prisoners selected by the prison authorities and entrusted with keeping watch over a prisoner. Only prisoners in the "strict-regime brigade" would normally be assigned trusties of this type. According to Chinese government Reform Through Labor regulations, a prisoner who "refuses to recognize his crimes and accept reform" must be locked up in the strict-regime brigade to undergo "enforced reform." This means being isolated in a tiny cell and having trusties who are all criminal offenders act as henchmen for the guards; it is treatment far worse than an ordinary criminal receives.

In Weinan Prison, where I was held in the strict-regime brigade for four years, from late 1985 to 1989, trusties were also a common phenomenon. Although United Nations guidelines on the humane treatment of prisoners state that political prisoners must be kept separately from those imprisoned for criminal offenses, in China employing criminal offenders to monitor political prisoners is common. At times, as many as thirty prisoners, divided into three groups, kept watch over me twenty-four hours a day, both inside and outside of my cell. They were not allowed to speak to me or show me any sympathy, and on one occasion, when a trusty broke the rules and spoke with me, he was severely beaten by the prison guards later. While in the strict-regime brigade, aside from sleeping, eating, relieving myself, and being allowed to stand up for several minutes every few hours, the rest of the time I was made to sit straight on a small folding stool. The seat of the stool was woven from several thin strands of rope that cut into my buttocks. During my four years of punishment in the strict-regime brigade, I was not allowed to speak or move, let alone read books or newspapers or get any other form of mental stimulation. The trusties would even form a tight circle around me in order to restrict my breathing and stifle any chance I had for thought or reflection.

In one letter, Wei writes to his brother and sisters that he has passed a relatively pleasant birthday because he was able to buy an old chicken and make Long-Life noodle soup. This might lead readers to believe that if a prisoner has money, he can buy anything he wants to eat or use in prison. As far as I know, this was not true of prisons in the 1980s. According to the prison regulations at the time, prisoners could only purchase basic necessities once a month, primarily items such as cigarettes, toothpaste, and washing powder. Only on important holidays such as New Year's or Spring Festival could one also purchase a limited amount of food items. But China is a nation where "individuals" rather than regulations rule, and prison regulations are enforced entirely according to the whims of individual prison officials. If a prisoner came across a relatively good-natured prison official who had sympathy for him or might just want to do a prisoner favors in order to entice him to change his attitude toward reform, the official could serve as a helper. The official might overlook the regulations and allow a prisoner to buy food items, and he himself might even help buy things for the prisoner; other regulations might also be changed or relaxed. But if the situation is the opposite, regulations can be done away with completely and a prisoner might be persecuted to the point where he can neither beg for mercy nor death; this is also a common occurrence. In my judgment, the fact that Wei was allowed to buy a chicken and cook noodles on his birthday was an example of the former kind of treatment and Wei was so beside himself with happiness over his good fortune that he wrote about it in his letter home.

Wei Jingsheng's love and care for rabbits while in prison is especially touching, as several rare photographs taken of Wei at the Tanggemu Farm Reform Through Labor Camp in Qinghai province show. He later told me that his time at this Qinghai *laogai* was his "happiest" period in prison because, as he explained, "I was allowed to eat hot food and I could raise rabbits." Whether Wei liked rabbits or not before, I don't know. He says that his intention was to breed an exceptional variety of rabbit, but I believe there were other reasons as well. During one period, I, too, was lucky enough to have the opportunity to raise rabbits. This was when, after a long period of strict-regime measures that had had no effect on me, the prison authorities tried adopting a kinder approach. I was still locked up in the strict-regime brigade and watched over by trusties, but I was allowed to move about and was no longer starved for food. I could even take refuge in the filthy, urine-smelling rabbit hutch, where I relaxed and watched the rabbits chase each other and bound about freely. Those, too, were my "happiest" days in prison, and to this day, neither Wei Jingsheng nor I eat rabbit meat.

Wei Jingsheng is currently being held in Jidong Number One Prison, also known as the Nanpu New Life Salt Works Prison. This is the same prison where he was held before his release in 1993— he is even being held in the same cell. In addition to the guards watching him, there are five criminal offender trusties keeping an eye on him. If his sentence remains unchanged, when he is released at the age of sixty, counting his two prison stays plus the period he was secretly detained, he will have been deprived of his freedom for thirty years—half his life. What is even more distressing is that Chinese society, as well as the international community, has reacted indifferently to the renewed persecution of Wei Jingsheng. It has received even less anger and attention than his first imprisonment in 1979. I hope that this is due only to the Chinese government's restrictions on information and that people simply don't know enough to make a judgment. I don't want to believe that, in their desire for monetary gain, they have forgotten the value of human life and dignity.

The Chinese government stifles human will and diminishes human value. If the publication of this book can inspire people to take action to stop the Chinese government from slowly killing Wei Jingsheng, then our goal in putting it together will have been achieved.

A Note on the Editing
and Translating
of the Prison Letters

Kristina M. Torgeson

In 1993, Wei Jingsheng learned that he would be paroled six months before the completion of his fifteen-year prison sentence. Suspecting that his early release was a diplomatic bargaining chip being used to boost China's bid to host the 2000 Olympics, Wei did some bargaining of his own. He refused to sign his parole form until he got the prison file he knew contained the many letters and statements that he had written over the course of his long imprisonment but that had never been mailed out. The writings in this book are excerpts of the more than four hundred thousand words contained in that file.

Soon after Wei's release, friends and journalists, anxious to learn more about the thinking of a man who had taken on the status of a living legend in China during his imprisonment, urged Wei to publish his writings. As he told Robert Bernstein, his literary agent, in early 1994, Wei had plans to write an autobiography based on his prison letters, but in the meantime—"just to satisfy my friends' curiosity," as he said—he decided to publish several of his later prison letters in a major Chinese newspaper published in Hong Kong and Taiwan. Knowing that overseas Chinese readers might not understand why his letters were addressed mainly to Communist Party leaders, Wei wrote an introduction that described how prison officials had frequently confiscated letters to his family and forbidden him to write to anyone else, but had encouraged him to write to government leaders to "discuss matters" concerning his case. Instead, Wei explained, "I took advantage of this opportunity to air some of my ideas to [the Party leaders] with the hope of giving them a better understanding of certain new issues so that they might make decisions on the fate of the nation more objectively and comprehensively for the good of the people and the country. If it weren't for this reason," he continued, "I would not have written to them . . . for writing to them was a very painful thing." Wei also apologized to readers for the crudeness of his language at times and remarked that the letters were "the fruits of only a small part of my thinking. Later, given the time and opportunity, I will explain my ideas in more detail."

Unfortunately, before his "disappearance" in April 1994 and his subsequent conviction in December 1995 to a fourteen-year prison term, Wei Jingsheng did not have the time to proceed with his plans to write a more extensive account of his prison experiences or his thoughts on democratization in China. After Liu Qing, the chairman of Human Rights in China, a New York–based nongovernmental organization, received the texts of Wei's prison letters, Wei Shanshan (Wei's sister), Robert Bernstein, and several of Wei's friends and colleagues in the Chinese democracy movement made a collective decision to have them translated and published. By doing so, they hope to make Wei's ideas and courage known to the world and draw attention to the gravity of his present situation.

Many of the letters that follow, particularly those addressed to family members and prison authorities, are translated in full, while space considerations required that most of the longer letters be excerpted. In excerpting these letters, I have tried above all to preserve the main points of Wei's ideas and arguments while reducing repetition and extended digressions into the finer details of Chinese politics and history. In the interest of increasing the readability of the letters for a general audience, I have not indicated where breaks in the translation occur although I have generally retained Wei's prose structure. The full original texts of the prison letters of Wei Jingsheng are held in the special collections of the C. V. Starr East Asian Library at Columbia University.

In addition to the prison letters themselves, several of the statements that prison political instructors asked Wei to write explaining his "thoughts" or "reflections" on specific topics such as revision of the Constitution and the Sino-British declaration on the fate of Hong Kong have also been included, as has one of several memorandums Wei wrote in 1992 as a record of his prison treatment. Notes appended to the texts of two letters that Wei presumably made while having the letters typed up after his release in 1993 have also been retained in the translations. Readers are asked to refer to the glossary in the back of the book for explanations of individuals, terms, and historical events mentioned in the letters.

The excerpted translation of the October 5, 1992, letter on Tibet is gratefully reprinted from *Tibet Press Watch*, published by the International Campaign for Tibet. Excerpts from the letters of September 5, 1990, and June 15, 1991, are based on translations provided by the U.S. Foreign Broadcast Information Service with some modifications. The transcript of Wei's 1979 defense statement contained in Appendix II is reprinted by permission of the Society for the Protection of East Asians' Human Rights and is based on translations by Amnesty International and the U.S. Joint Publications Research Service (74764). The translation of Wei's autobiography in Appendix III benefited from the very generous suggestions provided by Professor Ta-Ling Lee of Southern Connecticut State College and Miriam London, a researcher in Chinese and Soviet studies, and their earlier version of the autobiography published in *The New York Times Magazine* on November 16, 1980. All other translations are entirely my own, as are any errors that may have occurred in the course of putting this book together.

Upon publishing several of his prison letters in 1994, Wei Jingsheng wrote, "I hope I will never again have to resort to this method to discuss issues, for it is better to present them openly to the people so that everyone can debate them." Unfortunately, as this book goes to press, Wei has been deprived of even the freedom to write to his family—no letters have been received since April 1994, when he disappeared into the Chinese prison system. As one guard informed his sister in October 1996, "Not a single word written by Wei Jingsheng will pass through these prison gates without the approval of the higher-ups." Wei's heart condition has worsened and he is on oxygen; his reading materials are severely restricted, and he has no news of the outside world. Even a letter from the president of the European Parliament inviting Wei to accept the 1996 Sakharov Prize for Freedom of Thought was returned to sender unopened. The publication of Wei Jingsheng's prison letters will, I hope, aid efforts to procure the release of Wei and other prisoners of conscience in China so that they may work toward the day when all citizens of China can speak their minds freely without fear of repression.

the

prison

letters

魏京生

Following his March 29, 1979, arrest and October 1979 trial (see Appendix II), Wei Jingsheng was held in solitary confinement in Banbuqiao, Beijing's largest detention center. For the first two years of his imprisonment, Wei was not allowed to write to or see his family; thus the first letter in this collection does not come until the summer of 1981, near the time of his transfer to a solitary cell in the "strict-regime brigade" at Beijing Number One Prison.

August 25, 1981

Dear Members of the Central Committee Secretariat and the Legal Affairs Committee of the National People's Congress:

Thank you all very much. I have recently been allowed to visit with my brother and sisters, and the knowledge that my family is well and that my situation has not adversely affected their lives or work is a welcome surprise that makes me extremely happy. I am not sure whose idea it was not to implicate my siblings or father in my affairs, so I must thank all of you collectively and don't think I'll be too mistaken.

Of course, I would like to see you extend this spirit of tolerance by making a clean sweep of all your despicable old habits of brutal repression and allowing society to develop under a more normal political atmosphere. By doing so, you will unite more people behind you and decrease the number of innocent victims, thereby greatly diminishing social dissatisfaction and instability. This would surely benefit you as well as society. If you truly desire to carry out reform with "stability and unity" as you say, this is an essential condition. The lack of this spirit of tolerance is one of the primary reasons why minor problems in China have so often been magnified into larger ones.

You might not understand how I feel, as I'm still not very good at writing songs of praise. You might even consider this to be a rather insignificant matter, indeed I myself realize it is no great piece of news, but I am writing to let you know that people are capable of recognizing when you do things right, and I hope knowledge of this fact will prevent you from turning from right to wrong. For then, even more people will take this as a positive sign for the future. Of course, changing a tradition of political persecution that has taken shape over a long period of time cannot happen in a day or two, or by doing one or two small things. Therefore, I hope that you will persist in your present course.

There is also a small personal matter that I am writing to bother you with. Actually, I've already bothered you about it before, but because I haven't been able to communicate through the usual channels of late, I'm going to waste your precious energy yet again. Please bear with me.

During the summer of 1979, I wrote asking permission to read and study. My request met with your approval and the kind consideration of those working here, and thus the past two years were not a complete waste for me. Recently, however, for some inexplicable reason, my family has no longer been allowed to send me books or magazines.

From the newspaper I know that you are exhorting cadres and young people to study more theory and history. I too wish to study such things and love to read books of this nature and think your exhortation should apply to prisoners as well. I can't believe that, because I have become a criminal, even the books I read are implicated as counterrevolutionary materials. You say that I need to be reeducated and reformed. Well, then, since reading and studying are forms of self-education and reform and don't run counter to what you are recommending, why restrict me? If you say it's because "After this guy reads, he can't be reeducated," then I say, even if I don't read, there's no guarantee I'll be reeducated, and letting me read is unlikely to make me any worse!

Since revolutionary theory is said to be the "crystallization of all human knowledge," then studying all human knowledge should be even more advantageous to this crystallization process. It follows that crystallizing only a small fraction of this "knowledge" will not amount to "revolutionary theory," but to theory that at least won't be very "revolutionary." How, then, can placing restrictions on reading materials help a person better accept the revolutionary reality?

If you really believe in your own theory about the crystallization of all human knowledge, but feel that it is not yet widely understood, you would do well to encourage people to absorb knowledge more fully so that they can use their own minds to "crystallize" it into revolutionary theory. From what I understand, this is the very reason you did away with the deceptive policies of the Gang of Four period. I loudly applaud this action and hope to take advantage of this opportunity to enrich my knowledge and open up my own eyes. Not only do I wish to study all kinds of theory and history (Chinese history in particular), I would also like to read various memoirs and literary books, particularly some of the more recently published works of foreign and Chinese literature. But, as I understand it, all of the books in the prison library here are either from the Gang of Four period or are novels published shortly after its demise and are still thick with the "Gang flavor." I feel that such books are a waste of time and have no redeeming qualities whatsoever. I, for one, can absolutely not stand works of this type and formed an immunity to them long ago. Even if I did come into contact with them, they wouldn't infect me; but still, why should I waste my time on them?

I have decided to write you this letter in the hope that you will permit my family to send me books and magazines so that I can fill my head with the "crystallization of all human knowledge" rather than frittering away my time. Just as the cadre in charge here always says to us, "There will come a day when you too must return to society and take part in the work of revolution!"

Respectfully yours,
Wei Jingsheng

November 1, 1981

Dear Lingling, Taotao, and Shanshan:

Hello everyone!

During your last visit you forgot to bring me a pipe and rolling papers, and you didn't bring enough tobacco either. If I'm not careful I'll have to buy some cigarettes before the year is out. I still have some paper and tobacco left over from your last visit, though, so I can get by for a while. Taotao's shirt fits me perfectly, but it's so white that it's hard to keep clean—it's a good thing I have so much free time on my hands, and enough washing powder too! But please don't concern yourselves over my daily needs.

While we were saying good-bye following last month's visit, Lingling mentioned to me that during a meeting with some foreigners, Deng Xiaoping said that I could be released if I changed my thinking. I'm not quite sure when this took place, but if it happened prior to last year, then forget about it, there's no use bringing up old news. If it took place more recently, however, would you write and tell me the exact details of what happened and what the different views on it were? I'd like to get as realistic a picture of my own situation as I can. That way if I'm faced with any new changes, I can react to them more quickly and effectively.

Right now my mind feels a bit rusty and my reactions to things are slow. I'm completely cut off in here and feel so out of touch that I have a hard time assessing things people tell me. I've become both too trustful and too suspicious of everything at once—a bit like an old bumpkin who's just arrived in Beijing from the countryside. I'm unsure and hesitant, and have trouble understanding things; it's getting to the point where I can't tell the difference between good and bad anymore. I desperately want to understand everything around me, but I'm hampered by the restricted scope of my vision. Every so often now I'm able to watch a bit of television, but I'm very limited in what I'm allowed to see. The trusties assigned to keep an eye on me can even control what I watch because if they don't want to see the news, then I can't either and I can only go back to my cell and sleep. But this is beside the point; you can guess the rest yourselves.

Let me get back to what I was saying. I remember that when Lingling told me this bit of news, I replied, "It's not easy to change one's thinking." But this is not completely true. During the nearly three years I've been in here, my thinking and feelings have not been the same as before. The fact is, it's impossible for one's thoughts to remain unchanged—this is just common sense. In a general sense, my environment influences my thoughts and feelings; I'm capable of adapting myself the way Jewish people do to their surroundings. When I first heard what you told me, my initial reaction was that it was just Deng's way of placating foreign opinion. Over the past three years I've heard people say similar

ambiguous things many, many times, but I've yet to find that the actual results ever live up to the listener's hopes. People who believe such lines will always be duped. For example, in 1979 during the period before my trial, the court and the Procuratorate both really laid it on me thick, one time even going so far as to say they would rescind the charges against me if I cooperated. To tell you the truth, I nearly believed it when they lied that "nothing will happen to you if you admit your mistakes." But I never thought that any of the "mistakes" they wanted me to admit to were mistakes at all, so I decided to stick to my opinions and not sacrifice my princi- ←
ples to forge a deal with them. It later became apparent to me that everything they had said was a lie from start to finish. My case would never have been tried in the way they had promised, as even the length of my sentence had already been determined in a meeting of the Party Political Bureau. When Deng Xiaoping later published his opinions in the newspapers, it became very clear that I was "the chicken killed as a warning to the monkeys." When your goal is to warn the monkeys, you don't care what attitude the chicken has; even if I were to slobber with regret like Yang Guang did, the outcome would still have been the same. I just congratu-lated myself for not getting duped by them. I will never again con-sider abandoning my principles to strike a bargain. Even if a great opportunity is dangled before me, I will never regret this in the slightest. It's just like Old Mao once said: "All men must die, but death can vary in its significance." I don't want to be a hero, but I don't want to be condemned by history either. Why should I let others point to our family's descendants and say, "There's a rela-tive of that spineless so-and-so!"

A foreign trade cadre who was in prison here for accepting a bribe told me that the foreigners he did business with called me a hero of the Chinese people. "Foreigners used to think that Chinese people were weaklings and lacked the courage to stand up for prin-ciples," he once said to me, "but this time you've shown them that we Chinese have real guts." Even a police chief, who was in here for committing some crime and who never agreed with any of my views, called me a "hero." No one in the prison objects to such comments, but I certainly don't let them go to my head. I see them as cups of poisonous wine that they pour for me while they puff themselves up in front of others. Their flattery doesn't move me—I won't suffer just to be a hero. I'm not that stupid.

I stick to my beliefs, not only because I feel that they can help people, but because history is already beginning to prove that such beliefs are beneficial to the prosperity and happiness of our people. Today, even the mighty leaders of the central government wouldn't dare to openly deny the validity of the basic points I raised during what amounted to little more than a short-lived political movement in the late 1970s. Would they now dare to openly praise dictatorship and deny the necessity of democracy? Would they deny the necessity of reform and call for the preservation of a Soviet-style socialist economy? Would they deny that the days when dictators appointed local representatives have passed or that open elections are now needed to legitimize the government? Whether they are pressured into doing these things or they do so voluntarily, as long as they recognize them, then I believe we can begin to speak the same language. And if they actually put these things into practice, then I would even be willing to lend them a hand. Unfortunately, I can't determine exactly what, if anything, they've got up their sleeves, so I can't carelessly sacrifice myself for their sake. I must be completely sure first, so it's a good thing that nobody needs me for anything right now anyway and life in here is not entirely unbearable.

As far as them saying they will let me go if I change my thinking—that's completely ridiculous. First of all, as I said before, one's thinking is always changing. Second, aren't they just trying to turn me into a real "counterrevolutionary" by having me renounce democracy, reform, and the people? I know they would never admit this themselves, but there's no harm in you writing them for me and asking, or else you can just directly copy a few lines from my letter and send it to them. Third, will they release me only after I change those parts of my thinking that they don't like or agree with? If that's the case, then I might as well just prepare to die in here. No two people ever think exactly alike, and there will always be those who don't see eye to eye with each other. Even if I were a computer, I still wouldn't know exactly which person's thinking I should memorize in order to please everybody. This is just another way for them to say that they have no intention of releasing me.

This third scenario is probably the most likely, but there is also a fourth one. That is, they might feel it is more to their benefit to bring a slaughtered chicken back to life than to eat him, as that way they can make full use of my potential value as a means of demonstrating their great tolerance. But whether this happens or not doesn't have much to do with me, and there isn't anything I can do to influence things either way; the ball is completely in their court. At any rate, this is probably the least likely scenario of all and we shouldn't waste our time thinking about it.

I'll stop here and wait for your reply. If you're worried about writing the wrong address, maybe Lingling wouldn't mind delivering it here. This letter might be extremely important to me, so I hope this time you will come through for me. When you deliver it, if Secretary Zhao of the discipline section (he's the one who sat at the door during our last meeting) is not there, then look for Section Chief Huang—I've spoken with him before and he's shown some concern for me. You could also look for Leader Zhao of the strict-regime brigade (the one who sat by the table that day)—he's a cadre from the unit in charge of my daily activities and study. There's also Political Instructor Chen, whom you haven't met, but if the other three aren't around, you can try to find him. All in all I hope you can tell me what I want to know because it is not illegal and it doesn't break any prison rules. It doesn't hinder my "reform" either.

Say hello to everyone. Taotao, when you write to them, please pass on my good wishes to Weina's family.

Jingsheng

Evening of November 2

P.S. The workload here has increased these past few days and I haven't been sleeping well, so I didn't manage to copy over yesterday's letter until today. I'll ask the brigade leader to mail it out tomorrow. After going through inspection and the mails, I suppose it probably won't make it into your hands for some time, but I hope that you will write me back as soon as you receive it. You can imagine how I'm feeling, so I won't go into it further. Lingling, if you deliver the letter here, maybe you could ask the cadre who takes the mail whether he could pass my pipe and tobacco on to me as well. Of course, if you mail it, then there's no need to worry about that until December.

Also, when you see Shanshan tell her to take care of her health. Work is important, of course, but one's health is even more important. She can always make up her studies later, but it's not easy to recover good health once it's been damaged. I hope she waits until she is completely well before leaving the hospital; she shouldn't kill herself over grades. And tell her she shouldn't try to emulate the air of a "romantic artist"; she was not like that before and was level-headed and careful. She took after Mama in that way. How come she has changed so much? Nobody will respect her more because she puts on the airs of a "romantic artist" or admire her for her small-time intellectual snobbery. She would do better to focus her energy on developing her art and ideas. Of course, I'm basing all this on my impressions of her from before I got in prison, since I don't really know what she's like now.

November 19, 1981

Dear Lingling, Taotao, and Shanshan:

Hello everyone!

I was very happy to receive Taotao's letter (written on October twenty-fourth and mailed on the twenty-fifth) earlier this month. I haven't been allowed to watch television recently and then I was excused from work for two days because my knuckles were aching, so I ended up having even more time on my hands than usual. Since I don't have any books to read, I'll write to you for fun. Besides, it doesn't take too much of your energy to read a letter and it helps me to relieve some of my boredom.

Did you receive the letter I wrote on November first? I won't send this letter until I've gotten your reply. Once I do, I'll mail it together with the next letter I write, as I can only mail out one a month.

Taotao, you wrote the wrong character for a word throughout

your letter. Maybe this has something to do with the fact that you didn't go to middle school. You also miswrote the phrase "just the opposite," and turned "the length of a day" into "the width of a day." These mistakes all break the rules of common language usage. You must take care in the future to avoid showing your ignorance in public. It's hard to avoid sometimes, but try not to do it too often. Actually, even the so-called "writers" who fill the pages of the *People's Daily* display their ignorance quite frequently, just as they go on shaking their heads and declaring that "kids today just don't have any culture." The strange thing is that as of yet no one has called them arrogant, which can probably be explained by the word "old." In our country being "old" is a cover for doing all matter of bad things, even some really despicable ones.

Taotao and his wife say I am arrogant, but I'm not convinced. People often call me arrogant, but it's usually just when they can't come up with any better response to me. Whether intentionally or not, they always seem to forget one thing: I can talk to people from all walks of life, whether gentlemen and ladies of the high-level cadre stratum or old peasants from so deep in the mountain valleys that you can barely understand a word they're saying. No one has ever had misgivings about talking with me because of my "arrogance." Once in a while someone will admonish me for being "a bit pompous," but it's usually because what I'm saying violates their common sense of things. This has helped me to understand why Lu Xun said, "What a blessing it would be if there were more people with such personal arrogance!" and "What a disaster if there were more people arrogant only in the conformity of their 'patriotism.'" If a society, or even one person, is to progress, then one must abandon some of what is considered common sense and explore new things that have never been understood before. In short, one must pursue the strange and unknown. For if a nation stifles the unknown by relying only on the common sense of being arrogant in the conformity of "patriotism," then it is destined to lag behind in human progress.

This rule applies to individuals as well. Sometimes I think that the reason people are wiser than monkeys has a lot to do with the fact that they are more curious and their force of habit is less

ingrained; monkeys, for the same reason, are wiser than other animals and are categorized as primates. The swan, however, who floats
so proudly along, never deigning to pay any attention to others, has
such a strong sense of habit that even if several of its flock are
killed in a place, it will still go back there. If such a strong sense of
habit was not outweighed by the swan's ability to reproduce, then
I'm afraid swans would have been extinct long ago. Thus, the type
of arrogance that is truly intolerable is pride of habit and a tena-
cious defense of common sense without sensitive reaction to new
things. Just as Taotao's teacher once said, my "reactions are quick"
and this further shows that to call me "arrogant" is incorrect.

One of the greatest strengths possessed by all of the children in
our family is our ability to react quickly and cleverly to things.
We're good at adapting to new situations and accepting all kinds of
unfamiliar things. I can see this trait most clearly in Shanshan and
Taotao. But after Taotao was in the army for a while his "son of a
cadre" attitude got so strong that even I could hardly stand him any
longer. But this isn't the reason why I didn't write much then. It
was more because during that period I was heavily influenced by
the thinking of Lu Xun and had lost my confidence in the Chinese
"national character." I was trying to escape from reality and no
longer felt like discussing anything. Also, Taotao's "son of a cadre"
snobbishness grated on my own optimistic personality, so I didn't
even feel like writing. Over the last few years I've discovered that
Taotao has gradually returned to his old self and from his letters I
can guess that this is probably because married life and the semi-
tropical beauty of Xiamen both agree with him. But please don't
assume that the stubborn, arrogant impression I've given you is
caused by the four white walls enclosing me so opressively. I still
feel that I'm quite an optimist and could adapt easily to "semi-
tropical beauty." Or at least in my own imagination!

Some people writing in the newspapers lately have been clam-
oring about being "eager to help others," and saying that China
lacks the backbone for "self-sacrifice." I hope you will all be sure
of who it is you are sacrificing yourselves for. It's better to "make
sacrifices for oneself" than "self-sacrifices." That is, to sacrifice
for the interests, convictions, and aspirations of all of our "selves,"
so that the human race as a whole will benefit. It goes against

human ethics to sacrifice for something other than the "self" in this context. "The basis of morality is egoism, and if the proletarian were not acting to benefit himself, then he would have no need to resist oppression." (See Lenin's "Philosophical Notebooks.") By this, of course, I'm not saying that egoism equals selfishness, or that the basis of ethics is ethics itself. Even Lenin himself went on to clarify this, so you see, sometimes even Lenin and I agree.

Actually, people's opinions are basically alike on most matters; it's only when people try to second-guess each other that problems arise. For example, one of the guys in prison with me is serving eight years for murder because he acted on his second-guesses of others at the beginning of the Cultural Revolution. He used to be a Party member of strong "national character," and when he shared a cell with me in 1979, he still approached everything with extreme caution and was always trying to interpret the intentions of others, from the brigade leader on down to the other criminals in the cell block. His opinions never wavered from those being published in the newspapers or whatever the Party's current political movement happened to be. But the recent trend toward social freedom has made people more willing to speak their minds. There isn't a single wall that remains uncracked—lately even this guy has dared to make such offhand comments as "That old revolutionary Song Renqiong, there he is at another fucking banquet." Saying such things would once have been considered taboo "loose talk," so doesn't this go to show that he is enjoying his newfound freedom? Everybody does, and he's no different, but at the same time he continues to disapprove of this kind of freedom because he is intent on figuring out what "others" are thinking and what they in turn think the "others in power" are thinking, and then adopting this thinking as his own. Even though he realizes he has no personal freedom whatsoever, he feels safer this way and objects to anyone who tries to fight for individual freedom or the freedom of others.

Do "those in power" dislike this freedom? Once, during my trial, my interrogator struck up a conversation with me and proudly pointed out that one could already "freely express individual opinion" in society. He said that even during the processing of a case, he could voice opinions that ran counter to those of his superiors without any negative consequences. He grew exuberant as he proclaimed: "Our party's policies are more relaxed now. Respecting the rights of the people is democracy, isn't it? What other party has such confidence in the people?" He was quite satisfied with the freedoms the Party had so kindly bestowed upon the people. I suppose "those in power" do not consider such freedoms to be a mistake either. It's a pity, however, that they aren't any bolder than their own subjects when it comes to trying to second-guess what "others" really think.

Instead, "those in power" ask the "others": "You see, such freedom doesn't suit the customs and habits of the Chinese people, does it? Perhaps we've even given them a bit too much freedom?" The "others" then immediately take such words as a hint and do their best to come up with reasons and evidence to prove just how too much freedom runs counter to the will of the people. They even dream up ways of showing how the interests of "those in power" are hindered by these freedoms. In the course of everyone trying to second-guess one another in this way, freedom turns into an element of extreme evil in their minds. Everyone starts saying "Just get rid of it, then we'll be happy," and nodding unanimously from the top levels to the bottom. But this unanimity actually runs counter to everyone's original desires and even goes against human nature. Only by repressing human nature can such conformity be brought about; it represses not only the nature of the "others," but "those in power" as well. And the reason is all because they repress the nature of their "selves." This, then, is the tragedy of a nation of second-guessers.

My observations in recent years (particularly since leaving the army) have made me realize that our nation is not at all as dismal and hopeless as Lu Xun and I once described it. The people have great reserves of self-confidence, self-respect, and self-consciousness stored away. In recent years these feelings have been mounting rapidly, and this is why I am now willing to sacrifice some of my own personal "happiness"—that is, if being alienated from rights that are "inalienable" can also be considered "happiness." I often think that, as far as Chinese people today are concerned, it is becoming less and less possible that a social system as violent and brutal as that which existed under the Gang of Four could be tolerated again. This is the only reliable guarantee that such a tragedy will never occur again; all other promises are undependable. Human enlightenment is the sole guarantee that humanity will escape from repression. As Eugène Pottier wrote in the "Internationale," "No faith have we in prince or peer, / Our own right hand the chains must shiver . . . / And give to all a happier lot." What, then, is happiness? It is nothing less than realization of the full potential of humanity. Full and free development of personal will is the highest goal of humanity. Even communism teaches this! I first came to an understanding of this fact by studying the classics of communism, not the texts of "Western capitalist freedom." Of course, there are some "communists" now who aren't accustomed to hearing such things. This is because, even though they may call themselves communists, they too are impostors—the "second-guessers" of communism.

I'll stop here; this is getting too long. I'm becoming like an old lady who doesn't know when to shut her mouth. I won't be able to fit everything into the envelope.

I never had a pen or pencil to write with while I was in Cell Forty-four, so I composed some poems and hid them away somewhere in my brain for safekeeping, but now even I can't find them! I'm afraid I'll have to wait for Scotland Yard to use their hypnosis techniques on me before I can remember them again. In the meantime, I'll copy out a poem I recently came up with for your "enjoyment"!

On November 6, I saw the end of a television program about the folksinger Jiang Ge's suffering before and after the Cultural Revolution and how he "brought honor upon the nation" when he went abroad. I returned to my cell and wrote "To Jiang Ge":

A small house, filled with music and song, suffering and happiness,
In the arts, must we pander to foreign tastes?
Let us be intoxicated with our thunderous laughter,
Let the curses and swears pass like a nightmare.
Life is no more than a dream, and I have just awoken,
Worldly affairs still have their ups and downs.

When the entire Chinese nation becomes aware of this,
What a bounteous harvest we will reap.

Jingsheng

November 21, 1981

P.S. I've decided to stop waiting and go ahead and send this letter off. First of all, I'm afraid if I keep it under my bedding, I will continue writing and make it longer and longer, and secondly, I don't want to miss my chance to send out a letter this month. Finally, and most importantly, I've given up hoping that your reply will contain any good news. After reading my November first letter to you, the brigade leader here told me firmly that I "shouldn't fantasize." He's wrong about me ever harboring any fantasies, but I do take his words as an authoritative response to the questions I raised in my letter. He probably has access to official documents and knows the intentions of the higher-ups pretty clearly, so his estimation of the whole situation is undoubtedly much more reliable than my own.

Taotao urged me to stop saying "I won't die" so much because he's afraid it just makes me feel more lonely. But that's nothing. I once thought I was condemned to death and I had prepared for it. After spending half a year on death row, death began to seem about as inevitable as life. Still, I never felt lonely. Sometimes I think if I had died, it would have been better for me and all of you. A quick death is better than lingering around like this half dead, half alive, waiting for death. At least it's not as painful. That way I could also have relieved you of a burden and lessened the dark cloud hanging over your heads. Better yet, dead people are more likely to obtain a "reversal of a false verdict" and you could at long last rid yourselves of the "relatives of a counterrevolutionary" label. I often feel sorry for having caused you to bear such a label. The dead might not be able to directly thank those who helped them, but their deaths can bring the living more tangible benefits. If I were already dead, it would also be easier for those high officials whose reputations I've sullied to cast off my shadow. My death would be better for myself and everybody else. A loss could turn out to be a blessing in disguise, so what does being "lonely" matter? It's human nature to resist death, and I am only human, so it looks like, unfortunately, I'll be around to burden you all for a few more decades!

Jingsheng

December 2, 1981

Dear Members of the Central Committee Secretariat and the Legal Affairs Committee of the National People's Congress:

I am writing to trouble you yet again. Please accept my deepest apologies, but I have no alternative. I didn't want to bother you, as I know you must be so busy that such a trifling matter as this is hardly worth your notice; you probably just overlooked it in the shuffle of catching up on your large backlog of work. That's why if you want to get something done in our country, no matter how big or small it may be, you've always got to give it a "shove."

Several months ago I wrote you a letter concerning my family sending books and magazines to me. To date, I have received no reply. Although there is a library here, it doesn't have many books and even the cadres say, "It's just that way." Two months ago one of them was considerate enough to borrow four books for me, but I still haven't been able to exchange them for others. They are all pretty mediocre books from the Cultural Revolution, but even books like these are rare commodities in here. Since I'm not allowed to select books myself and the cadres don't know what I like to read—particularly since they seem to feel that I've read most everything already—they are just blindly choosing books for me. They are doing the best they can under the circumstances, but it's difficult for them and I feel it is too much of an imposition. I'm embarrassed to constantly badger them to borrow more for me. My brother and sisters don't mind the trouble and are willing to send me books. They will all be inspected by the cadres so you needn't be worried, and besides, my brother and sisters know what kinds of books I like to read and what I've read already, and they can even send me some of my old ones. They are all conscientious members of your Party, so there's no need for you to be concerned. This will not only save trouble for the cadres here, but it will allow me to obtain more appropriate study materials. You can satisfy everybody at once, so I can think of no reason why you shouldn't do so.

I've heard the explanation: a person's incorrect thinking is closely related to the books and magazines he's read, and if you want to reform, your reading materials must be selectively restricted; we can't allow you to read whatever you like. While this hypothesis is somewhat similar to Marx's famous theory that "man's social being determines his consciousness," it also bears a close resemblance to that famous view of Goebbels that "lies repeated a thousand times become truth." Or, perhaps, this theory is somewhere between the two and might be considered an amalgamation of both. If people's thinking could really be controlled the way you force-feed a duck or teach a myna bird to talk, then there would be few problems in the world and our newspapers wouldn't have to waste so much ink and paper over discussions on the topic of "how best to undertake political thought work." Yet the reason experts in "political thought work" complain is that people don't always believe what they are told and even go so far as to distrust and loathe what they hear. People's thinking always follows the basic rules of human understanding and they will believe what they come up with on their own. The way peasants fatten up ducks by forcing food down their throats can't be applied to humans for it spoils the appetite. Perhaps we should consider this one of the great human weaknesses. But thank goodness for that; otherwise, whenever the government disliked "proletarian revolutionary thought," what would they rely on to carry out the "proletarian revolution"? When the Gang of Four shackled all modes of thinking, did anyone but the disobedient few like myself manage not to become ideological accomplices of the Gang of Four? No, that was not the case. "Political thought workers" should investigate how this old question relates to new situations. As the venerable old Marx once said, "Before you can change the world, you must understand it."

But there are always bumps and grinds along the road to happiness. It's not bad if you come up with something after all that grinding, but beware: No matter how much you grind coarse grain, you are still left with the inedible stuff when you're through. Nevertheless there are still people stupid enough to try grinding it into gold, ivory, or jade. History is not lacking in examples of such fools and there are certainly people today who are equally stupid; perhaps I am just such a person myself. That's why with all my tongue-in-cheek apologies I still "grind" on you rather than the brigade leaders here. Actually, it's because my own "stupidity and arrogance" tells me that these matters have nothing to do with them and it would be wrong for me to blame them. Even though they say that it is a prison rule that books may not be sent in, I have sound proof that many of the other prisoners receive books and magazines from their families. Stating that it is a "regulation" is just their way of dealing with me since they have no alternative. So, as a "special" prisoner, I've got to do some special "grinding." It's a nuisance, but I have little choice, there's nothing else for me to do. I urge you to bear with me a bit—a noble minister's heart should be broad. The Cultural Revolution criminals like Kuai Dafu and Han Aijing both receive special treatment, so why is it I can't fight for the same? As they say, "It's not that I have *not* done anything good, but that everything I've done is not wrong!"

I was deeply moved to read in the paper how you've been having heart-to-heart discussions with young people, illustriously "showing concern for misled youths." It inspired me once again to take up "dissident political views" from yours, so please allow me to now take the liberty to express some of my dissatisfaction toward certain people and matters, in spite of my restricted vision and shallow understanding. I welcome your comments.

To borrow the words of a critic writing in the *People's Daily*, "Even members of the landlord class can love." The exploiting class also has its love and fine manners, just as the proletariat class has its "ruffians, idiots, prostitutes," and the like. There's plenty of evidence for this in the classics of your party leaders, but what are the repercussions for society? You have personally witnessed how the so-called "pillars of the dictatorship of the proletariat" have suppressed humanity in the past, so how do you feel about it? Class is only one aspect of humanity; everyone might be "branded" by it, but that brand doesn't extend to one's belly button or every hair on one's head. The landlord class has its "open-minded gentleman" Li Dingming, the Communist Party has its "inhumane pile of dog crap" Jiang Qing, and even the mother of "public enemy" Chiang Kai-shek was from the "poor middle peasant" class. There are many among you sirs who defected from the exploiting classes or enemy forces for the side of progress and I refuse to believe that before your defection you were so thoroughly shameless and vengeful that if you had an affair with a "concubine of a landlord," it couldn't be called love or be considered respectable. But please don't mistakenly think that I'm arguing on behalf of the landlord class in order to appease some old grudge—my own grandparents were thrown into a river and drowned by "home-going" landlords seeking vengeance for lands confiscated before the Liberation, so I have no love lost for them. But I do think that class is a matter of status and interest and does not determine a person's morals or personality, or his ability to love. The goodness or badness of a person's character, the nobleness of his feelings, his integrity and sense of justice are not absolutely determined by what class he was born into.

Citing "concubines" to make an argument or using phrases like "our cadres, our commune members" and ominous-sounding words such as "our Party, our people" to put on an intimidating front is like displaying a sheep's head in the shop window but selling only dog meat. It's not being done for the "liberation of all humanity" as you say, but in order to incite prejudice and stir up political fervor. To persist in a politics based on discrimination is a shameless and cruel way to satisfy a few bloodthirsty souls. It's like trying to feed starving people with the ashes from a Buddhist temple.

Those who practice this type of politics of discrimination come to no good either. There is ample evidence of this in history, particularly in the experiences of people from all levels of society during the Cultural Revolution that have taught everyone painful lessons. Why should we forget the pain before the scars have healed? In recent years writers have been told to write less about the "scars." Is this suggestion intended to help people forget about the pain? I don't know if there is any logic to this, but I do know that if you want to avoid getting more scars, you've got to remember where the old ones came from. It won't help matters to "forget about the pain once the scars have healed," for dealing with them openly is still the best cure.

People today have learned from their scars and are much smarter for them. As the common folk like to say, "Once you've squatted in the outhouse, you know what color shit is." Literary critics are especially good at the game because politics in China has been so inextricably bound with the arts since the early twentieth century that the arts have become a small window into political trends. Despite the famed reputation of the "iron curtain," it's difficult to shut all the windows in one's own house. By closely examining small clues and hints, most people can guess what's going on, and nine times out of ten they're not too far off.

I'm writing you about this because I hope you will not tread that old path again. Although it is often said that a prodigal son who returns home is more precious than gold, do you really feel that two years ago you were "prodigal sons" but twenty years ago you were not just fools? You gave yourselves up as scapegoats and yet you still say of Mao, "After all he was a great leader." It's just like when Ah Q mistook the master's slap for a sign of affection and even relished the swelling it caused as a wish for good health and wealth. I don't want to see you trying to reason away your past mistakes or back away from the good things you're doing now and will do in the future. Of course, there are always bumps and grinds on the road to happiness, but wouldn't it be better to have just a few, or none at all?

I know that in my situation, I shouldn't be writing such things to you. At the very least, it won't do me any good to do so. But I am unable to stop myself; and even though you don't like to read such things, I still can't keep from writing them. It's not as if I were just feigning "concern for the nation and the people." At least I don't think you are all that bad; if I considered you to be as hopeless as the Gang of Four, then even if I weren't a lowly person whose words carried little weight, I wouldn't be talking to you like this—after all, even I realize it's foolish to scratch a tiger's ass. I hope that my words won't make you lose your self-control and explode in anger.

Just think them over calmly and then carefully consider whether there might be a grain of truth in some of my opinions.

Wei Jingsheng

February 27, 1982

Dear Lingling, Taotao, and Shanshan:

It's already the twenty-seventh and our visit still hasn't been arranged. It looks like our meeting this month might take place in name alone. I've heard that there have been a lot of other visitors lately, so there's nothing to be done. It's a good thing that I can still write twice a month, so let's use our letters to chat.

Since you don't like it when I talk about "national affairs" and I'm not supposed to discuss politics in my letters, I'll just write about culture and art and hope you won't object. Taotao and Shanshan are both very artistic, and even Lingling can bear with us while we talk about it for fun, although she may care more for other things, especially the movies. I'm not sure if she's the one who subscribed to those movie magazines you sent me or not, but I do remember how much she always liked the movies. I even remember how much she used to like that Pingju opera actress Xin Fengxia. Do you still have time for such luxuries, Lingling? Now that you've got a child, you're probably too busy. You ought to send her to nursery school soon. It's good for the child's development and will help you save time and energy. It makes me laugh to think that even though we are all adults now, we haven't really changed much since we were kids. But there are many times when I wish I were still the easygoing and carefree child I once was; adults' brains are terribly complex, or maybe it's better to say they're annoyingly complex, and much more vulgar, dull, and insincere than a child's. But this is all a natural consequence of the struggle for survival, so who's to blame?

When I saw the advocates for "intensifying art criticism" writing in the newspaper, I thought it a whole lot of nonsense. I've recently had the chance to see a few of the new artistic works on television and read about them in the magazines you've sent. Although, of course, they shouldn't even be discussed in the same breath as the rubbish produced twenty years ago, some of the works are still little more than fisheyes being passed off as pearls. Even a few of the "advocates" have called these works real hack jobs, mechanically produced. To get to the true root of the problem, though, it's not just that they "lack life," it's actually more like they lack artistic ability and show no sign of anything realistic at all. This goes to show that although the Gang of Four "line" has now been discarded, the pollutants their ideology created have yet to be cleared away completely and even continue to influence the thinking of comrades who thoroughly loathe the Gang of Four.

Perhaps my words are again too harsh, but I think that opening up criticism of the arts and analyzing such questions will do a great deal to help break down the ideological barriers blocking the path to democracy and reform. If we don't get rid of this feudal ideology, then democracy and a new civilized society will never succeed and will simply meander off course once again. The kind of criticism I am talking about, however, is not exactly the same as that which the "advocates" are calling for. They are frequently exhorting people to, on the one hand, carry out "self-criticism" in a "calm and peaceful" fashion, but on the other hand, they go on disregarding all reason in order to punish those whose opinions differ from their own. It's not true to say that they are just lashing out at random, for they certainly have ulterior motives and are more than capable of taking advantage of a given situation. It's my hope that today's critics will begin to really learn from both friends and foes alike and engage in heated and spirited debate while remaining honest and civil, and playing by the rules. In this way, not only will the arts develop, but social progress might avoid many possible setbacks, slowdowns, and regressions. The truth always becomes clearer the more it is debated, and besides, nobody can ever really claim absolute truth. The people are neither stupid nor blind, so what is the need for such critiques to remain "internal"? Public works of art should be critiqued publicly. The truth is, most of the self-proclaimed "experts" in many fields are no wiser than ordinary people.

I feel that the main problem with art today is the same problem that existed during the Gang of Four period: It's false and unrealistic, and too blatantly political; in short, it's "fake and shallow," as they say. The problem is actually not that serious, although it's still six of one and half a dozen of the other, and there hasn't been much real improvement in quality. An examination of the script to the movie *Lu You* shows that these problems are not negligible and we are not entirely out of the woods yet.

The biggest flaw with *Lu You* is that it is not very authentic and distorts historical fact as well as an historical figure. A true rebel against feudal Confucianism (although not a very successful one), Lu You is altered beyond recognition into a "fine young man" that any conservative old fogy could accept. These old fogies even got uncomfortable watching the quaint British television version of *Anna Karenina* and were only able to accept the Lu You script because it deliberately distorted history and replaced the real characters and historical events with more conventional impersonators in order to promote certain dubious customs of decorum. You can see how it is wrong for those who say that "art for art's sake" means you can completely disconnect art from reality.

What kind of a character is Lu You in the movie script? Simply put (but not necessarily completely accurately), he is a cross between a model Confucian gentleman and Romain Rolland's "mad artist" character, Jean Christophe. He's a strange creation who's got the countenance of a Jia Baoyu from *Dream of the Red Chamber* and the insanity of a Christophe. That's why the author didn't hesitate to tamper with the most enduring fact of the poet's life—Lu You's tragic love affair with Tang Wan. From what I have read in the annotated collections of Song dynasty poetry, the couple spurned the pressure of moral codes, their families, and society and lived together for many years. Finally, these pressures became too much and Tang Wan married a merchant and Lu You another woman. But to satisfy the tastes of these moralistic old fogies, the screenwriter took out this ancient love story. This in itself wasn't too moral an act, something even the moralistic scholars of old never dared to do. This shows that not only do people today no longer fear incurring the wrath of the ancients, but the screenwriter doesn't understand the poet's works or the other writings of the period.

Throughout his entire life, Lu You's mental outlook was colored by a strong defiance of feudal customs and mores. But the screenwriter heard only the word "mad" and took his image of a disturbed personality lifted from foreign novels he's read and mixed it together with a traditional Chinese gentleman to create the crossbreed who appears in the script. Actually, the blind worship of things foreign prevalent among young people today comes out clearly in the screenwriter's misunderstanding of the Christophean type. He created a distorted character by forcing the image he has onto that of the Chinese "famed mad genius," which he knows even less about, to produce a nondescript character. This type of error has become a common failure of historical novels and movies of the past few decades.

The "famous mad geniuses" like Lu You in ancient times were mad because feudal customs were simply too intolerable. It was more convenient to move about under the cloak of "madness" in order to resist these customs or to simply numb oneself to them. But they weren't really mad at all. They were acting this way for the benefit of others; it was more like a battle tactic or a suit of armor put on to protect oneself, and not a real illness. Lu You became this way because his personal experiences in love, politics, and national affairs produced in him a natural aversion to feudal customs and the corrupt habits of officialdom. But if he wanted to go on living comfortably in society, he could not simply confront these customs head-on and be a moral "backbone of China." Yet, the poet's natural love of humanity and life also kept him from easily accepting this state, so just as one gets drunk to ease one's troubles, so Lu You feigned madness and flaunted the rules of social decorum in order to relieve some of the dullness he felt, and to make an attack, however small it may have been, on feudal customs.

The fact that traditional China could be so dictatorial and at the same time pass down so many anti-feudal elements in its literary classics has a lot to do with literati intellectuals feigning madness in order to resist social mores, as well as an increasing aspiration and admiration for the "famed mad genius" style. It was no less than a Chinese struggle against feudalism undertaken by the intellectual class that was later echoed in working-class struggles against feudalism. It was these struggles that saved

Chinese civilization from being completely strangled by despotic tyrants and ensured the preservation of such a rich and magnificent traditional culture. This all confirms the depth, force, and enduring tradition of humanism in Chinese culture. Portraying a "famed mad genius" as a one-dimensional character who shows his resistance to feudalism with lines like "Mom, you just don't understand!" is about as tasteless as dried fish and shows a real misunderstanding of traditional Chinese culture.

Does this screenwriter understand the European "mad artist," then? No, he doesn't, for the mental state of the European "mad artist" has since the Renaissance actually been practically the same as that of the "famed mad genius" of traditional China. In order to resist vulgar social customs, the "mad artist" too has clothed himself in a coat of arms. Both the European and Chinese versions rose from the cultural and artistic arenas and their activities are more or less similar. It's just that Chinese people in the early twentieth century were biased and felt that foreigners were completely different from Chinese and thus began referring to "foreign devils" and "barbarians," concepts which later gave way to the theory of Chinese uniqueness. If we were to take off these tinted glasses and have a closer look, we would find that Chinese and foreigners are actually completely alike. Taking all the races of the world—from black skin and thick lips, to yellow hair and blue eyes, to flat nose and round face—into consideration, there is no exception, so what makes any one uniquely different? If it hadn't been so distorted out of proportion, we would see that the so-called "unique Chinese mentality" derived from nothing more than reactions to different times and environments. This doesn't, however, prove that a people are unique. And only by understanding this reasoning is it truly possible to understand the different mentalities people have in different historical periods and different countries. "Man's social being determines his consciousness"—it's a pity that people forget this so often. Actually, people often have similar reactions to similar environments, which is what Stalin meant when he said that things happen "independent of human will." I really admire these words and think this may be the one true thing that Stalin said in his entire life; it's no less true than Marx's old Jewish adage: "Suspect everything."

Taotao, do you still remember how the two of us acted back when we were staying in our ancestral hometown? I had grown disgusted with the false niceties and affectations of southerners and began self-consciously modeling myself after the "famed mad geniuses" of ancient China and abroad. I said that I didn't understand all the local rules of decorum and was more easygoing, so if people couldn't take it, then they shouldn't have anything to do with me. As a result, we ended up being the only members of the entire Wei family who went to gatherings empty-handed and left the same way. How much trouble this saved us! And it saved Cousin Jingren a lot of worry too! But not Papa. He spent several hundred yuan each time he went home and he still ended up with a reputation for "transforming social traditions," so he would have been better off not spending anything at all.

You and I were the ones doing the real transforming and the more word of our behavior got around, the more legendary we became in the village. Add to this your talent for sweet talk and my own ability to wag my tongue and persuade others, and I figure the impression the two of us left on the villagers was really that of "mad geniuses." I heard that up until 1979 we were still a popular topic of conversation at local gatherings, probably for this very reason. But what do you think made the two of us "mad"? We weren't really mad at the time but were actually more clearheaded than all of those people who were doing the "Mao loyalty dance" and plastering photos of Mao all over the place. People label things that they can't understand or that make them uncomfortable to talk about "mad." In hindsight, the fact that during that period of "class struggle craze" you and I were able to stand up at gatherings in front of everyone and openly rattle on about the scandals of Jiang Qing and others without getting in trouble was because the villagers thought of us as "mad geniuses." How we benefited from that image! If it weren't for that, I wouldn't have had to wait until now to be branded a "counterrevolutionary"!

People were honest in their relationships with us. Even those people who didn't have any family blood ties with us became close friends just because we used the tactic of the "mad genius" to peel off the customary polite shell that masked our own and others' spirits, and allowed everyone to open up to us. The fact that the

principal of the Wang Family School who had once been labeled a
Rightist and one other guy that you don't know—the former hospital head who was labeled a Rightist and transferred to Jiang-
xinzhou, where I met him—were both willing to associate with us
and accepted all of our nonsense without worrying about getting in
trouble was also thanks to our "mad genius" armor. I will never
forget the doctor in particular. He himself was a model "mad
genius"—shabby clothing, wild hair, barefoot, and with a delirious
laugh. People often said that he came and went without a trace like
a ghost spirit; the only problem with this being that if you needed
him in an emergency, he was hard to find. But he and I were like
old friends at first sight and got along well right away. He came to
see me every day as regularly as only a trained soldier or doctor
could. (He actually had fought in North Korea and received a cita-
tion of merit.) But when he made his wife go out and we took refuge
in his shabby little grass hut to discuss and critique things, he
turned out to be a keen observer of people and a deep thinker.
The intensity with which he analyzed things wasn't informed by the
slightest bit of "madness"; on the contrary, he was more like a
crafty old fox. Of course, I mean this in the positive sense of the
phrase. He is one of the really close friends I've had in my life.

When I left the town, he accompanied me all the way to the
river's edge—a forty-year-old man with a scraggly beard covering
his face. Even I got pretty choked up because we both knew that
we would probably never see each other again. At the time, the
Li Bai poem "For Wang Lun" floated to mind. I bet if we had
told people we were making a film about the Tang dynasty and said
that I was Li Bai and he was Wang Lun, everyone would have
believed it. Our emotions were no less than when Wang Lun saw
off Li Bai, and it just so happened that I too was leaving on a boat
on the river—me with my round, pale face and he with his full
beard. It's too bad that people today are so stiff and no longer have
the spirit to break into song or present a poem when seeing
someone off.

But let me stop here before this gets any longer. If you have any
disagreements or find fault with any of my views or arguments, then
please write back and challenge me; there's no need to be polite. I
don't have any reference books here at hand, so I'm sure I've made

some mistakes. If you write back with a vigorous critique, it might help me break out of my apathetic mood and would be good for my health as well. You shouldn't miss such a great opportunity to kill two birds with one stone!

Say hello to everyone!

Your brother,
Jingsheng

NOTE: On April fifth, I was told that this letter would not be mailed out.

March 16, 1982

Dear Prison Warden Xing:

There are several small matters that I probably shouldn't bother you with, but it seems that I must. I'm not entirely to blame for these and there's no real need for blame at all, but things are already such that I still had better discuss them with you.

I haven't been sleeping well for quite some time now. There are several reasons for this, but the main thing preventing me from getting a sound night's sleep is the light that shines in my eyes all night long. My principle is: If I can make do, then I won't bother the people who work here. I know that work of any kind is not easy, and all jobs have their difficulties. That's why I went ahead and fashioned the aluminum foil from a few packs of cigarettes into a shade in order to block some of the bright light that is reflecting off the ceiling and into my eyes.

Who would have known that not only was this prohibited, but when I tried to explain that it wasn't interfering with the brigade leader's work, I was told that as I didn't "listen to reason," there was no need for them to be reasonable; they even joked about my age. This left me at a complete loss. I feel that even in prisons today, all actions should be explained. Saying there is "no need to explain" to those who don't understand your reasons, and explaining things only to those who do, is a bit unreasonable in itself, wouldn't you say?

I would like to request that you pay some attention to this matter. It's not that the others' words are so unbearable—everyone in prison has learned to listen, after all—but because they can't always say things so directly. I've thought about writing you before this because my health and spirit can no longer take the prolonged lack of sleep and the depression I feel from staying in this tiny cell and never seeing the light of day. I heard that when Wang Guangmei was in prison (not here, of course) she lost her mind for the same reasons. Although this has been openly denied by some, I still believe the "rumors" coming from people close to her are more reliable than the lying newspapers. Besides, there is no longer any reason to cover up for actions taken by the Gang of Four. Things are much different now and I don't want to be the first to follow in Wang Guangmei's footsteps, no matter what. I don't feel that asking to have the light turned off at night and going outside for some sun and exercise now and then with the brigade leader's permission can be considered unreasonable requests.

As far as I can tell, filling such requests does not constitute "special treatment" here. In the cell next to mine and all the others I can see outside my door and window, the lights are off at night. Besides, I haven't gotten into any fights and I'm not plotting an escape, so isn't the fact that I have been locked up in the strict-regime brigade for so long "special" treatment enough? I asked unsuccessfully to be dealt with in the same manner as political prisoners connected to the Gang of Four, but I was sent here just the same. Why, then, can't I at least be treated like an ordinary political prisoner? I don't understand why I should receive special punishment, for even if there is someone who is abusing public power to retaliate against me, no enmity exists between you and me, so can't we find a way to talk this over? If this is not something controlled by the higher-ups, then I would like to ask you, Secretary Zhao, Political Instructor Chen, and Brigade Leader Zhao to contemplate my request in a timely fashion. I also hope that this request will not interfere with my family visits, because today, for some unknown reason, I was not allowed to see them.

Wei Jingsheng

March 21, 1982

Dear Lingling, Taotao, and Shanshan:

Our visit this month was so rushed that we didn't get a chance to finish discussing a few matters, two in particular.

The first concerns Ping Ni. I wrote you about this once already in a letter that was confiscated. First of all, we must consider this matter from a political perspective. It wasn't easy for her father to get his job back, and if it hadn't been for the downfall of the Gang of Four and the implementation of so many new policies, it would have been difficult for him to get out of prison, let alone return to political life. Their family has suffered for many years, and now they should be allowed to live, work, and study in relative peace. They can't make up for the past, but they should at least be able to have the same chance for happiness now as others do. Her father should also take this opportunity to realize his own political aspirations. I have no right to let the unlucky cloud that hangs over my head cover her entire family as well. You ought to realize that a family with a political background like hers could face unforeseen problems for having ties with me. This is quite different from your situation, as you are involved only in ordinary work; you simply can't judge them in the same way.

Second, from a personal perspective, she's already twenty-eight or twenty-nine and not that young anymore. Why should I make her wait for me until she's an old lady? The thought alone makes me feel uncomfortable and I don't want the added mental burden. I already discussed this with her when I was preparing to go to prison and even though she said she wanted to wait for me, I never felt that it was the right thing to do or that it was good for either one of us. It would be better if we made a clean break and parted unattached. This is what I wanted to speak to her about face-to-face when I requested permission for her to visit. She doesn't always see things in perspective.

As far as feelings go, we were together for so many years that, of course, I could never deny having them. But feelings change as well; they are, in Engels's words, "constantly renewing." People should not hide themselves behind a tree or sacrifice their own chance at real happiness for the sake of feelings that are dead or in cold storage. Poets always love to write of the most intense feelings as if there is no possibility of happiness without them. But that's not true. Of course, the most intense feelings are the best, but in general there are only moderately intense feelings and just because they aren't the best, we shouldn't write them all off as bad. It's better to be aware that feelings can sometimes lead one down a dead end so as to avoid taking that path. This way there's no chance of casually renewing your feelings or having feelings that linger on. This is not only appropriate for lovers and friends but also for close comrades, because in all relationships between individuals, feelings are always living, changing, and renewing themselves; there is no such thing as feelings that never change.

You and I are siblings, so beyond feelings we have an inextricable bond and you have no choice but to share in my "achievements." But she is different. She can and should extricate herself from this relationship and search for happiness. At the very least, our feelings for each other have in a concrete sense already been severed from both sides, so why not make a complete break? If you see her, you can pass on my wishes to her and tell her she doesn't need to come anymore. I wrote a poem entitled "Encouragement" and some parting words for her, but unfortunately they were confiscated with the last letter. Please tell her to study hard and to overcome her bad habit of always paying too much attention to the past and the future instead of seizing the present. Tell her to help her father do meaningful and good things for the Tibetan people as well as for the people of China and the world. Wish her happiness.

The second matter I want to discuss concerns what you call my "scientific fantasies." You are mistaken; I'm not doing these things to try to "reduce my sentence." Whether that is even possible or not is something I've never even considered. If it's too much trouble for you, I can always present my scientific projects directly to the prison authorities and not bother you to help me find channels to bring them to fruition. The truth is, all of these fantasies and plans began long before I had the slightest inkling that I would be a "counterrevolutionary" languishing away in prison. The earliest ones would be the windmill, the turbine engine, and the flying machine. These were the "topics" that I began thinking about way back when I was a student with no interest in politics. At that time I had already thought of using a current converter recycling mechanism to improve work efficiency, but I hadn't figured out exactly how to do it. Finally I came up with the idea of a "reverse axle," and I first began to fully understand such questions. When my living and eating conditions here improve and I get my energy back, I'll be able to overcome the last hurdles and complete this project.

All my theories on aerodynamics are the result of past thinking as well. Solar energy is something I started contemplating when I was still in the army and have continued thinking about since I was demobilized. After noting the ample sunshine and rivers in northern China and the terribly impoverished lives of the peasants there, I began thinking about ways to harness solar and hydraulic power. When I got out of the army, I gave up the chance for more exotic work and chose to be an electrician because I had fantasies that I could make some contribution to research in this area. But, of course, the reality wasn't quite as beautiful as the fantasy. Half of the beauty of human life is fantasy; reality is never quite as pretty—sort of like the news photos on television.

I came up with the idea for the "spring-activated hoof-style wheel cart" while I was still working with horses in the countryside, so I guess it is one of my earliest inventions. The latest ones are the "vortex gas separator," the "vortex gas separator liquefier," the "vortex coal gasification furnace," and various types of "parachute wind harnessing devices" such as the "parachute kite." I thought about these last two types of inventions for several years after I got out of the army and came up with the basic plans for them while I was in Cell Forty-four at Banbuqiao and then here. As you can see, not a single one has anything to do with "putting on a show" to get my sentence reduced or, as you suggest, "building castles in the sand" that I shouldn't waste my time and energy thinking about.

I spend my time and energy, as well as my money, on books, in order that I might do something to benefit human life and happiness, but it's also because I have a curious mind. When I was in school I wasn't so clear about what I wanted to do with my life, but I was curious and everybody around me said that young people should have some purpose. What exactly my purpose was wasn't too clear either, but I did have some vague notion. I remember how, when I was in middle school, I read in *Reference News* that some young boys in the United States had launched a small rocket and sent several white mice dozens of kilometers into the sky. My friends and I talked about catching up to and outdoing them, and that's when I began to study aerodynamics. Unfortunately, Lingling threw out all the books and plans I bought back then. I walked home rather than taking the bus and even gave up my bad habit of snacking—a habit I still have—in order to buy those books. Of course, nobody supported our plan and it was never completed despite the money we saved for two years. We only managed to buy a few little things like books and some crucibles and beakers. Even our teachers and parents said that we were "reaching for stars" and not following the "proper track." But I still believe that if nobody tried to "reach for stars" and everyone stayed only on the "proper track," then we'd all still be back gathering wild berries and walking around naked with no more than prophetic visions of wearing tanned animal hides. Because, for primitive man, gathering wild berries was the "right track" while hanging a hide over a flame to tan was "reaching for stars." What we might consider to be "reaching for stars" today could turn out to be the "right track" of the future.

The vague notions I had in my student days turned into the clear goals I have now only after I lived in the countryside and was in the army. I realized that, for peasants without a morsel to eat or a stitch to wear, sending rockets and satellites into the sky was more harm than good, so I turned my thinking from rockets to windmills, hydraulic energy, cars, and so on. My goal is to give people access to better tools and energy sources. This is one of the fundamental ways for us to relieve poverty and harness our natural resources.

Of course, there were many problems in the beginning and I just followed behind everyone else. The only thing that I managed to accomplish is my present condition, and that is far from "complete" either. But as there will still be problems in the future, when you send my ideas to some places that might develop them, it would be best if you used one of your own names, not mine. At least you might avoid a lot of unnecessary political interference and allow these things to help people sooner. The amount of political interference in modern Chinese history is appalling. I heard that Wang Hongwen postponed the announcement of the Tangshan earthquake for a dozen crucial hours because it "interfered with the criticism of Deng Xiaoping"—I guess those tens of thousands of corpses weren't worth postponing it for! Even death is too good for people who did things like this in the past, and yet the possibility of them happening again still exists.

There are some people who might be scared off by my name. Unfortunately, there's no way to get around this, so it's better to use one of yours. These projects are all too ambitious and there are a lot of problems; I'm aware of this. I ask only that you take the matter to heart and not be afraid to make inquiries and sound things out. Maybe there is some possibility for them. Shanshan, please take the plans for the "energy-saving pressure cooker with timer" that I gave you last time and the "wind-resistant lighter" that I will give you this time to somebody at your publishing company. Perhaps with some editing they could be submitted in a small invention contest and might even succeed. Don't worry that they are small and not "sophisticated" enough, because they could make everyday life more convenient and economical for people. But don't forget to put your name on them; "model youth" and "counterrevolutionary" don't exactly go well together!

Jingsheng

As part of his "reeducation," prison officials periodically asked Wei Jingsheng to read and comment on articles published in the People's Daily, the official mouthpiece of the Communist Party. Instead of writing the formulaic responses expected of him, however, Wei used these opportunities to organize and express his political ideas. In the statement below, Wei offers his "opinions" on the 1982 draft revision of China's Constitution regarding the rule of law, political restructuring, and the causes of the Cultural Revolution.

May 6, 1982

My Opinions on the "Draft Revision of the Constitution":

All the citizens of the country are currently engaged in a discussion of the nation's Constitution. Before the May Day holiday, I had a talk with Prison Warden Sun in which we touched upon the draft Constitution, but I didn't discuss my ideas fully. I basically only commented on its good points and did not point out its shortcomings. To give one's opinions on the revisions of the Constitution means to correct its shortcomings, not just to lavish praise. Songs of praise on a matter of this kind, other than providing the singer an opportunity for flattery, have very little benefit for anyone else. Therefore, I intend to omit my opinions on the strengths of the draft Constitution and discuss only the parts I find inadequate and inappropriate. I say this in order to avoid any misunderstanding. Warden Sun asked that I take myself into consideration and his concern for me was obvious in his remarks. I feel that, for a Chinese citizen, to care about national affairs is to care about oneself and others, and that this is both a right and an unshirkable duty of every citizen. I would, therefore, like to fulfill my duty. My opinions are in four main parts and I will discuss them accordingly.

1. *Description of the state system must be comprehensive, clear, and precise.*

All laws and regulations stem from the Constitution, and all clauses contained in the Constitution are determined by the clauses concerning the state system. The accuracy of these clauses has enormous consequences.

Our country is a people's republic—a fact expressed even in its name. In our country, therefore, the people are the mainstay of the nation. This is the fundamental definition of any democracy. A society wherein the people are the mainstay of the country is also following the original aim of socialism. On a theoretical level, then, the implications of both democracy and socialism are essentially the same; the only difference is semantic. But when such expressions are employed in a document like the Constitution, they are being used imprecisely.

The concept of "socialism" has been used so indiscriminately by people that it almost takes on different meanings—sometimes ones that are completely at odds with each other—depending on who is using it. A dictionary devoted solely to the meanings of the term "socialism" would be no thin book. Lately, even the self-styled "masters of socialism" have begun admitting that "socialism still needs perfecting." Expanding the usage of this term to the realms of politics, economics, and even ethics generates even broader definitions of the concept, turning it into an ambiguous notion encompassing too many contradictions and meanings. Using such a notion to convey the nature of state sovereignty and to express the legal character of the state system makes it not only likely but inevitable that misunderstanding, confusion, and distortion will occur frequently. Impreciseness of this kind also opens many doors for those who want to distort and tamper with it. All one need do is take hold of power, don a "socialist" overcoat, and everything is legitimized. Thereby, this impreciseness makes the state system unstable by nature, and in the long run increases the possibilities for danger and turmoil.

There are always power-hungry people in any age and the Constitution should be a lasting assurance against their greed and designs on state power. In this regard, society cannot trust anyone too easily and must not entrust the most fundamental power to any person without having certain safeguards in place. Nor can society rely solely on the judgment of particular individuals; it can have faith only in its own judgment. Therefore, the Constitution must formulate the state system clearly, completely, and precisely so that the entire citizenship has the ability to monitor the persons they entrust to exercise their authority. The history of our country makes this an all the more serious question. It is possible for the Chinese language to be written much more precisely, so why say things in such a roundabout way? Establishing the people as the masters of society is to realize the true essence of socialism. Why must the Constitution establish "socialism"—a word with so many interpretations—in such an elevated position? Is that because you're not satisfied with the practice of socialism, but only eager to fetishize the name? I myself approve of socialism and have always hung out its signboard, so it goes without saying that I am not opposed to others doing the same. But things have become so serious that those who claim the label are not really all socialists. True socialists seek guarantees only for the interests of the people, not for the privilege of their own beliefs.

The concept of "the people" is used very adequately in the realms of political theory, academic discussion, and elsewhere, so much so that it has no replacement. This is because in these arenas it is being used to express a range of meanings rather than to demarcate a definite boundary. In the arena of law, however, it must be used precisely in order to include and determine the position of every single individual. The term "the people," therefore, is insufficient for this purpose. If it is to be used, it must be clearly defined as a legal term with a very precise meaning in this specific context. Instead, I propose using "all citizens of China" or "all residents of the Chinese territory as well as all immigrants holding Chinese citizenship" or some very precise wording to explain the concept of "the people," or to replace its use in the Constitution altogether in order to make the concept fixed and accurate and leave no room for distortion. Of course, there are still other ways of expressing it even more precisely. I am merely offering some examples.

I also feel that the use of the wording in the draft Constitution of "led by the working class, and based on the alliance of the workers and peasants" is inappropriate. In a democracy, the basic right of all citizens is the right to lead in all aspects of society. This right to lead can be divided among three larger powers—legislative, executive, and judicial—that are entrusted to appropriate representatives selected by the people at regular intervals. But the main power remains in the hands of the people; those entrusted with power never possess complete authority over everything, otherwise they are usurpers. Therefore, this basic right to lead society is held equally by all citizens, and no citizen or class should possess special privileges over others. A social system in which any class or social group holds special "leadership authority" is nothing more than a feudal dictatorship or a variant of it. This is an essential distinction from a democratic social system in which all the citizens enjoy equal basic rights.

A dictatorial social system in which a single class enjoys special privilege is certainly no guarantee that the rights of the working class will be protected either. Just look at "socialist nations" such as the Soviet Union, Eastern European countries, or our own country, that continue waving a banner that the "working class and the proletariat lead everything." But does the working class in these countries enjoy even the equal rights that citizens of a democracy do? Let alone any special privileges? This lesson of both history and reality clearly explains Marx's famous thesis that the proletarian must emancipate not only itself but all mankind, for only then will it be able to achieve true emancipation.

If a country is "based on the alliance of the workers and peasants," does this mean that no other classes take part? If the country protects the interests of certain people and requires these people to support the country's existence, then these people are *all* the basis of the nation. A democratic people's republic is a nation of all the people, and it protects the interests of all the people and has the support of all the people; therefore all the people of the nation are the basis of a people's republic. Doesn't the above statement imply that the People's Republic of China only represents and protects the will and interests of this "basis" and fails to represent or protect the will and interests of its other citizens? What are the equal rights and responsibilities of the citizenship? Must not citizens of other classes also carry out the task of protecting and supporting the existence of the nation? The people of a country who must perform duties but have no power are serfs or slaves, and not real citizens.

2. *The specific content of particular political lines and policies undertaken at specific times always bears the imprint of the political*

terminology specific to a given system of thought; therefore it is
better off not written into the Constitution.

The reasoning behind this item is extremely simple and obvious;
even the autocratic emperors of ancient China understood the truth
in maxims such as "Laws of an earlier dynasty need not be continued in the next," and "Do not be partial to the doctrines of one
school of thought," and "Establish a government for all under
heaven, not for one clan alone," and so on. But in recent years only
lies, boasts, and falsehoods have been the rage, as if all foreign
wisdom has never been learned, and the teachings of our Chinese
ancestors has been lost completely as well. It's as though even a
document as serious as the Constitution is incomplete without a
few words of contemporary jargon thrown in. By doing this, the
Constitution turns into little more than a collection of choice
examples of current popular language, and will be short-lived. Just
take a look at the three constitutions promulgated during the last
thirty years—their brief life spans are in direct proportion to their
political trendiness. If you take into consideration that the Constitutions of 1954 and later existed in name alone, then you realize
that the life of a constitution was shorter than that of a textbook,
and the constitution formulated when a child entered high school
would be replaced by a new one by the time he graduated. This is
really too frivolous.

There are many reasons for the short life span of a constitution.
During the dictatorial political atmosphere of the past, the constant
reshuffling of upper-level leadership was the primary reason. The
detailed inclusion of specific political lines and particular policies
of a certain period is another reason. Each time the line or policy
changed (or was improved) it was necessary for the Constitution to
undergo revisions as well. Political lines and policies are constantly being changed (or improved), so that with every change, the
remnants left behind in the Constitution become a hindrance to the
revision of the political line and policy development. A constitution is never as powerful as people, so in order to cater to people's
interests it is best to discard it; but after being scrapped two or
three times, the reputation of the constitution is scrapped too, and
people begin to say it is "no more than a piece of waste paper." The

scope and direction of change in the verbal expressions of what is called the "Marxist" system of thought are especially difficult to predict, and might be revised several times in one year. A constitution pieced together with such expressions loses its fundamental solemnity.

The Constitution regulates the basic relationship between the country and its citizens, delineates the country's and society's basic political structures, and determines by legal means the enduring rights and responsibilities of the most important and basic relationships between individuals in that society; it is like a permanently binding contract between two people. This, of course, is simply a metaphor. But specific political lines and fixed policies are means of continually advancing that contract and obtaining benefits for all by undertaking concrete management and technical methods. These two things need to be kept separate. If you tie flexible and changing political lines to permanent basic structures, rights, and duties, then when society faces changed realities or newly discovered strengths or weaknesses, it will be too restricted and won't be able to alter its original structures to obtain more benefits or correct unexpected shortcomings.

Politicians and thinkers have the bad habit (I am no exception to this rule, even though I am not qualified to be either) of always believing that their ideas and principles are the "absolute truth" and should be passed down unaltered for generations. Therefore, they always attempt to place their ideas in a position of supremacy. But no mode of thought can ever be supreme, or there would be no need for further development.

Have our people not suffered from meaningless domestic struggles over such matters for long enough? Even if leaders want nothing more than to gain empty reputations for themselves and their ideologies, it is still not worth the trouble. They would be much better off doing something more productive. I've yet to hear of an ideology having a reputation that lasted generations, but have only heard of individuals who have made contributions beneficial to the people whose reputations have gone down in history. If an ideology is to last generations, it must constantly develop itself and continually make contributions toward the people's well-being.

Fettering an ideology that once had the potential to make a contribution to society by placing it on an insurmountable pedestal only helps it to go down in infamy and drag everyone else down suffering along with it.

3. *Legislative structures should be comprehensive and executive mechanisms streamlined.*

There are some people who object to the endless discussion without resolution that takes place in legislative bodies in the West. They prefer the decisiveness of the absolute powers of the emperor. Therefore they try to keep legislative bodies as streamlined as possible so that they can make policy decisions quickly and decisively like emperors once did. In these people's view, executive powers in democratic countries are frequently held back by this "endless discussion without resolution," therefore legislative bodies that can unanimously "wave through" any motions are the most ideal "streamlined legislature." But an overly streamlined legislative mechanism often leads to flawed policy decisions. Because people are unaware that the flaws are due to hastily enacted legislation, such mistakes are too often blamed on excessive executive power or a problem with the executive officials themselves. There are some who devise ways to divide executive power in order to break up the authority of the executive bodies, for they think that if brilliant men like themselves restrain the power of the executive, then all mistakes can be avoided. Hence an irrational and divided situation such as we have now is created, where policy decisions and legislation are carried out hastily and imprudently, while the executive bodies are so bogged down with restraints that it is difficult for them to be effective.

The discussion without resolution that takes place in Western legislative bodies is not a bad thing; in fact, it is a very good thing. Only after comprehensive discussion can legislative policy decisions be made as carefully as possible. When policy decisions are discussed, the pros and cons and all potential repercussions must be fully considered, and as many interests as possible be taken into account. This is because all policy decisions should be "overly prudent" in character. When it's momentarily impossible to fully consider all the advantages and disadvantages and all the possible interests involved, indecisive discussion is still safer than carrying out matters too hastily. Legislative bodies that are too decisive and hurried can frequently produce mistaken decisions, and can also foster dictatorial executive powers that have the potential to cause all kinds of evil—a repercussion that spells no good for either society or the nation. Precisely because of this, representative institutions in democratic countries are comprehensive yet still considered inadequate and therefore spawn many nongovernmental institutions, such as "advisory bodies," "quasi-representative groups," "monitoring councils," and the like, to supplement the legitimate legislative bodies in order that policy decisions are made even more prudently and comprehensively.

Executive power should be the opposite. It should be characterized by swift and firm implementation of policy decisions without allowing for any dispute. Too many overlapping executive mechanisms disperse authority so that those responsible for taking care of certain matters do not have adequate authority to act swiftly and effectively in the best interest of society.

Can executive powers foster dictatorship? Let us look at examples from abroad. The power of the presidency of the United States is quite concentrated—it probably has even broader powers than any Chinese emperor ever did. Yet it would be next to impossible for someone to climb into the seat of the U.S. presidency and impose a dictatorship. This is because no matter how great the office's powers are and how much freedom to take action it has, the president's power must constantly meet with the approval of the entire citizenship. In addition, his actions are always monitored by representative organs specifically assigned to do so and which are independent. There can always be mistakes, this is natural, but any intentional dereliction of duty or overstepping of the limits of presidential powers is prohibited. And it goes without saying that this is true of a usurpation of dictatorial powers as well.

Based on the principles of what I have said above concerning legislative bodies being comprehensive and executive mechanisms being streamlined, I feel that the legislative mechanism in our country is too simple. Its authority to examine and carry out policy-making decisions and to monitor executive power and even voice opinion and criticism is too small. There is simply no way for it to function as a genuine legislative instrument, let alone act to limit or veto executive power. If you want to know on what grounds I say this, the reality of our country from its inception until now is the most powerful evidence. Since the founding of the People's Republic of China thirty years ago, there has never been a decree, no matter how commonplace, that has not originated from the Communist Party or the executive powers. In thirty years, the main legislative body has never overruled executive authority or made a proposal for society's benefit independent of the executive. In fact we've never even seen it undertake any form of disagreement, and where there is no disagreement, there is no discussion; and a legislative body that does not discuss policy decisions is nothing more than an institution in name alone. How, then, can such a legislative body carry out its duty and fulfill its responsibility to the people? Hence the country does not run as it should and any person who grabs hold of executive powers can arbitrarily violate the popular will of the people's republic. This is the most important lesson our country has learned over the past decades.

I propose that, in addition to the Standing Committee of the National People's Congress, there be established at least one other legislative body with equal powers that are no less than that possessed by legislative assemblies in the West. The most ideal situation would be if, after analyzing the experiences of democracies in the West, in addition to the Standing Committee of the National People's Congress, which is a house of representatives with seats allotted by population, we should establish another institution in which seats are based on provincial administrative districts, in order to form a senate in substance. If we decide national policies according to population density alone, then the special interests of particular areas would frequently be overlooked. The country must do its utmost to show consideration for the interests and will of all parts of society and not simply submit the minority to the will of the majority.

The basic character of a country's political system should be to mediate, neutralize, and balance all different opinions and interests; the minority should not have to submit to the majority in ordinary matters unless under special circumstances when no compromise can be reached. The meaning of democracy is not majority rule over the minority. Indiscriminate abuse of majority rule only leads to social disunity and the widening of divisions already in existence.

In addition, the interests of different elements of society, the opinions of various parties and factions, and even the concerns of different occupations (such as industry, agriculture, commerce, military, cultural, education, and so on) should be considered more fairly. Therefore, besides the representative bodies based on region and population, our country's unique Political Consultative Conference should be considered as a third body possessing a higher legal status than the grassroots private, consultative organizations. This would be distinct from a typical technical advisory board, as it would play a more comprehensive advisory function representing all sectors and discussion would therefore be different from that which takes place in the legislative bodies. This body might have a slightly more limited jurisdiction and exist more as a "consultant" to the main legislative bodies.

Finally, state planning should not set strict quotas for business, nor should the government assign people to directly manage business. By adequately monitoring and charting development trends and industrial activities, as well as changes in the market, government should play only a guiding role in coordinating business relations. This will require development of the government's role as a mechanism for distribution, as a promoter of research and as a monetary regulator. In other words, the relationship between the current overbearing government and the subordinate commercial world should be reversed, and government should serve the interests of business, not the other way around. Political authority can represent the will of the people and control the social and economic atmosphere, but it need not directly manage business. Business serves society through the market, not through the government, and when the government tries to control the economy, it controls the market. When the government interferes in business, it fails on both the governmental and economic fronts.

4. The military should not have independent authority, otherwise it can endanger the country and the people.

The "Draft Constitution" raises the Standing Committee for Military Affairs to an independent status equal to the chairman and the State Council, and directly under the jurisdiction of the Standing Committee of the National People's Congress. I feel this is inappropriate. At a time when there is no war, the management of the standing army is an executive matter. As the nature of executive power is actually different from that of the legislative body, the legislative body cannot manage and command the army. But, as Sunzi's *Art of War* explains, once a general is engaged in battle, "There are commands from the ruler that are not accepted." What this is actually pointing out is that the nature and requisite character of military affairs are very different from legislative and executive affairs, and they should not interfere with each other. Therefore the management of military affairs should follow the great tradition of "civil officials shouldn't act as soldiers, the military shouldn't participate in government." This can avoid interference between the civil and military, and avoid the impetus for military leaders with different political views from carrying out military coups.

It is no small matter whether a legal system and social ideology follows the prescription that the "military shouldn't participate in government." It is actually one of the decisive factors in determining whether or not the military has the potential to interfere in domestic politics. Without the custom of military noninterference in government, when internal political discord reaches a dangerous point people will naturally first turn to force to settle domestic political matters. Even if they don't stage a full-scale military coup, using the military to decide political affairs is already a blurring of right and wrong and has a harmful effect on the country and the people. There will always be conflict and dispute in politics, and if you want to ensure national security, you must have armed forces; but military actions are not always the most reasonable actions; therefore, separating military affairs and domestic politics is one of the most important means of preserving the health of domestic affairs. It is also crucial to the establishment of democracy and rule of law. The mentality of "violence solves everything" is a direct threat to democracy.

In recent years, our country has nearly abandoned the old custom of "the military should not participate in government," and recent political struggles in our country have even resulted in military coups. In 1966, when Mao Zedong launched the overthrow of Liu Shaoqi and undertook an individual dictatorial movement, would he have dared to have done so without the support of Lin Biao, who then controlled the military, or without eventually transferring all military power into his own hands? Or to put it another way, would leading-level cadres like Liu Shaoqi and Deng Xiaoping all have acknowledged his superiority? Why were his illegal activities so easily accepted by people? Why, when a political movement started, did he immediately use the army to take over control of the schools and all levels of political institutions? In reality, this was a successful military coup. But his technique was more brilliant than those of other bare-fisted "third world" military governments and he clothed his military coup in a political movement and incited the fanaticism of the masses who were unaware of the facts. Such a smooth seam did he sew that by his not calling it a military coup, most people failed to recognize it as such.

The three main reasons why a phenomenon of this type was able to occur are: (1) Politics were not democratic. As a result, people could not exert their will to influence the political tide before the event, and after the event they could not overturn the actions that had violated their rights, nor did they have any means of upholding fairness, justice, and truth. The people were in a powerless position, and even politicians had no safeguards. The lack of safety was much more serious than anything that mere hoodlums or thieves could create. (2) Politics were not open and were only conducted by a handful of people who claimed they "fully represented all the people." When the accounts of these people differed, people could only believe whoever was in a greater position of authority. This allowed those in authority to generate an atmosphere in which the truth could be twisted to incite the masses. When politics are not open, this creates fertile ground for dictatorship and even those accomplices who helped to deceive the masses will sooner or later get a taste of their own bitter medicine. (3) The military habitually participated in politics, but military officers didn't know the rights

and wrongs of politics as well as politicians. Add to this the deception created by a lack of open politics and the way military leaders
were used as political tools of the commanding officer to break
down political life and establish a dictatorship. Using deceptive
and unreasonable violence to oppose a handful of rulers who were
never democratic in the first place and therefore never had the
support of the people is like using a rock to break an egg—a
guaranteed victory.

Therefore, I suggest first that the Constitution state that the military must not participate in domestic politics, and military personnel must not participate in political parties, and special actions
wherein the military is called on to quell domestic armed rebellion
must be approved of by an absolute majority (a two-thirds or three-
quarters majority) of the National People's Congress; and finally,
military officers cannot hold offices in any legislative, executive, or
judicial government offices in any locale. Domestic public security
should be the responsibility of the security mechanisms and institutions under the jurisdictions of the president and provincial
leaders. The military must not act in the name of maintaining
public security as a way of directly interfering in politics and
depriving citizens of their rights. They must not declare direct
military takeovers and all emergency situations should be handled
by an equal coalition of the legislative, executive, and judicial
institutions and by the people directly; the military should have no
authority to control any agency outside of the military. Only after a
vote in the legislative body is passed can the armed forces assist
the government in handling a crisis; neither the judicial nor executive bodies have the authority to call for military assistance. The
purpose of the military is to resist foreign invasion; it has no right
to suppress the people.

My discussion of these four points is still very superficial and not
necessarily completely correct, but I've already gone on for far too
long. I would have liked to be a bit more concise, but these points
are very different from those commonly discussed in the newspapers, so I'm afraid if I don't go into some detail, others might
have a hard time understanding. Nevertheless, I am afraid it will

be difficult to avoid misunderstanding and misrepresentation. But I have little talent or education, and I've done my best, what more can I do? There are many people in China with knowledge and the ability to think, so if everyone felt a sense of "we all bear responsibility for the success and failure of the nation," and researched and discussed these questions together, then I believe the "Draft Revision of the Constitution" could be revised even better and we could produce a Constitution that will bring happiness, not evil, to this and future generations.

Wei Jingsheng

June 30, 1982

Dear Prison Warden Sun, Secretary Zhao, Political Instructor Chen, and Brigade Leader Zhao:

Quite a few things have happened recently, so I'm going to spit them all out at once for the sake of speed. I've said before that I don't want to make any trouble, and no matter whether you believe me or not, let me reiterate it one more time. I've always felt that most problems can best be solved through discussion, but there are times when this is not always the easiest way. Sometimes it can be useless and frustrating, and difficult to pursue. Can you accuse me of being impatient? Can you call me unreasonable?

The first matter concerns the television. I recall that Political Instructor Chen and Brigade Leader Zhao attended to this matter last year and with the approval of the "upper-level leaders" told me: From now on whenever the trusties watch television, you can watch along with them. I was, of course, very satisfied with this and was grateful for the concern and understanding of all involved, and had no additional opinions on the matter. For a period of time this decision was carried out very smoothly. I sat behind everyone and watched along with them, enjoying a lot of cultural programs and learning many useful things—there was no problem whatsoever. But then, I can't remember from exactly when, the trusties started prohibiting me from joining them at times and eventually the "permanent resident" prisoners stopped letting me watch altogether. After languishing away in a tiny cell from morning till night, being able to watch a bit of television now and then takes on a special importance that you, who live with your families and in society, would be unable to fully comprehend. Naturally, I tried to feel the situation out by "talking things over." I remember how on several occasions in the past, when the brigade leaders have forgotten about this "lone stalk" and I have written notes reminding them, they have never gotten angry. But now when I want to write to the brigade leader on duty I am unable to pass it on, and I am told even the trusties might get in trouble if I do. I simply don't understand what the hell all this confusion is about. I refuse to believe that the cadres or the trusties, for that matter, are intentionally making trouble for me, and I have never discovered any material on the television that was inappropriate for everyone or improper in any way. So what should I think?

The second matter concerns writing letters. After my arrival here, Political Instructor Chen, Brigade Leader Zhao, and Secretary Zhao all told me, one after the other, that with the approval of the cadres and leaders, I would be permitted to enjoy the regular prisoner privilege of corresponding with my family, and all restrictions regarding prisoner correspondence were explained to me. Although I didn't completely understand the reasons for these rules, I planned to follow them—every occupation and activity has its rules and customs, after all. People inevitably have to go along with the local customs wherever they are and can't just stubbornly adhere to personal views. But now my correspondence privilege has been basically cut off and not only was I never notified of this, but I have still not received an explanation as to why. If you say "No explanation is necessary," I must reply that you are mistaken. All matters should be explained; even a criminal must be told why he is being arrested, so why shouldn't taking away one's legal right to correspondence require an explanation? The rules prohibit discussing one's case in letters, so I didn't (besides, those in the outside world probably know more about my case than I do anyway); I was told "it's better not to discuss politics," so I simply refrained from discussing politics, even though this runs counter to the Party's own policy of "politics first." But if letters that discuss literature and art or family matters, and even those concerning science, are confiscated as well, there is simply nothing I'm permitted to write about. Or is this what is meant by the slogan "all work concerns political work" and, therefore, anything I write about concerns politics? But what I am not clear on is how an ordinary person and an ignorant young guy like myself, even if I were to scream out as loud as possible, can be such a nuisance to our great leaders. Can they really be so afraid of letting people discuss politics? And science and technology, even if a government is not desperate to obtain them, will cause it no harm and can only bring benefits. Can it be remotely possible that since the Four Cardinal Principles have been raised, you're even afraid of talking about science and technology? Even in my wildest dreams I never would have imagined anyone could interpret Deng's Four Cardinal Principles in such a negative way.

I don't think that all my inventions are useful or that all my opinions are necessarily correct, and I certainly don't think that I am such a threatening figure. To retreat ten thousand steps back, even if I was so threatening, concealing news from me wouldn't make me any less threatening, so what's the point? Now that people are beginning to discuss the rule of law, the legal apparatus should never again become the weapon anyone in power can use to vent personal anger. If I write fewer letters and watch less television, will anybody really gain anything for it?

These are my main points; other trivial matters like emptying my chamber pot and lighting cigarettes I don't need to write and disturb you with. I can sort them out by speaking to the trusties. There's nothing unbearable and my health is still good; thanks so much for all of your care and concern.

Wei Jingsheng

July 20, 1982

Members of the Commission for Discipline Inspection of the Central Committee and Members of the Standing Committee of the People's Political Consultative Conference:

I am not sure where I should direct several "insignificant" matters I would like to discuss. After long deliberation, I thought it best to ask you esteemed leaders and exemplary officials to be the judges.

It's difficult for me to know where to begin. I never wanted to bother anybody with these matters, but planned to just go on patiently and try to forget about them. But things often exceed even my expectations, and now there are some additional issues that it wouldn't be right for me to keep from you. Therefore, I must set aside my original resolve and "seek lenience in confession." The matter is more or less like this:

While in prison, I often try to think of what kinds of things I can do to be of benefit to the people. Although I've been stripped of almost all of my other rights, it seemed I still had the "right" to undertake scientific investigations. So I racked my brain to think of ways to experiment and invent some useful things. Of course, my "inventions" are not necessarily all useful or practical, nor are they all definitely new either; there could very well be places where they overlap with others, and some may even be rather absurd. But it's not very likely that they have no redeeming value whatsoever. The important thing is that they be tested so that I can follow through with the good ones and make changes in the unsuccessful ones. Even famous scientists must go through this process. Considering that the cadres at the prison here are not scientific researchers, forcing them to carry out such tests would be rather difficult and I don't want to impose on them. And, since I am not doing this as a "meritorious service" to atone for any crime, I decided to turn the bothersome matter over to my brother and sisters to take care of and was preparing to let them try to help me find a way to put the projects to use. Of course, they would have checked with the appropriate government bureau before submitting them anywhere for consideration.

At first I was told that letters concerning technical and scientific subjects would not be confiscated, and I was even encouragingly told that it would be good for me to make a contribution to the country and the people. I was so happy and excited to hear this that these words are still engraved on my memory very clearly. But things rarely turn out as beautifully as we imagine. Under these difficult conditions (without access to any reference materials), I spent a great deal of time and energy writing out my ideas, drawing up plans, and sketching figures—but nearly every single one of my projects was confiscated. Only the two that I myself actually thought were the least original and complete projects—one concerning solar energy and the other on calculating oval-shaped dimensions—were sent out to my family. And now recently I have been informed that: "According to the regulations, this type of thing cannot be mailed out. There will be no exceptions." They also said that my projects had "already been handed over to the appropriate bureau for investigation," which had subsequently reported that "they have all been published in magazines before." The cadres here seem to feel it was unnecessary to tell me any other particulars. Now, if they were to tell me that one or two of my inventions overlapped with those of other people, that would be entirely possible, but to tell me that over a dozen of them were duplications is clearly impossible and shows me that something isn't quite right. It would be ridiculous to claim that I had copied the work of others, as it was only a short time ago that I was finally allowed to have my family send books and magazines to me and everything that they have sent has been inspected by the cadres here, who can vouch that there was nothing in them that pertained to any of my "hobbies." Obviously, it's impossible to plagiarize someone's work before you've seen it and I'm afraid I don't have that superhuman power. It would also be highly unlikely that anyone could plagiarize my work since the letters that were sent out were read only by the cadres here and the "appropriate bureau." Who among them would dare to stir up trouble right under the nose of the Public Security Bureau? Frankly, this theory doesn't have a leg to stand on.

Perhaps my scientific projects had actually been prohibited by the "appropriate bureau" long ago, but my superiors here chose to use sweet words of encouragement to mask this decision out of consideration for my feelings. Nevertheless, I still feel that those in positions of authority in the "appropriate bureaus" are not always the final word on anything. There are numerous examples of scientists whose progress was blocked for a period by misunderstanding and conservative thinking. There shouldn't be dictatorship in science any more than in politics. The views of the authorities today will someday be looked back upon from a position of much more advanced science the same way chemists of today now regard ancient alchemists.

Or perhaps someone said: "There's nothing to your inventions, you just wanted to smuggle some other message out inside them! Otherwise, why are you so conceited as to insist that you must publish them rather than just taking notes and hanging on to them? Aren't you afraid that others will laugh at your shoddy inventions?" My response to this is, what could I possibly have that others are so afraid of and that I would need to smuggle out? Even if I had developed a secret code, is it likely it could be so superior that even the Public Security officers could not break it? I would never dare to think I was so smart, and besides, I don't have any need to do things in such a roundabout way.

My reason for being anxious to have my inventions published and put to use is not out of a desire for fame or profit—I don't attach much importance to such things and would even rather others plagiarized my inventions than to have wasted my time in vain. As long as they can be useful to people, that's fine; this is my only "criteria." I am anxious simply because our country's energy resources are very scarce and people in rural areas are in an especially desperate situation. I think that the several types of windmills I have invented (including the miniature "revolving-parachute" windmill that was returned to me several days ago) might help them relieve their state of poverty, or at least be of some use. Naturally, the sooner I can see my efforts be beneficial to the country and the people, the happier I will be. They certainly won't cause anybody harm, so why shouldn't I try to hurry them up? I'm not afraid that people might laugh at me; I've always done things in this manner. Even great inventors make mistakes, so why not me!?

But Lu Xun was right when he said, "In China, no matter what you do, you must do it as deftly and quickly as a somersault, otherwise . . ." This is still true today, when everyone must speak so indirectly that when I say things too directly, nobody believes me. It's no wonder, for how can a "counterrevolutionary" like myself dare to think that he can do something beneficial for the country and the people? On this point, I've already reached my wit's end. In our nation, as somebody once said, "You need status even to be a successful brown-noser." Naturally a "counterrevolutionary" locked up in prison can't have much beneficial influence on the country and the people, since he certainly doesn't have the prerequisite status to do so.

This reminds me of another series of issues. For several thousand years, China was the acknowledged leader in the human sciences. Today even, when overseas Chinese scientists are successful, it is considered capturing the gold for the "Chinese people." We can say unabashedly that the Chinese people are full of talent, but then why is it that in the last few centuries we have fallen so far behind? Why are there so few people inside China capable of "capturing the gold"? There are, of course, numerous reasons for this, but the most important one is that the standard for judging everything is power and influence. Little emphasis is placed on developing other types of talents, so they are all considered secondary. In short, anyone who has authority at any level in society practically has omnipotent "powers" over virtually everything else below him. Whatever people try to do, it is judged on the basis of power: If it is deemed unbeneficial to those in power, even if it might be of great use to the people, or especially if it might help the people at the expense of those in power, then those in power have the authority to veto it.

"Power" is abstract, but those who hold this power are living human beings with actual "omnipotent" powers. Therefore, all decisions are based on personal standards of power, and the scope of their authority to overrule things grows ever greater. Only a small portion of the population has such power and what they feel is beneficial and what they are even capable of recognizing as such is extremely minuscule; therefore many new things (including scientific inventions) that might benefit the people are not very likely to meet with their approval. This power is like a great pair of pincers clamping down on the neck of the Chinese people so hard that they can barely gasp for breath, let alone have the life force to develop vigorously.

All you have to do is glance through the newspapers of late to find numerous examples of formerly "suppressed talents" who have now been set free and you can understand the force of these great pincers. Someone who has ultimate authority over a factory or workshop has the power to suppress important inventions, discoveries, or scientific activity by simply "deeming" that they are of no use to him. Between the ignorant "deeming" and the omnipotent power of those in positions of authority, how can there possibly be even a single path left unhindered for the development of new ideas and science? There are people of talent all over China, and there are many, many with aspirations to science and progress, but under the pressure of these pincers, all their efforts are as futile as looking for fish in a tree. Science does not emit spontaneously from the brains of scientists, but is the accumulation of many people's smaller efforts. The famous ones are just those who have taken a greater role and are seen as representative. But in a situation where each and every brick has been pressed flat by a great pair of pincers, and the very existence of the bricks is now in question, there is no hope for building a great tower. Nothing can grow without soil; where scientific knowledge is not widespread among the people, how can there be great science or great scientists?

Fatheadedness has so reduced everything but politics into matters of such insignificance that the sole factor determining human existence in China is politics. Therefore, people have little choice but to waste most of their energy on politics, which has been blown way out of proportion for far too long. This has served to increase both the intensity and complexity of political disputes, and caused the vulgar ruthlessness of politics to infect and disease science and culture as well. To use political standards to judge science and culture, not to mention people of talent, is as worthless as breeding a donkey with a thoroughbred. It blurs the lines between right and wrong, and good and bad in science and culture, and breaks down the natural process of weeding out the inferior and choosing the superior. This is chaotic enough in the short term, but in the long term you will find that science and culture lag behind. You shouldn't feel too pleased with yourselves just because one Chinese satellite makes it into orbit, because in an overall, unbiased evaluation, if you're not making progress, then you're falling behind, there are no two ways about it. Judged on the basis of international progress in science and culture, our nation has been consistently falling behind throughout the twentieth century. We can't go backward any further or it will result in further "suffering of the revolutionary masses," and the "revolution" will have done little to help them.

The stifling of the development of science and technology today is something even the ruthless first emperor, Qin Shihuang, would have trouble accomplishing. The current "politics first" attitude actually doesn't mean any value is placed on politics, but is just a repeat of Qin Shihuang's old trick of employing only bureaucrats, not creative thinkers. In essence this is a dictatorship. If this type of dictatorship over every facet of existence is not wiped out and a healthy balance of government, agriculture, commerce, and science is not established, then it will be impossible for any reform measures to be truly and thoroughly realized.

This is what concerns me most and is the real reason why I hope you will make rational decisions. Are you really satisfied with simply busying yourselves rectifying misjudged cases from the Cultural Revolution? Persons with a sense of responsibility should apply themselves to even greater tasks.

I've been unwell lately so my writing is rather disorderly, please excuse me.

Wei Jingsheng

In his September 1, 1982, speech to the Twelfth Party Congress, General Secretary Hu Yaobang called for a number of reform measures that Wei Jingsheng considered similar to ideas espoused by democracy activists like himself in the late 1970s. Wei wrote a long letter to Hu, excerpted below, offering encouragement and advice, as well as a warning to guard against the conservative forces within the Party.

October 1, 1982

Dear General Secretary Hu Yaobang:

The speech you made to the Twelfth Party Congress was full of new ideas and very exciting, and as a result, it didn't put everyone to sleep despite its length. What I noticed in particular was the second part concerning reform of the country's educational, scientific, and planned economic systems. I don't want to critique the "great significance" of these reforms as history will be the judge of their success or failure and people today shouldn't start boasting too soon. I only want to explain the positive contributions their future implementation will make, as well as my own opinions on several inadequacies. Some people might think I am speaking a bit too presumptuously, but that's okay, that way a general secretary of such power and influence as yourself won't mistake my words for flattery.

In all fairness, many of your new ideas are not really that far from the ideas of so-called "hostile elements" like myself. At least the differences are much smaller than from the thinking of those conservatives who hold on stubbornly to the centralized dictatorship and feudal serfdom of the "state-controlled" economy. We are not the blind fools that the lackeys and brown-nosers around you describe us as, nor do we "blindly worship Western capitalism" or "plan to overthrow socialism." As for socialism, we have our own views and our own understanding. These might not be identical to yours, but we too are earnestly and sincerely trying to "seek truth from facts" for the benefit of the people, and our differences will eventually grow smaller. "All roads lead to Rome," as they say, and socialism is just one among many such roads, isn't it? So let me ask first that you not be scared off by my "counter-revolutionary" taint and don't use this as an excuse to read my letter with tinted glasses, otherwise you'll be thwarting my good intentions. In my present situation, I know I shouldn't necessarily be sticking my nose in your "business," as in the past I have been reprimanded for it.

I was especially excited about the part in your speech expounding upon the new concept of the "planned economy." Your thinking on the economy has for the first time broken away from the conventions of the "planned economic system" and you have begun to explore a true "Chinese-style socialist path" (I've read the September 6 article in the *People's Daily*, but due to the "socialist control" system here, I haven't been able to read any other articles about it). Actually, this should really be called a "general socialist path," as these are questions that countries undertaking socialism in every corner of the globe are also facing.

"Soviet-style socialism," in a basic theoretical sense, is not socialism at all. There is no democracy in its politics and its economics are nothing more than a hybrid of Western serfdom and Asian bureaucratic commercialism, which ends up being the type of feudal socialism that Marx once said was still "tattooed on rear ends." Both the peoples of China and the Soviet Union have been seriously harmed by this variety of fascism and it has been hindering socialist development for a very long time. With all that we have learned, we should once again explore the contributions of the nineteenth-century pioneers of socialism. The new concepts in your speech are, from what I can tell, precisely the "dawn" of this type of exploration, and they feel truly epoch-making! How can one fail to be excited to see that, after so many setbacks, there is a first ray of dawn illuminating future progress?

But it's too early to celebrate; there is still the possibility that this "first ray" might be blocked by clouds and problems incurred due to the lack of guarantees on democracy. It appears that the curtain has already risen on the struggles over this, and that they may go beyond debates on paper alone. The sounds of counter-attacks from the conservatives can now be heard. What is of special concern is that those socialist "dissidents" in the Party are

very different from the young dissidents in the democratic movement who have no power whatsoever and are actually imprisoned.
Those conservatives who maintain a belief in the "traditional
planned economy" are precisely the ones who hold the greatest
amount of power, are entrenched in higher positions, and can rely
on old tricks to resist the force of reform. You absolutely must not
overlook their influence; it is crucial that these conservatives be
thoroughly unmasked. Many of your comrades have already made
efforts toward this goal, but I still feel they are not adequately
forceful or thorough and that your thinking is still not open and liberated enough. The conservatives in the government will take
advantage of these weaknesses and drill holes in your plans and
this makes me very uneasy. One billion impoverished people in
China cannot allow you to hesitate, and this hesitation is dangerous
to yourselves as well—those old conservative "dissidents" won't
let you do so for long.

According to the "socialist morals" of "public first, private last,"
it's only right that I leave my personal matters for last. There are
some unusual restrictions in the prison here: Petty criminals and
hooligans are allowed to have family visits once a month, but
political prisoners are only allowed one visit every two months. I've
also heard that most *laogai* prisoners can have their families send
transistor radios and musical instruments, but when I wanted to
study some English and listen to the news broadcasts, I was not
permitted to have a radio; when I wanted to review my Russian, all
of my Russian textbooks were impounded (officially nobody has
ever stated that they could not be brought in). I am told that
musical instruments are not allowed in the strict-regime brigade
cell block (the prison inside the prison where I live), yet I often
hear the sounds of flutes, guitars, harmonicas, and so on. Even the
leather shoes I wore here from Banbuqiao Prison were confiscated
after I sent them home to be repaired and I was subsequently told
leather shoes are prohibited (although I've seen others wearing
them). I don't understand what restrictions of this kind do to help
"reform" me.

In what you call the "most democratic of countries," if I write a
letter that is merely asking for things but that you think is too

long, the letter is confiscated in its entirety. On paper, we are allowed to write letters, but in practice it's prohibited—what high-handed nonsense! In fact, even books written by you Party leaders have been confiscated. It's as if they can smell the stink of counter-revolution on them, otherwise why does it take them so long to "inspect" each group of books? Even magazines like *Biography* containing articles introducing you great leaders are confiscated. I know that confiscating letters is not your doing, but I am also aware that, even though you tried to keep it secret, the outcome of my case was determined by members of the Party Central Committee like yourself. That's why when I have something to say, I think I should address it to you.

Enough already; I've been waxing on for too long and should wrap it up. Even just to smoke a cigarette or go to the bathroom, I have to knock on the door, make a report, and wait my turn. And then my train of thought is always broken by the slamming of the iron gates, so this letter is wordy and it's taken me an entire ten days to write. For the time being, I'll call it the "Ten Day Forum."

Whether friends or enemies, we should still shake hands at parting.

Your most devoted hostile element,
Wei Jingsheng

December 4, 1982

Dear Brigade Leader Zhao:

A brief explanation of two questions we discussed last time.

First of all, on writing letters. I don't think that when Hu Yaobang reads my letters he will be as angered over my caustic language as you say. In fact, just the opposite, the biting words might have a kind of psychological effect and prompt him to consider more carefully what I have written. If I don't do this, he might totally misunderstand the intent of my letter and overlook what I am only allowed to discuss superficially. A politician at his level has a thick skin, and the only thing that matters is the quality of what's in the letter. Actually, I'm not the one who invented this method; it's an old device that people of ancient times called "sharpness drives home criticism." Besides, what do I care about taking a risk? If he were really angry, he wouldn't bother merely taking away the pitiful right to books and meetings with my family that I have now—a move of that nature could only come from you.

Anyway, even before you came to bring me my books, I had already decided not to write any more letters for now (unless there is an absolute necessity). I've already said just about everything I have to say. I also think that I should try to give you less trouble. You've always been very tough on me, but I am not a small child who does whatever he's told. I recently saw something about a model public security officer in Anhui province, so perhaps that's a sign of things to come here. Beijing is of course very different from Anhui and it's never vigorously taken up the teachings of the Third Plenum and made a clean sweep of the remnants of the Gang of Four. The only model leaders you might find in Beijing are among those in the Party's democratic faction. But to you, your job is just a job, no different from that of a worker or farmer, so it wouldn't be right for me to ask you to take on an added burden and get caught up in my affairs. I've decided, therefore, that the distaste and anxiety you feel over the letters I write is reasonable, and if I still need to write, I will be more careful. Yet I remain at a loss to understand why you want me to discuss each letter with you before I write it. I take full responsibility for whatever I write and sending letters out is a legal act in accordance with your regulations, so you don't have to take any responsibility. Anyway, if I do anger those big heads of state, it certainly isn't because of the tone of my letters, but because of the content, and since I don't think you'll be drafting that out for me, you would be better off just standing aside. As for Deng Xiaoping, Hu Yaobang, Chen Yun, and Zhao Ziyang, they are not as thin-skinned as you think, and my ideas are not as useless as you imagine. But I don't want to stray too far off the subject.

As for the second issue, concerning speaking to other prisoners through the window, I am well aware of your view; you already made it clear in your memo, so there's no need to be repetitive. If I encounter this problem again, I will simply explain to them that they should speak with me less in order to avoid trouble and everything will be fine. This way, not only will I satisfy your request, but I can do so without making them think I am too proud or condescending to speak to them. After all, they are people too! If they don't talk to me, I won't talk to them; it's that simple.

Wei Jingsheng

April 12, 1983

Dear Hu Yaobang:

My health is deteriorating and I don't have much energy, so let me get straight to the point on several matters.

I've got coronary heart disease, high blood pressure, and at times I've shown symptoms of cerebral hemorrhaging—all of which I've written to you about before. I would like to receive competent medical treatment and be placed in an environment more conducive to recovery than I have here in prison. I don't know what you think of my requests. Are they too excessive?

If not, then why have I been thrown into the "self-reflection" solitary cell again? People with my illnesses must live under better conditions in order to recover. Spending month after month, year after year in the gloomy atmosphere of this cell is extremely detrimental to my health. That is why I have continued to write letters and make requests, but they've resulted in nothing but my being shut up yet again in the tiny space of this three-by-four-meter cell. And those trusties (all reliable old Cultural Revolution era criminals) open and slam the doors all night long and constantly make some kind of noise (such as coughing loudly and so on), making it impossible for me to sleep. They're as skilled and efficient as if they were trained psychological warfare experts, so that even while I write this short, simple letter, my head feels like it is filled with lead. I would like to take a walk along the corridors to stretch out my limbs a bit, but I am not allowed to. They keep telling me "No special treatment," but what I would like to know is, isn't being locked up alone month after month, year after year considered "special treatment"? Doesn't being sick and not being taken to the hospital amount to "special treatment"?

These past few days my health has taken a sudden turn for the worse: I'm vomiting and I have diarrhea all at once; I feel dizzy and my chest is tight; my rotting gums have swollen and all my teeth are so loose I can't even chew soft fruit any longer. I have sent notes to prison officials at every level, but all to no avail. It seems as if I am deliberately being forced to take a step further, but exactly where to and why I don't know. No matter how much I think it over, I am still at a loss to understand how much benefit can be squeezed out of a single prisoner like me. Even if you were to finish me off once and for all, what purpose would that serve? The drunkard's mind is never just on the cup—there must be some ulterior motive. But then again, it's not like things haven't been this way since the very beginning!

Wei Jingsheng
Writing from solitary confinement

July 1983

Dear President Li Xiannian:

This insignificant person who has never written to you before and now takes up his pen so boldly to compose a letter to you asks first that you forgive him for "bothering" you. I'm not like those ordinary people who shower you with praise and wishes of good fortune—there are too many others diligently plodding that route and I have never had the pleasure of counting myself among them, so I'm not going to start now. Nor do I have the inclination to pretend to be refined and talk in big words, as I did when I wrote previously to General Secretary Hu Yaobang and Premier Zhao Ziyang. People have long ridiculed me for doing this as "making underhanded attacks to solve his own problems" or as "a complete waste of ink." Their words all make sense and I don't want to make such mistakes, so in this letter I would simply like to ask your help with a difficult problem.

For a variety of reasons, matters concerning me must all be decided upon at the very top, although the authorities as high as the Party Central Committee don't seem to care much for doing this in accordance with the law. That is why I am now forced to write thanking you for your kindness in still allowing me to write letters at all, but also to let you know that letters I have written dealing with scientific questions that have absolutely nothing to do with politics (all of which were sent to my younger brother and sisters) have been confiscated. After writing asking for some explanation why for over a year, I have still not been given one. ("There's no need to explain" is not an explanation.) Of course this isn't all that important and it can wait until the 1990s when I get out, since science and technology in our country progresses about as fast as a rickety cart pulled by an old ox. That's true whether my projects can even be considered "science and technology" or not. Now I cordially request your attention on another more urgent matter; at least for me there is nothing more urgent.

My coronary heart disease has been getting progressively worse over the past years. It has been extremely bad since the attack last winter and it continues to flare up often. Seeing that the conditions for treatment here are limited, once the "suspected criminal" was definitively diagnosed at the end of June as coronary heart disease (this after being taken to the Beijing Public Security Hospital), not only myself but the doctors all agreed that my living conditions, the food, and the medical treatment I receive here are "life-threatening." At first I thought that if I relied on my optimism and the doctor's medicine there would be no problem, but the doctor disagreed: "All else aside, the stress of not being allowed outside for months and years at a time is bad enough." In addition to this, there's also the incredible level of noise here, the poor food, and all other types of annoyances, intentional and not. It appears that there is some truth in the doctor's words. The past month's treatment hasn't had any apparent effect. I believe that perhaps the only effective way to a cure is to have a change of environment, to stay in the hospital (of course, not the prison hospital, which I hear is even more tightly controlled than where I am now) or to be moved closer to my family to recover for a period. The doctor also tried to console me, saying, "Relax, perhaps before long there'll be a special amnesty." Apparently, while he is very well intentioned, he doesn't pay too much attention to politics. Anyway, I don't harbor such lavish hopes; but I can't deny that I still hold out for the possibility that I might stay in a hospital isolation ward like I did during the Cultural Revolution, or else be released on temporary medical parole in accordance with the law. Moreover, this is not my only illness—my health is poor in general and my teeth have begun to fall out as well.

I therefore entreat you to be fair and help provide me with a better environment for recovery. I realize that the person who is currently making the entire country read his selected writings won't be too happy, but I don't see why this should trouble him. What threat can a little guy like me pose for a "great leader" like him? Even if I was somebody, that was four years ago. During my trial, he already had his hand in fabricating what was clearly a misjudged case and stretching the already flawed judicial system to an unlawful degree. (I've already banished most of the illegalities that occurred during the process of my arrest, interrogation, and trial from my mind, otherwise there would be no way for me to remain an "optimist" until now. After all, these all have long precedents in the People's Republic of China, so there's no need for me to place blame on the Public Security organs, the Procuratorate, or the Court.) Since then, I have fallen into the depth of illness from which I have no way out. I simply never imagined that the people I once held such high admiration for could really be so small-minded. But everyone has their moments of blindness, especially when they are young and inexperienced. What can you do? Life is always full of surprises. Nowadays, however, I am forced to seek help from even elders like yourself whom I have never held in very high esteem. I can only ask that you behave like a person with an ordinary sense of conscience and act in accordance with the law to help me.

Now let me turn to another topic. I want to recommend an extremely good article to you. (I've attached a newspaper clipping.) The cadres here in prison have the authority to determine what is "appropriate" reading material for me, so why shouldn't I have the right to recommend a good article to you? We're all people after all! Even if some of us have tasted a bit more of the salt of life than others. In recent years those "eulogistic" authors haven't written much of real interest (even less so than in the past), but Liu Binyan's two articles on Zhang Haidi and Zhu Boru are real treasures (that is, they're valuable because they are so rare). They are good because Liu Binyan has captured the kind and upright nature of "good people," and aren't full of the unreadable nonsense about "unselfish devotion of heart and soul to the Party and the people." There are good people like Zhang and Zhu everywhere you look, thousands of them, but there are few articles praising them in the manner of Mr. Liu—there are lots of horses around, but few champion stallions, as they say. The fame may have gone to their heads by now, but these two guys really come alive in Mr. Liu's piece. Some people might think that his article undervalues their worth, but actually there's no need to "inflate" good people. The phrase "nobody's perfect" isn't entirely correct either. Just as long as a person is multidimensional, then he is genuine. Somebody blown out of proportion by political pundits, however, becomes little more than a puppet. Capturing the true essence of what makes a good person good the way Mr. Liu does is much more convincing. Calls for people to "study" such-and-such a political movement are just fine-sounding attempts to get people to do good things. Of course, encouraging people to do good is not a bad thing, but the results are dubious because good people don't do good things just to fill a party "statistic." If you take a look at the numbers of model "Lei Fengs" around, most of them are fakes just currying favor. Why are these lessons ignored and not taken seriously?

Please excuse my immodesty! This is really too trivial a matter to trouble such a noble mind as yours with, so please forgive me.

Wei Jingsheng

In the following letter to his brother and sisters, Wei Jingsheng makes the first of several references found in the prison letters to hunger strikes. Wei undertook a number of hunger strikes during his imprisonment to demand better treatment for himself and fellow political prisoners and to have his case reexamined. The exact dates, reasons, and resolutions of this and subsequent hunger strikes mentioned in Wei's letters are not known.

October 22, 1983

Dear Lingling, Taotao, and Shanshan:

Hello everyone!

Lingling, I just received your letter of October 19 and I understand your concern. Nevertheless, you don't entirely understand my situation. For one thing, this is because I am not at liberty to write about it; for another, there are certain matters I've been unwilling to tell you about because I am afraid of the burden it might put on you and the negative effect it could have on the family. That is why you don't fully recognize the dangers to my health that the conditions here present. But now I want to let you know something else: Since the day of your last visit, I have stopped eating. This is something you will probably find even more difficult to understand.

You tell me to be patient and wait for things to be resolved through official channels. I hear you, but do you realize that I have been waiting for nearly a year for a response? The cadres here have told me that they've never confiscated any of my letters requesting an "official resolution" of my situation, so I'm beginning to think that if it were ever going to be resolved, it would have happened long ago. I haven't had any appetite for over six months, but I've forced myself to put down a few spoonfuls of rice each day so that I could have the strength to wait for the "official resolution." Over the past year I've had frequent heart palpitations, but I've tried my best to remain calm in order to help the medicine do its work. All my teeth are so loose that I can't even bite a piece of soft steamed bread; I have to wait until I can soak it in water. If I weren't so stubborn, I'm afraid I wouldn't have been able to remain patient for this long! Why would I be doing this if not because I am trying my best to resolve this situation without making too much trouble for people? Have I not been acting out of good faith toward your "Party organization"?

But what has come of it? The fates of thousands upon thousands of others who put their "trust in the Party organization" serve as a warning. In other words, we Chinese people have gotten into our current mess because we're too good and too willing to believe the kind-sounding words of others. But now my heart condition is worsening with each attack and I'm afraid I might not make it through the winter or next spring. In the past I depended on you to bring me jam and milk powder to supplement my meager diet, but now I don't even have this, and if I can't eat, what can I do? Whether I complete this hunger strike or not makes little difference. I might as well make a clean break of it. These past few days I've stopped forcing myself to gnaw on those coarse rolls or hard vegetable roots and my teeth have actually been less painful! It's a welcome side effect. Today when the doctor measured it, my blood pressure wasn't that high either, so it looks like even if I can't persist in my hunger strike for the one hundred days I would like, I will at least be able to keep it up for one or two months without any problem. If I wait until the point where my condition is so bad that I can't take it even a few days more, I'll just end up like Chen Yi or Liu Shaoqi, who were dragged off to the hospital when they were nearly dead so it could be said that they had "died of natural causes." I might be stupid, but I'm not that stupid yet. I know this trick. And with an illness like mine, I could be stricken down at any moment. I'm undertaking this hunger strike now as my last effort to go on living and so that I don't end up in such a stupid situation. I won't take the risk Chen and Liu did. Besides, you needn't worry, the cadres here have told me that with the advancement of science today, they have all kinds of ways of keeping me alive—there's one more assurance for you!

The point Lingling raised about the letters I have been writing is something I have long been aware of myself. If you had seen those letters you would know that the tone is no less polite than when I write to you. It's true, however, that once somebody becomes a politician, if you don't add a few lines of flattery in when addressing him, not only he, but others will think you're being disrespectful. But I am simply unable to flatter people and there's nothing I can do about it. If you must know, the letters I've continued to write to the leaders over the past few years are even more detailed than things I published in the past. I've made things so black and white that just about anybody in the world could understand them clearly, so I don't know why those who should understand even better have so much trouble. But if a wolf wants to eat a sheep and there are plenty of them around, what can one little sheep do to beg for "mercy"?

Truthfully, all I want to do now is recover my health. I don't care to haggle over old disputes with people. In my letters to them I have also pledged repeatedly that "during my recovery, I will not voice any political opinions." I'm reduced to begging them, but to no avail. What more can I do? I'm asking everyone in the family for advice. At present I can only "follow the example of the old revolutionary generation," but I also want to hear your ideas. I still hope to get direct word from the higher-ups on their opinions as well. Perhaps you should be the ones to pass information about my situation along to the "Party organization" because all of the cadres here want to avoid trouble and don't dare to speak on my behalf, so naturally there are a few discrepancies between their reports and my actual situation. If you told them, perhaps it would be more complete and accurate. When you get my letter please reply as soon as possible; better yet, come and discuss it with me in person.

Say hello to everyone for me! Say hello to little Fanfan for me!

Your older brother,
Jingsheng

P.S. I never was good at flattering lovers either. It seems that I'm an incurable case! Ha ha!

November 9, 1983

Dear Deng Xiaoping and Chen Yun:

Let me begin straight off by telling you that this letter does not concern my request to be released on medical parole. As for the state of my health, I discussed it very clearly in a previous letter and there is no need for me to repeat details of my condition here. Although everyone seems to feel that my receiving medical treatment is contingent upon the resolution of my "thought problem," I feel the two matters are entirely different and shouldn't be confused.

This letter is prompted by the self-criticism published by Zhou Yang in the *People's Daily*. In the past, self-criticisms were either tactical maneuvers used in political struggles or forced confessions written by those "bowing their heads and admitting their crimes." Zhou Yang's self-criticism, however, seems genuine, showing that the atmosphere for self-criticism and general critiques has normalized a bit of late. I say only "a bit" because I've still seen quite a few of both the forced and tactical types of self-criticisms in the newspapers recently and any true expression of personal feelings is still pretty rare. Even the hard-liners looking for chances to stage a comeback see this as an opportunity. These problems persist mainly due to flaws in your planning. But I will address this later.

Let me start again. Since the atmosphere has normalized a bit, I too want to "imitate the sages" and do a little self-criticism of my own. Of course, I would never be able to do so if it weren't for this new relaxed atmosphere; otherwise the hard-line conservatives might think I was capitulating and it would only serve to fan their arrogance, while others might get a false impression and fail to see their own shortcomings. Trying to solve a problem through excessive self-criticism is not good for anyone. While the individual himself might gain some immediate benefit, he can harm society and others by doing so. There is very little actual significance in the resolution of his problem and he won't gain the admiration of those around him either. In addition to my self-criticism, I plan to discuss a few things you do not know about. Let me start with an analysis of some matters concerning the Democracy Wall Movement.

During the more than one hundred days from December 1978, when I first got involved in the Democracy Wall Movement, until March 1979, when I was arrested, I went through three significant phases. They can be summarized as: Engagement, Direction, and Turning Point. Due to several incorrect appraisals of the situation, particularly regarding the direction you in the leadership were heading, I made a series of mistakes in handling certain affairs. These mistakes have had far-reaching implications, and it is not possible for me to be vague about them.

ENGAGEMENT

A lack of democracy is the principal reason for China's many problems. Reform and democracy are the preconditions for modernization. This is my basic view of China's problems and was the subject of my article, "The Fifth Modernization: Democracy." Modernization of the people is the precondition for all modernization. Thus it was with great interest that I followed the beginnings of the Democracy Wall Movement, although I was dissatisfied with its unclear focus at the time.

Long before Deng Xiaoping's interview with the American journalist Robert Novak in November 1978 (I don't think this text was included in the latest edition of Deng's selected works), I had come to the conclusion that everything went through a certain process of development: Things invariably matured at a steady pace, staying basically in the right direction, and it was only a matter of time before they arrived at their goal. That's why I didn't plan to get involved in the democracy movement initially and certainly never imagined that I would end up in my present state.

Actually, I had felt quite discouraged by politics and distrustful of politicians ever since the failure of the anti–Jiang Qing movement during the Cultural Revolution. In fact, I was a bit disillusioned with the world in general. Although I wasn't yet considering becoming a monk, I had thought of remaining simply an ordinary citizen, or maybe a detached hermit or self-content sage. Looking back at this today, my vain hopes of becoming a modern-day hermit seem pretty ridiculous. After all, even if you have only the slightest sense of justice, when you come across something that you absolutely cannot tolerate then you must get involved. Otherwise, what's so "sagely" about you? Escapism is just one form of ludicrous "snailism." It is an irresponsible act of cowardice both to oneself and to society. Every person has a share in the fate of his country; one shouldn't think this is the duty of just a few. Even if you don't care about politics, politics will still care about you.

In his interview with Novak, however, Deng Xiaoping clearly took a different view of things. He made it known that as long as a small number of people in power were responsible for China's affairs, there was no need for ordinary citizens to voice their opinions; everything could be decided upon within leadership circles. He even hinted at the suppression of any grassroots democratic discussion. Not only was this completely wrong in principle, but it also served to heighten people's sense of distrust and anxiety. Everyone (including your trusted followers) began to feel that this time would be just like all the others; the promise of reform and democracy would be little more than old tricks dangled before the people to distract them in troubled times. With this, many people involved in the Democracy Wall Movement began packing their bags and preparing to head underground. There were even some who declared anxiously: "The Central Committee decides everything and ordinary people needn't bother themselves by saying a word about it." (These are the people I later gathered together as the editorial staff of *Exploration*, proving that they didn't really feel this way, but were scared and wary of the situation.) As a result, curses were soon heard everywhere, some even going so far as to say: "Chinese people! What spineless good-for-nothings!" People had lost faith in the movement.

But it was precisely this kind of cursing that provoked my interest in Democracy Wall and I began rethinking my stance. I deeply regretted the fact that the first clear call for democracy and reform to come from the grassroots in several decades in our nation had already suffered such a setback. After careful consideration, I decided to take a chance and try to remedy a situation that was pleasing only to the bad guys and discouraging to the good ones.

I don't doubt that there is a democratic faction in the leadership. This is historically inevitable. But I feel that according to history, any reforms toward the development of democracy and socialism will be defective and abortive without the strong backing of the people. When a person in a position of power gets too high, he tends naturally toward dictatorship. The thrill of having your every word followed is just too intoxicating; that's human nature. In addition, hasn't China been plagued by the evils of dictatorship for thousands of years? Without the stimulus of a strong grassroots movement backed by popular sentiment (what is also called "public opinion"), the temptation toward dictatorship is irresistible. The French Revolution ended up by establishing an emperor and in our country, a democratic revolution nearly reinstated a new emperor on the throne. These are lessons of history that people don't soon forget. Each and every citizen has the responsibility to make an effort to guard against and prevent such a tragedy from recurring.

From a Marxist point of view, the socialist movement is the direct successor of the early phase of the old democratic movements; it is a movement to realize democracy and humanist ideals throughout society—that is why it is called "socialism." For this very reason, there is no socialism without democracy. So even now I feel that my involvement with the grassroots democratic movement was the correct and responsible thing to do. The fact is, when the democratic faction within the Party is struggling against the forces of conservatism and dictatorship, without the backing of democratic public opinion, it will never succeed. The dictatorial and conservative factions also have their strongholds in all levels of power. I'm thankful that I didn't fall under the influence of the evil fog of "snailism" or dictatorship that permeates society.

DIRECTION

Originally, the Democracy Wall Movement had been a purely spontaneous, leaderless outpouring of popular feeling. But following setbacks and resurgences in late 1978, it gradually began moving more quickly in the direction of concerted action. It became stronger theoretically, more focused, and took on a broader relevance. The big-character posters written to the leaders about the misjudged cases of individuals became nonessential accessories. This all caused a great change in people's views and interests in the democracy movement. To a certain extent, it had an effect on the depth and scope of thinking by people of all kinds. People began to see Democracy Wall as a unified entity and before long, what was once a jumble of small democratic groups in Beijing was transformed into a coordinated movement with weekly joint meetings. The primary question facing the democracy movement at this time was the direction to be taken. People were needed who could take on leadership responsibility and direct the movement.

It was precisely in this area that I made many serious mistakes, proving that I am completely unqualified to be a "leader." First of all, I did not promptly recognize my own influence and status among the various groups that made up the democratic organization, partially because I was afraid people would say I had personal ambitions for power. In addition, I was unwilling to take on responsibility for others or to waste my energy on what were sometimes trivial debates. Therefore I never accepted the responsibility of leadership, and at times didn't even attend the Joint Council meetings, wasting too much energy instead on miscellaneous everyday tasks. I allowed other organizations and individuals to do as they pleased and felt satisfied with this decentralized situation. I remember how during my trial I even proudly described the situation as being like a tray of loose sand, thinking that this proved my "democratic style." But looking back on it now, this was a foolish mistake. Of course one shouldn't infringe upon the freedom of others, but if you know something is not right and you refrain from criticizing it or offering the necessary intellectual challenges to actions that are clearly incorrect or bad, it is not only wrong, but lazy. By not taking this responsibility, I allowed all kinds of mixed-up elements to find their way in, and spurred the development of a number of flawed tendencies. In the end this was not only harmful to everybody, but it also got me in trouble personally, and gave people a false impression of the democracy movement. At the time, there was no one other than myself who had the influence or ability to take on this crucial task, so I cannot deny my responsibility in making this mistake.

Despite this, *Exploration* magazine did play an influential and leading role among the democracy groups and society at large at the time. The pain suffered by the masses for years had made a deep impression on me that was virtually ingrained in my flesh and bones. In addition, like many others at the time, I lacked faith in the changes taking place within the government leadership toward democracy and reform. In this way, I followed the tendency toward concern with the people's current suffering that naturally developed within the democracy movement. We focused our efforts on criticizing the darker sides of society, while overlooking a question of equal importance: namely, what strategy the country and the people should adopt in order to leave behind their present state of poverty as soon as possible. Simply proposing democracy and reform as the right route to take was far from enough. There were many complex and concrete problems involved in putting this general policy into actual practice, and it was very different from what many young people at the time imagined would be smooth sailing and immediate success.

Although I recognized some of the complexities involved, on the one hand, I was influenced by everyone's impatience for democracy and reform, while on the other, I still lacked confidence in the credibility of the efforts toward reform that you and others were taking. As a result, I reacted in an overly sensitive manner in dealing with several concrete issues and tasks. For example, the tone of my criticism grew more and more intense until it began to get overgeneralized and exaggerated. Everyone has a conditioned reflex to resist repression, and I could also defend myself by saying that I "took full responsibility for my actions" or that it was correct and necessary to expose the darker side of society. But because this was a biased approach and because *Exploration* was in a leading position, our attitude and tone had a lot of influence and was taken as the unified message of Democracy Wall. Therefore, if you look at it objectively, the widespread social reaction it generated and the fact that it was regarded as the central activity of the democracy movement eventually all combined to have a negative effect. It exacerbated the lingering distrust between the grassroots democratic movement and the democratic faction within the Party, widened rifts that should have been mended, and deepened a generally distrustful mood in society. But I was several months late in realizing this, and by then the situation was irretrievable. Although I later made some effort to do so, the conditions were not right and I had little success. In addition, you pressed us to the point where we were forced to resist and this widened the rifts even further and deepened the psychological pressure on both sides. A pernicious chain reaction.

Such rifts and mutual distrust made those fighting for democracy feel very much like "paranoid victims," and this produced an invisible but unrelenting psychological pressure that caused people to easily make the mistakes I mentioned above. They tended to radical extremes and had little hope for seeking discussion, cooperation, or consultation. It caused us to focus too much attention on resisting suppression and not enough on preventing the dubious influence of all types of far-fetched ideas from seeping in and polluting the ideals of democracy and reform. Some confused people even sought to form a "united front" in directions they shouldn't have and tolerated any strain of thinking that held up the banner of democracy. Even before my arrest, when a crackdown was still just a rumor, such tendencies had already emerged and even people calling for "free love" began showing up at Democracy Wall. If we hadn't been paying so much attention to the possibility of being suppressed, we could have established a more coherent stance and taken appropriate measures to resist such tendencies. Instead, while we occupied ourselves with an unnecessary battle, we were distracted from attending to a necessary one.

In addition, this rift and mutual distrust created a "suspicion craze" within the government leadership that made them react in an overly sensitive fashion as well. They felt insecure, as if anyone with opinions different from their own were an "enemy force" planning to usurp their power. They were unable to believe in the possibility of finding common ground or holding talks with those in society who held dissenting views, and they refused to consider the prospect of cooperating with a "democratic faction" or "dissidents." So it was inevitable that they eventually gravitated toward the old peasant philosophy: "You can only trust what you can hold in your hands." Such an overreaction caused you to divert your attention away from the conservative hard-liners and the bootlickers and parasites around you, and to focus your energy on countering this fictitious "democracy movement enemy force." In this way, while you were preoccupied with an unnecessary battle, you were distracted from attending to a necessary one. You probably would not admit to this, but it is a fact.

At first, I put all my energy into using every means possible to try to establish contact with the two of you, even informally. I wanted to get a more reliable picture of what your plans and positions were, so I would not have to make judgments based on official propaganda alone. But all my efforts failed. I discovered that those acting as your "eyes and ears" unanimously felt that there was no way you would agree to a meeting, as you already felt that the democratic groups were your "irreconcilable enemies." I went on actively seeking an opportunity for discussion even though most people thought this was ridiculous. For centuries in China, the great leaders of our nation have always been regarded as almighty emperors, so why would they deign to consult or discuss anything with ordinary people? This is not just my personal grievance, but an irrefutable fact. You might not necessarily see things this way yourselves, but even here in prison people find it very funny that I write a few letters to you each year. They act as if I must be mentally ill or just plain delusional to even harbor such a wild fantasy that you might reply to my letters. This clearly demonstrates how the burden of a tradition that has perpetuated a deep estrangement between the people and their leaders continues to exert an influence on people's thinking and actions.

During the past few years I've been under strict isolation in prison, to the point where I'm not even allowed access to information about my own case. But I can still see that the rift and rejection between the democratic factions within and without of the Party has had a great influence on the country's political structure. I can also see that this mutual distrust has created many obstructions to democratization and reform in our country. These unnecessary struggles have made it hard for everyone to carry out unrestricted reform and reconstruction. Instead, they have given opportunities for all matter of forces, including the various dregs of the Gang of Four forces who are still hoping to make a comeback to exploit these differences. Although the responsibility for bringing this political situation about is not entirely my own, as one of the characters who played a key and detrimental role in fomenting these differences, I realize I cannot relinquish all the blame. This is the main point of my self-criticism.

When you made the decision to use extreme measures, the democracy movement faced a crucial turning point. Some people wanted to go into hiding, but most people knew that this was clearly impossible. Judging from the precedent set by your policies in the past, the possibility of this never really existed because you would never have tolerated us going into hiding unless we had hid all the way abroad. If we had done so, the situation would undoubtedly have caused the process of democratization in China to suffer interference from external influences, creating enormous stumbling blocks and a much more complex situation. China's affairs are still best solved by the Chinese people themselves; no one else should be allowed to give the government an excuse to carry out a crackdown or hand a bargaining chip over to external powers. Furthermore, I was still unwilling to give up on any last chance of expanding the momentum of democracy and reform, so I pressed hard that we should remain in Beijing and continue our efforts as a way of setting an example. Instead of weekly meetings, I proposed many legal activities such as joint interviews and appeals to the Public Security Bureau in order to reassure people. This way we could attract the greatest amount of publicity and prove to people that everything was okay and there was no need to run away.

Some radical factions, however, felt that we should go underground immediately and head for the hills to start a guerrilla war of resistance. There had always been elements in the organization that had hoped to undertake armed struggle, but after seeing that the policy of legal action followed by the Democracy Wall Movement was not entirely hopeless, they had been attracted to it. But these people had made their preparations early on and, with the first gust of a cold wind, they were ready to take to the hills. If we had not put a firm stop to their activities, they would certainly have pressured others into guerrilla action. As Democracy Wall had from the outset always been more of a national movement than a local one, this faction had the potential to influence many small organizations from around the country with different tendencies to join them. Since people looked to me to some extent, I eventually managed to put them off temporarily and they finally said to me reluctantly, "Okay, we'll follow you, but if you do take some action, don't leave us hanging here."

It was hard to convince the militant faction, however, because when repression began looming more definitely, the possibility of a lawful struggle diminished. The debates to try to convince them were heated and often continued loudly from meeting hall to restaurant and back out on the street again with everyone practically cursing at each other. There's nothing unusual about this, though—it's not easy to convince people on matters of life or death! Even those who were usually moderates began doubting my judgment. But many people continued to believe that you in the leadership wouldn't do anything too extreme. I told them, "If the sky falls down, there's always a tall guy there to hold it up. If I am arrested, there'll still be time for you to run." The fervor to take to the hills then died down.

The reason I tried to control the situation and not allow it to go on taking its natural course was not because I didn't believe you would arrest people—much extremely reliable information had early on confirmed for me that reports of arrest and repression were more than just rumor. Otherwise I wouldn't have burned all of our lists and documents and made it so difficult for your henchmen to render "outstanding service." It also wasn't because I thought that it would be entirely impossible for us to hold our ground if we had indeed taken to the hills. On the contrary, China's great size and the fact that the people's knowledge of guerrilla warfare had been nurtured by years of Communist propaganda, in addition to widespread discontent and a general feeling of turmoil at the time, made conditions ripe for guerrilla action. Three or four million soldiers could not have destroyed the guerrillas; as long as they could have hung on for a period of time, they might have caused a national upheaval. It's difficult to say what might have happened.

But inciting national upheaval and widespread guerrilla warfare would have aggravated other complex social problems and meant complete social chaos. With everyone doing things their own way, some of these different factions would definitely have turned to sources outside the country for support. This would have been unavoidable in such a life-and-death situation. At that point nobody would have been able to control the situation any longer; once it had gained momentum it would have been out of control. Such chaos would have multiple consequences, with repercussions extending far beyond this small group of people. The fate of the Chinese people as a whole would have been hard to predict.

What would the future have held for the Chinese people? Could they have withstood such turmoil? Nobody has the right to lead them into a war of such severe and disastrous proportions ever again. That's why even while I waited for you to arrest me, I was still doing my best to discourage the guerrilla tendencies. I was aware that hiding would be better than sitting in jail—there were plenty of hiding places and I have enough experience to escape the mostly inept searchers, I'm also not such an idiot that I wouldn't have been able to survive abroad if I had to—but I just couldn't get away because I felt that my disappearance would be a signal for others to take to the hills. This responsibility was simply too great and I could not think of myself alone. I figured that it was inevitable that if you were going to make arrests you would make many, but since so much of your anger was directed at me, if you got me, others might be let go. Even imprisonment or execution was better than watching millions of people fall prey to a hopeless situation. This would also allow those who would follow in our footsteps some room to maneuver by not blocking all avenues toward the peaceful development of democracy. Even if not everyone understood this at the time, ensuring the future of our movement was also our responsibility.

All in all, of everything that happened during that period, two things out of three were done correctly; that's about a seventy-thirty or sixty-forty ratio. But that's not good enough because the overall goal—the promotion of democracy and reform—was left unattained. As my mistakes hindered progress toward this goal, they were critical mistakes. Although such a failure is almost imperceptible and difficult to assess, its effect is long-lasting and its influence widespread. I may not be the only person responsible for it, but this does not lessen my share of the burden.

I haven't eaten in over twenty days. I don't have much energy, so my writing is disorganized. I ask no more than that you do your best to read it. Please pay careful attention to the "connotations and implications."

Wei Jingsheng

December 6, 1983

"Reflections" upon reading Standing Committee Chairman Peng Zhen's Speech on the Importance of the Constitution:

Actually I don't have any reflections to speak of because there is nothing really new in Standing Committee Chairman Peng Zhen's speech. Nevertheless, it does contain an old cliché that is not only necessary, but extremely important to reiterate again and again as often as possible. People shouldn't just talk about the Constitution, but, as Chairman Peng points out, take steps to implement and strictly enforce it so as to avoid retreading old paths. Words like these ought to be repeated in our country constantly. The past few decades have bred a certain complacency in people; they no longer take the Constitution very seriously or believe it is of much use. In general, the authority of the Constitution is rather low, and it is often considered little more than "a scrap of waste paper." Various past tragedies, both large and small, have occurred because of just such a lawless and chaotic situation. If we hope to prevent such tragedies from happening again, we must first, as Chairman Peng says, practice adherence to the Constitution.

Implementation is no easy matter. There has been a Constitution in the past as well, but various tragedies and problems have still occurred because the current political atmosphere or the latest political jargon is always used to distort the words of the Constitution, sometimes even displacing it altogether. What can we do to keep the Constitution from being meaningless? There is a need for political trends and jargon because things are constantly changing and developing and politics must be able to adapt to these changes. But there are also aspects of politics that change relatively little, and the Constitution and the law are the elements that keep these stable. Tacking on lots of faddish jargon when implementing the Constitution or using current political lines to interpret or replace the Constitution is basically the same as not having a consistent and secure apparatus like the Constitution at all. This is the fundamental cause of political instability and distrust.

I can't say for sure what things are like in the outside world, but judging from the situation here in prison, a consistent and accurate rule of law has yet to be established. Therefore, it is always good whenever Standing Committee Chairman Peng chooses to raise this point. It is especially significant that he should reiterate it now when the latest three political campaigns, "Strike Hard," "Eliminate Spiritual Pollution," and "Clear Out Three Types of People," have come in rapid succession. For without an extremely strong Constitution and rule of law, they could meander off in the wrong direction. Constantly changing political and social movements are necessary, but implementation of the Constitution is even more necessary. If putting the Constitution into actual practice and gaining the people's trust are not possible, then nothing else can be accomplished successfully. Fine words repeated too many times become hollow. You can see it as two sides of the same coin; you can't have one without the other. This is my opinion; I am unable to come up with any real "reflections."

Wei Jingsheng

Immediately following his conviction in October 1979 on counter-revolutionary charges, Wei Jingsheng lodged an appeal with the Beijing Municipal Higher People's Court. His motion was turned down and Wei did not file another appeal until the one below, in March 1984. Although it too was denied, Wei wrote similar unanswered appeals for a reexamination of his case in 1986, 1987, and 1992.

March 10, 1984

Appeal Submitted to the Supreme People's Procuratorate:

It has now been five years since my arrest in 1979 and I continue to feel that the verdict on my case was unfair. I lodge an appeal on the following grounds:

1. I had no access to state secrets, and there is absolutely no evidence that I secured state secrets or furnished classified information. How, then, was the so-called "crime of furnishing classified information" formulated? The two verdicts of the Beijing courts were unjustified.

2. The so-called "crime of instigating counterrevolutionary propaganda" is also groundless. All of the statements I published in *Exploration* magazine that centered on reform and democracy are basically in accord with policies that have been pursued by the Communist Party and the government during the five years since the Third Plenum of the Eleventh Central Committee. Even if not identical, the goals are similar or the same and any differences between my statements and the central government's guiding policies on reform and democracy are not as great as those between it and the dissenting viewpoints currently being expressed in the newspapers. There is absolutely no evidence to prove that I incited people to "overthrow state power." To rely only on quotes taken out of context to falsify grounds for upholding this crime is, I believe, extremely unfair.

3. The public criticisms I made in *Exploration* of upper-level leaders in the central government should bear no relation to any

crime, regardless of the fact that my words may have been strong and not necessarily all accurate. Yet during the trial, I distinctly felt that the court was somehow being pressured and would not dare to issue a fair judgment. Even the court itself failed to deny that the verdict had been decided on earlier outside of the court and information that came out after the event proved this to be true. After the court-appointed lawyer told me "Due to political reasons I have no way to defend you" and requested release from my case, the court concealed the fact that my relatives had hired someone to take on my defense and only announced it after the trial, making it impossible for me to exercise my right to defense. When I later made an appeal to a higher court, I was again prohibited from hiring a defense lawyer. I don't have adequate evidence to make charges that retaliation for an old grudge played a hand in this series of illegal actions. As your court has the authority to investigate such matters, I request an investigation into any illegal activities in the trial process.

Having realized that this case involved high-level figures and that it was therefore difficult for any one department to have control, I have not requested a reinvestigation of my misjudged case during the past few years. But now my health is poor; I have coronary heart disease, periodontitis, stomach trouble, arthritis, and a number of other illnesses. Living in long-term isolation, the conditions for recuperation are extremely bad, therefore I am requesting medical treatment in a hospital or a release on medical parole. I am told that due to my "political problems," however, such decisions are made by the higher authorities and that is why medical parole or hospitalization are prohibited. For this same reason, it seems, undertaking scientific projects in prison and mailing them out for further research and experimentation are prohibited as well. In short, redress of this misjudged case will bring about resolution of all these other problems. I must maintain some degree of hope in your court. I hope that you will reexamine this case fairly.

Respectfully,
Wei Jingsheng

March 27, 1984

To Members of the Political Bureau and the Standing Committee
of the National People's Congress:

I am writing to you with the hope that someone among you
will uphold justice. In the appeal I recently lodged with the
Supreme People's Court, I explained the reasons I am asking that
justice be upheld. The matter is actually very simple and clear: No
counterrevolutionary activities or selling of classified information
existed—this was an absolutely misjudged case. The reasons for
this wrongful case are obvious to most people; there is no need
for me to mince words out of respect. Since I was put in prison for
offending Deng Xiaoping, it is very difficult for my case to be
redressed. This is precisely the reason why I have not lodged an
appeal during the past four years. Under certain conditions, the
"rule of law" is little more than a decorative ornament subject to
the ruler's will—I've still got enough common sense to see that.
Having offended a mighty leader, I'm lucky I didn't lose my head
and must be thankful for His Excellency Deng's "generosity."

In passing, let me mention that I feel General Secretary Hu
Yaobang's formulation of "A First Proposal on the Unity of Ethnic
Nationalities" is incorrect. Even in a "purely" minority region,
most problems still arise from the contradictions between democracy and dictatorship, and reform and conservatism. Therefore, the
best way of resolving this question is to promote democracy and
advance reform. When improvement is made in these areas, the
"ethnic nationalities question" will resolve itself naturally.
Whether you are talking about the Uighurs or the Tibetans, their
ability to live dignified and fulfilling lives is much more important
than the "problem" of what ethnicity the county Party secretary is,
for example. I nearly married a Tibetan woman, and I once had a
Uighur "auntie"; in the army my best buddies were of all nationalities: Han, Hui, Tu, Zhuang, Miao, Tujia, and so on; and there was
even a Hui member of *Exploration*, so I believe my observations
can't be too far off the mark. I suggest that in the future you raise
the "ethnic nationalities question" less and stop creating a sense of
racial division; we are all Chinese, and that is the way it should be.
Widening racial differences does nothing for anyone but a dictator.

I haven't been eating or sleeping well lately, I have no books to read, I've had headaches and dizziness and I know my writing is a bit sloppy, so I have to bother you to tolerate it. I'm afraid I might even pass my headaches and sore eyes on to you, so let me finish up. The ancients said "The man of fortune and prestige is short on words," so it might be that the source of my misfortune is that I talk too much. As another saying goes, "If you speak too much, you're certain to make mistakes," so I never know what others might grab on to and attack me with later. But old habits are hard to change even in this day and age when "sticking to old ways" may be a fatal shortcoming. So in the last, let's all hope we can work together to change our bad habit of talking too much!

Wei Jingsheng

April 15, 1984

Dear Hu Yaobang and Zhao Ziyang:

This letter concerns only public matters, not personal ones.

Among the uncultivated lands in our country are large expanses of saline-alkaline wastelands, including those found in the plains of the Liao River, the Hai River, and Shandong, the Huangtu plateau, and elsewhere. And nearly all of the lands suitable for cultivation on the plains have been harmed by saline-alkalization. Of particular interest is the great salt flat of the Loulan Basin in the eastern section of the Talimu Basin (about one hundred thousand square kilometers) in the Northwest. In ancient times this was the territory of a great nation, but now it has become nearly desolate, no doubt due to its destruction by alkali-desertification. How to transform these salt plains into land where the people of China can live is a question I have been looking into for a long time.

While in prison, I have come up with several inventions and projects—a few of which I mailed to Premier Zhao the year before last. But due to the fact that in prison, any official's personal whim takes precedence over regulations, I have been unable to send them out to be researched and put to use. Only through the kindness and consideration of lower-level cadres was I able to show them to my younger brother to look over. Whether he was able to remember every detail of the entire manuscript correctly or not, I'm not sure. But what got me especially excited and prompts me to write you another letter promoting my inventions is that after looking at my wind-powered alkalinity control plan, my brother pointed out the weak link in it: the desalination mechanism. It so happens that one of the newest products devised by his work unit (the nuclear engineering department at Beijing Number Five Research Institute) can remedy it. Their ion desalination film has a high water permeability and the price is only five yuan a square meter, which is much better than the ceramic desalination mechanism described in my plan. This drops the cost of my plan to a truly feasible level. This is very encouraging and exciting, and I can't keep myself from writing to you and letting you know how much promise this project has.

I am sending you a slightly revised version of the plans I showed to him with the hope that they may be of interest to you. I am also requesting yet again that I be allowed to voluntarily go to the Northwest to work on controlling the salinization problem there. I've heard that the living conditions there are even poorer than on the *laogai* prison farms, so you might just consider sending me there to be a form of *laogai* in itself. I can see absolutely no reason why this shouldn't be possible. Unless, of course, the only way for me to satisfy you is to be worn down for years here in solitary confinement. What harm would it bring you to let me go and do some useful work for the country? In addition, I could be free of what, from a medical point of view, is an unlawful living environment (by the way, I'd like to point out that Marx himself said that putting anyone in solitary confinement for more than three months was an inhumane and illegal act). The chance to do some work would also ease my mind and it would certainly be very good for my heart condition. I have severe gum disease and stomach trouble, yet in here I am forced to eat hard wheat cakes, corn biscuits, and such. As far as I am concerned these conditions can't be any worse than what they are in the Loulan Basin, so I sincerely hope that I can be allowed the opportunity to participate in working to open up the area.

Of course, I understand that you too have your difficulties. If you are truly unable to send me to transform the desert, then please forward my plans and drawings to an appropriate or interested department. Please don't delay; after all, do we Chinese people still have time to wait?

Wei Jingsheng

September 30, 1984

Thoughts on the Signing of the Sino-British Joint Declaration on Hong Kong:

The current method of handling the Hong Kong question is certainly the most ideal. It takes into consideration the "face" and interests of both governments, as well as the interests and wishes of the Hong Kong people, thereby managing to meet the criteria of paying the smallest price to resolve a major problem. This solution will also benefit our country's development and security, and it's entirely possible that we will begin reaping these benefits from the moment the declaration is signed. During the current transition period, as our country frees itself from poverty and builds a new economic structure, this agreement is a vital condition to stimulating increased development. At the same time, it also removes a latent danger that could have the potential to explode into an international dispute.

But the joint declaration is still no more than the critical first step toward a complete solution; the final solution will begin in 1997. The only guarantee of this final solution is that in the decade or so before and after 1997, the policies set out in the declaration be followed to the letter and be coupled with the advancement of reform and democracy inside China. Otherwise it is still possible that harmful collapse and turmoil can occur. But no matter what, the present success is something every Chinese person should be happy about.

Many say that this provides a model for resolving the question of Taiwan. This is very incorrect. For sure, if the Hong Kong declaration is carried out conscientiously and reliably, it can increase our government's political credibility. This is an important condition for resolving the Taiwan question as well as many other domestic and international political problems. But this is absolutely not a model or an outline. The question of Hong Kong involves the return of land occupied by foreigners; the question of Taiwan, on the other hand, involves the reconciliation and cooperation of two different domestic political forces. It is also absolutely incorrect to phrase this problem as "the return of Taiwan to the motherland," for the underlying premise of this wording is that "Taiwan is a breakaway country from China." This formulation is unacceptable to both the Communist and Nationalist Parties and to the Chinese people, and it does not tally with the facts. Taiwan was already returned to China by the Japanese forty years ago, while the Taiwanese regime is nothing more than a domestic political power in opposition to the central government within China. It is one country with two political systems and not two separate countries; this is a basic difference.

The reunification of China is a question of domestic political forces moving from opposition to reconciliation and cooperation so that the two political powers can merge into one. It's not like Germany or Korea, where a country of a single race has split into separate nations that must be reunited.

There is nothing new about more than one antagonist political power existing in a single country. Examples from abroad might seem remote, but our country has been in this situation throughout the twentieth century. There was the father and son team of the Zhang warlords in the Northeast, the Soviet base areas in various regions, the "local government" of Yan'an, and numerous other examples. Yet if someone said that the Northeast at the time was a separate country or that Shaanxi, Gansu, and Ningxia provinces were once part of the Soviet Union, people would have good reason to think that he had lost his senses.

Taiwan is currently governed by a Chinese government. Once this is understood, then negotiations on political unification can be carried out and steps taken toward a gradual reunification. There is no need to wait for negotiations to be completed before undertaking these steps; they can be started today. The various policies on Taiwan that have already been announced are in fact steps toward reconciliation and cooperation; there is no necessity for negotiations with any foreign government. Naturally, a nation's central government possesses not only the power, but the prime responsibility for forging domestic political cooperation and unity. At present, however, many of the political and diplomatic policies toward Taiwan are not in keeping with a conciliatory approach, but actually might diminish the opportunity and atmosphere for reconciliation. The possibility of resolving the confrontational situation with the Nationalist government through contention and containment will lead to nothing in this century and probably nothing in the early part of the next one either. Military threats and containment can only cause the atmosphere to deteriorate; this will be disadvantageous for both sides, but in the end, it is the Chinese people who will suffer the most. For example, no one benefits when discriminatory measures are implemented that concern the protection of different types of Chinese nationals abroad; it only gives foreigners more opportunities for discriminating against all Chinese. If Taiwan is isolated diplomatically and economically, the result will be a loss of face for the Chinese people as a whole. It will also serve to force the Nationalist government in Taiwan to rely on foreign countries on an even greater scale. A divided China is not necessarily a bad thing for foreign countries, and this is obviously not our aim.

Actually, many of our current methods are holdovers from the past. Many were formulated under the premise of "extinguish the Nationalists" and are naturally not in step with current policy. I am being held in a state of isolation at present and don't have access to any national publications, so, of course, I know even less of what the situation is like behind the scenes. I can't judge whether the intent and reality of current policy are in harmony and can only speak as if they are. Naturally, when the intent changes, all concrete actions should change accordingly.

For example, when the Nationalists first attended the United Nations General Assembly, their delegation contained a representative from the Communist Party. Why don't we follow suit and give the "Chinese Nationalist Party" a speaking seat in our delegation to the United Nations? Of course, there is still only one voting seat. We could even take it a step further and set up a Taiwanese "chargé d'affairs" office in each of our embassies abroad in order to coordinate matters pertaining to Chinese holders of either passport. To go even further, we could invite the Nationalist government to set up an "office" in each province and out of reciprocity we could set up a Communist Party office in Taiwan. In this way, not only do we create a positive atmosphere for reconciliation, but we begin to take concrete steps toward political reunification. Negotiation can take place later if at all. One shouldn't negotiate for the sake of negotiation, or get caught up in peace talk conspiracies.

You must first initiate and carry out open discussions of concrete issues. If at first they refuse to receive our delegation, they eventually will or they will risk arousing public indignation in the overseas Chinese and Taiwan press. I doubt that even Chiang Ching-kuo and the others are that stupid. If negotiations are successful, then the two sets of diplomatic structures that currently exist can be merged into one. This way foreign countries won't have a chance to exploit this conflict to their advantage. There's no need to consider whether this is consistent with international practices or not. Even conventional practices were original at one time, so if others could take new approaches, why can't we? As long as it benefits national unity and political reconciliation, then it is feasible. There's no harm in establishing a precedent.

These are just some of my unformulated thoughts for your reference.

Wei Jingsheng

In the fall of 1984, Wei Jingsheng was transferred from Beijing to Tanggemu Farm, a laogai *(reform-through-labor camp) in the remote desert region of Qinghai province in western China. Following is one of the "thought" statements that prison authorities asked Wei to write shortly after his arrival.*

December 1984

Some Recent Thoughts:

I've been in Qinghai for over two months now. Aside from the climate and some other aspects of life here that I'm not used to, everything else is bearable. My health has been relatively stable and I haven't had any major outbreaks of heart trouble. My stomach problems and arthritis flare up now and then, but it's nothing major; only my headaches have been terrible. The political instructor and brigade leader look after me and there's no major problem there either.

I haven't done a whole lot of thinking about my personal future—or it might be more correct to say I've thought about it all before. On the one hand, I should write appeals and letters requesting a redress of my misjudged case—I can't just accept a decision as mistaken as that. On the other hand, I know I should also respect the law and quietly serve out my sentence. But these are two aspects of the same matter and I can't separate one from the other. By appealing the case, I question the integrity of the law and treat it as arbitrary. It would also be wrong not to carry out the sentence because mistakes were made in trying the case. The correct attitude to take is to accept the sentence while at the same time employing legal means to redress any mistakes. Whether my case is put right or not and how in the end it will be corrected is the decision of the judiciary; my personal opinion can do little to influence it. Therefore, I haven't been giving this matter a great deal of thought.

Every person bears a burden of responsibility for the welfare of the nation. Even if it does sound a bit funny to say that prisoners shouldn't forget to show concern for their country and their people, if you asked me to disengage myself completely from the future of my nation and my people and not to "comment on politics," I'm afraid I would be unable to do so. In the last few years in particular, as our country has redirected itself toward development, and movements for reform and democracy have surged and resurged, political and economic trends have not only affected the well-being of every person in the nation, but have concerned the personal interests of each individual to such an extent that it is possible to say that nobody can be "unconcerned about politics."

The cadres here now show great care in looking after us, so even if there is any problem, it can usually be overcome. It's just that this area is cut off from all news and it is very difficult to even find a newspaper to read. There is no television and we are practically sealed off from the outside world. It is essential to have a radio to listen to, but it appears that this is a rather difficult question for the authorities to solve. One guy might want to hear the news, another a lecture, and if it were placed on a wall in the yard, nobody would be able to hear it clearly, and if inside just one cell, then the others couldn't hear. So to avoid stirring up any conflicts, there is no radio at all. Why couldn't each prisoner simply be allowed to buy his own? There is a big difference between the isolation cells for political prisoners and the large ward; political prisoners tend to be more interested in politics. Even Jiang Qing enjoyed the use of a television and a tape recorder, so why should we be prohibited? No matter what kind of a prisoner one is, it's always good for him to keep up with current events, and Party policy approves of prisoners receiving more propaganda, since it is good for their reform.

It is a terrible shame for me to waste over ten years of my life. In addition to being able to use this time for study, I should be allowed to do some work that my conditions and ability will allow. Originally, I planned to put in order some of the inventions and plans I wrote up in Beijing, but now it seems I won't be able to get accustomed to the climate here for a while yet. The lack of oxygen aggravates my headaches and I must put my plans off for a time and wait. Some of the projects are rather large in scale and need to be given to a bigger work unit to experiment with, but there are some that aren't hard to try out and with the right tools and materials, I could test them myself. I hope that the cadres here will consider letting me do so.

I can't do any major work, but I can do some smaller things. The brigade leader has already arranged the sideline production for next year, but I hope to have a long-range plan in the future, so that I can have lots of work to do. This would not only improve my life, but the frequent exercise would be good for my health as well.

Wei Jingsheng

Spring 1985

Dear Lingling, Taotao, and Shanshan:

Hello!

I received your letter as well as the books and tape recorder. I'm very happy! But in my excessive happiness I regret only that you didn't also mail along a few cassettes so that I could enjoy some music. There is no radio or television here, and it's been a long time since I've heard any music. Aside from the cry of the wind and the cooing of the rabbits when they're in heat, there aren't any other sounds to "enjoy."

If you send an English tape, definitely include the study materials to go with it. I've never studied English before and I don't have any textbooks or dictionaries handy, so I'll have to wait for you to send me everything I need. Send the plug and microphone for this tape recorder along as well, and another adaptor. We have electricity in the evenings from a generator at the reservoir here on the farm and before too long the prison will be connected with the Northwest electricity network and the electricity here will be stabilized. I'll be able to listen to music as well as study English and it'll be a lot cheaper than using batteries.

Don't send along any "serious" political music. I'd prefer some relaxing classical favorites like Schubert, Mozart, or Strauss. There are some good popular songs too, like the music from the movie *Heroic Youths*, for example, which are very beautiful. On the train here, I heard some new versions of Chinese folk songs and tunes jazzed up with a modern flavor that were also very good. Zhu Mingying's series of folk songs made a deep impression on me;

"Clouds Playing with the Moon" and "A Chicken in One Hand, a Duck in the Other" are especially rich, even though she's broken with the traditional way of singing and added a Western-style twist. They're really enjoyable to listen to. I don't know why, but I like Western classical music, all kinds of modern styles, and even folk songs and opera from all over, but I can't take that self-proclaimed "serious" stuff. To categorize music as serious or not is pure nonsense! Music is an art that expresses emotion, feeling, and so on—"content that can be felt but not easily described"—through sound waves over time. This is just the opposite of painting, which expresses the same type of thing but through the composition of images in space. The more "content" there is in a piece of music, the less content it actually has; if an art that "can be felt but not easily described" is incapable of expressing politics, then so be it! Political treatises cannot express artistic beauty, and art (discounting supplementary elements such as lyrics) cannot be a tool for the expression of political views. No matter how good a shoe is, it can't replace a hat.

In a society without standards of quality, art too will be misrepresented. This is why true art belongs to the people. Those who consider their art to be above worldly concerns are not true artists. In the past, the fact that people didn't accept "foreign" music wasn't due entirely to appreciation customs (what are often described as expressions of national sentiment), but because the proponents of "serious" music completely lacked any musical taste. Young people today are quick to enjoy modern music; nobody needs to teach them and they eventually learn to judge good from bad for themselves. And foreigners are also quick to appreciate Peking Opera! Who says there are such things as immutable habits of appreciation? The romantic style of popular music from Hong Kong and Taiwan actually grows out of our "national sentiments"; it's one of the things our country's traditional music can amply express, and is not a foreign import. So why, then, must we also produce such a harsh, militaristic "serious" style of music? People's lives are varied and their feelings are complex, so if minds are not homogenous, then art shouldn't be either. Uniform art is part of the degenerate uniform culture brought on by conservative influences. It's just as General Secretary Hu said recently: "Only popular music is good music."

There's another line Hu Yaobang said well: "Right now we are primarily waging a battle against ignorance, and not against the so-called 'liberalization.' " I don't know where he made this remark—could you find it so I can have a look? The letters I've written to Hu Yaobang and Zhao Ziyang over the past few years have contained similar ideas, but at the time were considered by some to be "reactionary thought" and completely disapproved of. Now, however, my words seem to have been proven correct!

In her letter, Lingling was completely right in saying that people can't always think of themselves—that's precisely why I have always acted on behalf of others. But in my present situation I face difficulties no matter what I try to do. Even the minor matter of my raising rabbits—something that is both beneficial and harmless to the people around me—would have been prohibited long ago if Commissar Zhang at the labor camp here had not given his nod of approval. Other things are even more difficult. The original reason I requested a transfer to the Northwest was because I once heard that there was much to do here and people were needed. In addition, some of my inventions and plans had relevance to the Northwest, so I thought I would come and do what I could; at least, I figured, I would not be just wasting my time! But who would have guessed that I would be placed in solitary confinement here as well, cut off from all contact with others, and left in this stifling cell month after month, year after year. The only difference is the "trusties" that once guarded me from outside have now been moved into my cell and disturb me so much that I can't read at night or sleep during the day. Oops, I got it backward. That should be: I can't read during the day or sleep at night. It's a struggle just to study, let alone do anything else. Right now it looks like the only thing I can do is put my inventions in order and give them to you to take to the patent bureau. Otherwise, when I die, these things will all go to waste. I'll only be able to hand over the fruits of my mental labors to Marx when I see him in heaven! But as Su Shi wrote, "I couldn't bear the cold in such high places, so I rise and dance, playing with pure shadows; for what can compare to this human world?" I think I'm still better off leaving these things for humanity.

Recently I haven't done much work on my inventions because my health and mood have not been good. My heart condition has not been as stable as it was last year, although my blood pressure is not as high (this is probably due to the low atmospheric pressure here). But my gum disease persists stubbornly; I've lost two more teeth in a row and my last upper front tooth is ready to go to its grave. Soon I'll start sounding like an old lady flapping her gums! Also, my bowel movements are always very dry and I really don't know what I should do about it. Since I can't chew my food well, there are large pieces of food and blood in my stool. In addition, I feel dizzy and have a ringing in my ears, so I haven't felt like working on my inventions. It looks like I'll just have to do it slowly. Anyway, there's no hurry.

The living conditions here are bad, and so is the food. It's a farm and on a grazing area, but there's still no milk to be had. I hear that even the cadres have a hard time buying meat and it's more expensive than in Xining. Other than the locally grown "giant" bokchoy that is barely the size of a fist, the cadres have to go to Xining to buy their vegetables. You wouldn't believe what the conditions on this *laogai* farm are actually like. I did manage to buy a little pot so that I can boil my food when I can't chew it, and the cadres sometimes help me buy other foods for a change.

All in all, my situation is not that bad. When I had my blood tested, the doctor told me that my veins were easy to find. I've had my blood taken for tests twice, but I don't know whether the second time was a liver function test or just routine, but the first time when I was sent to the Hainanzhou Hospital, I felt that it took a really long time to get the results of my routine test. It made me wonder whether there was a problem with my blood cells. Maybe they couldn't find any to count?! But then, I still don't know the answer because they haven't given me the results yet. I'm not quite ready to drop dead yet, but my health is not great either.

It was actually illegal that the Beijing prison didn't let you find a lawyer. You have the right to hire a lawyer to make an appeal for me, and the right to ask him to apply for a release on medical parole on my behalf; I learned this from a case in *Democracy and*

Law magazine. Physical condition does not fall into the category of confidential matters. Since my case was an open trial, the trial files should not be considered secret either and the lawyer can consult them. Liu Shufen, the lawyer appointed to represent me before, read them. When you submit the appeal, you can look for her; I felt that the woman had a sense of justice and was very well versed in the law. (She is from the first crop of lawyers schooled after 1949.) Even though her defense was completely ineffective (and couldn't be any other way), I still trust her very much. Of course, if you've found somebody else I wouldn't have any qualms either. Just do whatever you think is best! I don't know the situation. Also, if anyone raises any additional conditions, you can take care of it as you see fit, you don't need to ask me. Anyway, you know my personality and my outlook: Let people do their jobs as they see fit and always think of the country and the people first. Only on matters of principle do I positively refuse to "defer out of politeness"; opposing democracy, the rule of law, or reform are things I will absolutely not do.

When you come to visit in the spring, you must definitely bring my guitar, as well as some jam, pickled tofu, sausages, and any other food items. You don't need to bring tea; I drink brick tea now. It's good and cheap (about 2 yuan per *jin*). Also, bring some of my tools with you. Sometimes I can do a little handiwork here like fixing things, building rabbit hutches or feeding troughs or water containers, so it would be quite useful. Bring my cutting pliers, pincer pliers, small hacksaw, hammer, ax, metal file, mid-sized saw, planer, curved planer, chisel, large shears, and other tools with you. I don't know if my soldering iron is there or not; if not, just bring a regular iron and some solder and soldering paste. As for the breeding rabbits, please don't forget them and no matter what, bring two males and two or three females. Don't bring adult rabbits—they're too heavy—bring medium-sized ones of about two or three *jin*. On the journey here you just need to give them your leftovers or fruit peelings and enough water and they won't starve. If you can't find Large-Ear White rabbits, then Giants (a West German breed), Himalayan, or Danish White rabbits will do. You can ask a few people and have a look around. If you really can't find them, then Gray-Blue ones are fine. Our family used to raise these and there are a lot of them in Beijing. If you also come across Large-Ear Whites or Giants of mixed breed, that's even better. Raising rabbits and doing a bit of handiwork helps me let off some steam and it's good for my health too; it would be a good thing for others too if I managed to breed some excellent bunnies. My bunnies are pretty funny too; they'd rather eat fish skin than grass— just like little kittens, but with long ears!

As soon as you get this letter, send more medicine; I only have enough Chinese medicine and vitamins left to last another month or so. By the time you get this, they'll be nearly finished. I'm no longer capable of taking care of myself, so I have no choice but to bother you to help me. As the Japanese say, "I am very embarrassed!" I have nothing good here to offer in return except for a bit of the fish I dried myself. I'll send some just to give you a taste of something different. Don't forget to take two over to Papa as a gesture from me. There's nothing on the fish but salt, so you might want to put some ginger powder, soy sauce, vinegar, or other sauce on the fish and steam it before eating. See how our Qinghai sturgeon compares to dried salmon!

By the time this letter reaches you, it will probably already be the Grave-Sweeping Festival. The poem I placed before the urn holding Mama's ashes has been there a long time. I'm sending you a poem I wrote in the fall of 1981. Help copy it over nicely for me and put it in front of the urn in place of the old one. Mama always loved to read my poems.

Eight-Line Verse

(One night in November 1981, I saw Mama in a dream, she was gone in a moment, I cried out and wrote this after awaking in tears.)

> *Your face and voice appear in the land of dreams,*
> *I feel mournful and anxious, my heart in knots.*
> *You gave everything to life before departing,*
> *But I go on living, dreams unrealized.*
> *A loving mother's hopes for her son endure,*
> *A filial son repents, but I cannot.*

My tears of sorrow pave your way to heaven,
How can I someday face my guilt to see you there?

If you like, I can send you a few more of the poems I've written in recent years—unless, of course, Taotao has something to say about it. I'm waiting for your letter. When you write, please tell me more details about the situation with Taotao's new girlfriend. I can help you think it over too. However, I think that Taotao got tainted by some of Papa's gentlemanly habits, and an old-fashioned "virtuous wife and good mother" type suits him, otherwise they'll have to break up. Taotao, what do you think about my comments? I really want to know. Try not to be so demanding of others.

Say hello to everyone for me!

Your older brother,
Jingsheng

Fall 1985

Dear Section Chief Gu:

It seems that my attempt to breed rabbits is getting more and more difficult. Although I have no idea why, the matter is beginning to look hopeless.

For one, I still haven't been given the room you promised me, since Han Aijing hasn't been moved back to Cell Four yet. As you've seen yourself, my bunnies are getting very big, and I can no longer let them out in the yard. Rabbits like to sleep during the day and move about at night, and they can't sleep well with too much noise. As for the problem of the filth, that's no longer even a priority.

Second, food seems to be getting more and more difficult to obtain. The rabbits won't grow well eating only scraps. None of the cadres are willing to take me out to cut grass, and with everyone putting off the task, a week frequently goes by when I don't get grass even once. I don't have any bone ash left either, although there's still plenty of salt. The feed you supplied hasn't come, and even if it does, there won't be any green feed in it. Without any grass to eat, the rabbits have been gnawing on the legs of the tables and chairs and even my shoes.

I feel that if we really want to do this right, then essential items like a rabbit hutch, rabbit cages, feed, and medicine are top priorities. You are well aware of my situation here, so I can only rely on you. We should have an overall plan and implement each item one by one. As for my going out to cut grass, I know you've certainly given the brigade this order, so I just can't understand why it's so difficult for them to take me out to cut some. Didn't you make it clear to them? Or is there some problem within the brigade? You're the only one who can look into it and find out. I don't understand anything and have no idea what is going on.

My health has not been very good lately; my cough is terrible, my heart is not good, and my arthritis is acting up again. When you arrange a visit to Dr. Guo, please see if I can have another tooth pulled while I'm there.

Wei Jingsheng

January 29, 1986

Dear Lingling, Taotao, and Shanshan:

I wrote you back immediately after receiving the 170 yuan you sent. It was a "chatty" letter and I chatted on for over twenty pages. I don't know whether you received it or not. From what I can tell, letters coming in and going out pass through a pretty tedious inspection procedure and I don't know at which stage my letters get stuck. The truth is, I write letters more quickly than you do. On average I write if not two then one and a half per month, while you average only one letter every six months.

If you can't get that tiger-bone liquor, just forget about it and buy some other arthritis medicine for me! My arthritis and heart condition both act up when the weather changes. I agree that tigers should be protected, but I think there are still more of them in existence than you said. The tiger's greatest enemy is man, so the only thing needed is stricter prohibitions on poachers, otherwise the animal's own ability to protect itself is very strong. This is probably the main reason why nobody sets up a fund for them! Here in Qinghai we have a member of the large feline family that is nearly as rare as those in the Northeast; it's been called the "most perfect of felines"—the snow leopard. I often read reports of poachers in the paper. Actually, merely issuing a regulation is not enough; the routes for the private sale of tiger pelts must also be cut off. When a single pelt can sell for several thousand yuan, the temptation to poach is just too great. The brokers and consumers of prohibited animal pelts should be punished. Then no one would dare to use them and nobody would buy or trap them. Otherwise the regulation is worth little more than the paper it is written on and the great outdoors will not be protected.

I think Shanshan's aesthetic sensibilities may have been influenced by my own. Do you remember how often I drew tigers when I was a kid? Tigers too are fearless in the face of danger: powerful, but not ruthless; strong and yet clever; and they never act recklessly. When I was working in the zoo, I would frequently go alone to the tiger den to enjoy them. (Others all disliked the stench of the pen and would not go for several years at a time.) As I watched them, I would forget that these "great cats" had lived in the zoo for several generations, and I would find myself lost in their beauty. There was only one tiger who had been born in the wild. It had lost part of its tail struggling during capture, but it was the least worth looking at: a real instance of the saying, "Once a tiger leaves the mountains, even dogs can bully him." The other tigers, having grown accustomed to life in captivity, appeared much more self-assured and more readily inspired fantasy and imagination. Aesthetic appreciation is one way of molding character; coarse people (although they are not necessarily evil people) can't enjoy this pleasure. Raising the cultural level of the people is not only good for productivity, but for enjoyment in general, for only in pleasure can one fully enhance the quality of culture.

Shanshan, over the past few years I've observed that you (as well as the entire artistic community) have had a tendency toward hoping for quick success and instant profit in favor of cultivating your own artistic talents and enhancing the quality of your cultural sensitivity. But this won't buy you much time because it is merely like tugging at an old jacket to conceal its raggedness, only to expose your elbows—there are too many problems to cope with. Your work unit doesn't give any bonuses, so it doesn't make any difference whether you accomplish your tasks well or not. You should arrange more cultural activities for yourself; you can read more, see more movies (high-level ones, that is), and put more effort into cultivating your own artistic sensibilities. Even by just walking up and down Wangfujing to shop you can appreciate the different "flavor" it has from the Qianmen market. This "flavor" can't necessarily be put into words, but like the old story of the jockey who could pick out a winning horse no matter what its color, if you understand the true essence of something, then you will always have it for your own. You will never need to regret that somebody thought of something before you. Great successes never intentionally try to mystify and frequently leave people with the impression of simplicity instead, yet the thinking that went into it actually took a great deal of training, knowledge, imagination, perception, and so on. Of course, it also takes creativity. Inspiration is not a servant that "comes when you beckon, and leaves when you command." You have to pay a price for it. Those who don't pay in full end up mediocre. That's why people of talent are so rare.

I read about your "artistic wall hangings" in the *People's Daily*. The commentary said that the exhibition was "put together by three young artists," and right away I guessed that the "Wei Yaling" credited with the photograph was you and even suspected that you had written the accompanying article. The style was very much like that of our family: straightforward, emotional, and unpretentious. It was only later when I noticed how many other articles this woman wrote that I took the crown away from you. Otherwise, this case of mistaken judgment could have gone on for some time. I don't know what the production arrangement is for your wall hangings, or whether you could let us out here in the sticks soak up a little of the profits, but after you explain the situation to me, I can talk it over with the section chief and political commissar and see. They aren't in charge of production, though, and seldom pay too much attention to my suggestions anyway. It seems that people put more trust in those with a diploma. So be it. A "doctor" (that's what they used to call me in my old work unit) like myself is never considered to be as good as one with a real diploma. This is just the result of a lack of education.

Even if I do get to leave here, I still hope to achieve my goal of producing an exceptional breed of rabbit. Aside from those that have been eaten (all male) or given away, I have still got two relatively good males and seven females. They live outside and in an empty cell without heat (the one I used to be in) at temperatures as low as twenty degrees below zero Celsius, and are totally fine; their growth rate is just a bit slower. Their body size and growth, and the length and quality of their fur, is much better than the old rabbits. It's just that the conditions for raising rabbits here are too poor. There's little food except for leftover scraps; I'm not even able to get hold of the seed cakes or wheat grass that is grown locally for fertilizer. It's really a shame. Even Section Chief Gu can't do anything. Our brigade has been here for three years already, but funds have yet to be allocated. The office is even anxious over heating coal, so how could they come up with money for me to buy feed or make rabbit hutches! I'll just wait and see if things change later. In the meantime, I've formed a "Get By Club" here—the rabbits just get by; there's just enough coal to get by; and I just barely get by myself! However, when you come this summer, you must bring me breeding rabbits: two male breeders at least. The best would be if you can get ahold of a German or French breed; the German breed has thick fur and the French has a large body. If the government finally comes up with some money, I'll write again and tell you, and you can buy an even better breed.

I read in the paper that Shanghai invested 350,000 yuan to set up a rabbit breeding concern, but I believe that if I do things right here, I might even outdo them. The climate here is cool and dry, and there is plenty of ultraviolet light. Breeding rabbits already exist here that are accustomed to the climate and that others couldn't find even if they looked. The high plains rabbit industry can eventually overtake that of the Shanghai region. The first little bunny I was given as a promotional sample grew quite well;

everyone likes him, but he's just as mischievous as my other rabbits; he'll leap over a meter-high fence in one bound. When I
wasn't paying attention for just a moment, a large spayed rabbit
chewed off part of the ear of a half-grown one. They fight even more
fiercely than those wild rabbits on the TV show *Animal Kingdom*.
And when they do, they're more like dogs, rolling around in the dirt
and dust; but what can you do with them?!

After I received your 170 yuan, I asked Section Chief Gu to buy
me an electric blanket the next time he had to go to Xining. But he
won't buy it now that he's seen your letter and he realizes that you
can buy it more easily there. So when you get this letter please
send me one right away. The coal is in short supply this year, but
Section Chief Gu says that there won't be a need for me to use my
own money to buy coal before May; he'll figure out a way regardless
of what happens. It looks like, at the very least, I won't have to buy
my own coal before April, so I've asked him to buy me some food
and other necessities the next time he goes to Xining. The medicine took 100 yuan. If you haven't sent Lingling's canned meat
already, please keep it for yourselves. It's convenient for you to
carry when you're traveling. The meat here is fresher and I think
the price is even cheaper. It's not good for me, but I still like to eat
a lot of it. It's more economical for you to send me money than
canned food anyway. The guards here are not completely unwilling
to help me out. Guards are people too; over the years there have
been some unfriendly ones, but of course some very friendly ones
as well—no different from people you find in any other occupation.

Also, Lingling, please send that long-life battery you mentioned.
We don't have electricity here during the day, so the evening is the
only time I can study English. In a sudden burst of energy, I finished the first five lessons in one week. If I keep up this pace, I'll
finish three books in half a year, so when you come, don't forget to
bring the new textbooks and cassettes. There's a limit on how long
I can use my tape recorder because the parts are always burning
out. Recordings are often unclear. (It records the lessons too
quickly and the speaking is too fast; a beginner can't catch everything.) I'm learning English like Lenin: it's not British English, but
my own version. I'll just make do with it until you come this

summer and then I'll go over it again and correct myself. I don't want a British person to think I'm speaking a foreign language! Please bring or send some more tapes. Also bring or send a set of screwdrivers, a tape measure, a pair of point-nose pliers, a small pair of tweezers, and some soldering paste and solder. That way when the tape recorder breaks, I can repair it myself, since the basic tools I've fashioned out of wire here are clumsy. On average now, I have to fix it once a month, otherwise it goes on strike.

I spend too much money, but what can I do? If my diet is even a bit lacking, all my little illnesses act up. Now I can understand what Engels meant when he spoke of the importance of meat to human evolution. But I know this burden is too heavy for you. I'm still so dependent. If you can get some of the money that might be owed to me for foreign publications, then please do. There must at least be some portion that can be considered legal income under my present condition. At least this much of it should be obtained first. Having money and not using it is the same as not having any at all, and if I don't use it to eat, drink, and buy medicine and coal, then I don't know whether I'll still be alive to get the money! Besides, it will bring some foreign currency into the economy! You can contact the appropriate people and do your best to get some of the money now. If you need to, get a lawyer. I have to leave this matter to you. I hope you can send a pen, books, medicine, and a calendar soon too. I've "detained" Taotao's lighter, but the flint spring is shot, so please ask him to find a lighter for me or another little spring. If only the spring and gears were okay, this lighter could last a lifetime—it would really suit the tastes of Chinese consumers.

That dried seaweed is delicious. Please bring a lot of it when you come.

Let me correct two mistakes Shanshan made: The first character for the word "allow" is different from the one in the word "full." Also, greater pandas are not a family, but a species in the carnivore order. In Chinese their scientific name is "cat bear," even though they look more like bear-sized cats. Lesser pandas, however, are called "bear cats." The Northeast tiger is not a species either, it is one of eight subspecies of the tiger species of the feline family.

There are three subspecies in our country: the Northeastern tiger, the Chinese southern tiger, and the Bengal tiger (in Tibet). It's the country with the most tigers in the world, and we should take great care to protect them.

Wishing you all a happy spring!

Give my best to all the elders in the family!

Your older brother,
Jingsheng

May 20, 1986

Dear Lingling, Taotao, and Shanshan:

Hello!

It's been a long time since I have written and a long time since I've received a letter from you. How have things been lately? I look forward to your letter arriving soon.

The pen Taotao promised to send me has not arrived yet either. I've been waiting for him and Shanshan to send it, so I haven't bought one myself. As a result, the good one hasn't arrived and I don't even have a mediocre one to use; as the saying goes, not only did I lose the melon, but I didn't even get any of its seeds! I'm sure Taotao is the one holding everything up. What's he so busy with anyway? Is he preparing to get remarried? He's not getting any younger, so he should get on with it.

Today is my thirty-sixth birthday and I passed it pretty well. A few days ago, while out having a false tooth put in, I bought an old chicken and last night I stewed a pot of soup to make Long-Life noodles in chicken soup today—what good fortune! I've spent most of the money you sent except for a little more than thirty yuan. It was mainly smoked and eaten away, and I used less than forty of it to buy books. There aren't any good books or magazines to buy here anyway. Even if some good ones happen to make it here, I don't get to buy them, so I will still have to rely on you to send me reading material. Send some of the recent award-winning or controversial works (except for the "new poetry"—I can't appreciate that). Several of the cadres here and I would all like to take a look at Zhang Xianliang's controversial new book, for example. No matter what, one should always formulate judgments on his own and not just mimic what others are saying. I still haven't read it yet and there's nobody to borrow it from, so I can only count on you to send it so that I can judge this "old news" for myself. Although there isn't much intellectual life here and things are slow-paced (on average, about six months behind Beijing), I'm still interested in the changes going on in intellectual and artistic circles.

It's not that I don't have an interest in science and the reforms any longer, but there's no way for me to take an interest even if I wanted to! And now that my health is so bad, I've been feeling really frustrated. If they feel they don't need more people to participate and want simply to rely on their own old ideas to carry out the reforms, then so be it! Why bother putting my two cents in and annoying people? Anyway, when they slip up, I won't be responsible. I'll just suffer a bit more along with everybody else and no more. From now on I'm going to take after those smarter folks, and even if I can't learn to brown-nose, at least I can keep my mouth shut and pay less attention to others and more to myself.

Looking at China's overall situation, the setbacks of 1984–85 are no more than "tremors"—the main quake is still to come. There may be big problems in the near future. The economy is an important factor, but not the crucial one. I'm afraid that all the factors will combine together to produce a shake-up no less devastating in scale than the Cultural Revolution! But the reasons for it and the way it happens will be very different. One of the reasons for its great intensity will be that those old men who are drunk on their false sense of power and the flattery of boot-licking foreigners have completely lost their senses. They look at everything through filtered lenses, seeing only what they want to, totally ignoring anything else, and stubbornly sticking to their ways. In the face of this situation, I urge you to build your own "refuge"—cultivate more flowers and fewer thorns. This way you can survive the coming disaster, since there isn't much chance for the tide to turn. Even I don't have the power to change things and in this respect your situation is even worse than mine, so don't waste your time. There are many people in our generation who are talented but gutless; and there are many who have more guts than me but lack talent; and still others who have the guts, talent, and the loyalty and devotion to the nation but don't have the opportunity to form an effective social force to resist the spread of decay and the speed of its exponential reproduction. In the face of a future like this, it's better to be wise and play it safe. Keep this in mind.

Who will emerge to rebuild the country and restore China in the beginning of the next century? The rest of this century can only be left to decay and provide more fertile soil for growth in the next century. This incompetent generation of headstrong old men who think they are omnipotent are the products of nearly a half a century ago and Chinese history now resembles periods of ancient history; nothing can be done but wait for history to regenerate itself and life to start anew. My mistake is that I'm trying to treat a patient with a terminal illness and will have to admit defeat in the end. In a world filled with ignorance, thinking becomes a crime. Remember this point well. Learn from the great sages of the past who feigned madness and acted like fools! For if you don't act like a fool now, you'll end up being a bastard like the others later.

I don't know if you will be able to come this summer or not. Please write and let me know in advance. If you do come, don't forget to bring a pen, a tape recorder, and some books and magazines. The tape recorder I have now is already a worthless scrap of metal. If you can't come before August, please send me some "funds." Even if I only spend money on cigarettes, after July I'll be "operating in the red." If it's permitted, Taotao, bring along your girlfriend, and if Lingling's and Shanshan's husbands can come to see me too, I would be extremely happy. Of course, this depends on whether circumstances will allow, so don't force it. I'm only saying "I would be extremely happy," but if it's not possible or there's not enough time, I won't be unhappy. I am extremely fortunate to have two such good brothers-in-law. Taotao is lucky now too, so please come and introduce me to the mother of my future nieces and nephews!

Pass along my greetings to all the in-laws in the family!
Say hello to little Fanfan!

Your older brother,
Jingsheng

P.S. Don't forget to bring along an English-Chinese dictionary.
There are a lot of words in the textbook that aren't on the vocabulary
lists.

January 9, 1987

Dear Prison Authorities:

The medicine I got the last time I saw the doctor is all used up and
the shots are nearly finished as well. My health has improved a bit,
but it's still not that good and the pains in my chest continue to be
very severe. The treatment methods available here at our Tanggemu Hospital are limited. Do you think it possible for me to see a
doctor at a larger hospital, such as Gonghe or Xining? My attacks
are now coming with greater intensity; they're much worse than last
year and occur at any time without warning. As the electrocardiogram revealed clearly, the situation now is very serious; I could be
struck down by an attack at any moment. Secretary Liu and Secretary Wang can give you the details of the situation, and Dr. Lu can
explain it to you as well.

The immediate cause of my illness is the cold. Right up until
last November, my health was better than the year before, but the
colder the weather turned, the less coal was distributed. In
December and January we were given nothing but inferior coal
(half of it the stuff brought in the year before last and the other half
from last spring). Political Instructor He even said, "We've got to
be a bit tougher on you." This type of coal can only generate a limited amount of heat. During the day I can manage to warm the cell
up a bit (zero to ten degrees Celsius), but once the fire is out for the
night, the cell is like an igloo. Judging from the thick layer of frost
covering the inside of my door, it's about minus ten to zero degrees
Celsius inside the cell. The amount of coal distributed is so small

that I can burn it only about four hours a day. Even a healthy person wouldn't be able to take it, let alone a person on the sick list like myself; after two or three months, it's impossible not to get sick.

If things are like this year after year, it looks like I won't be staying with you on your farm for long. When the farm leader told me to take better care of my health, I could do little more than chuckle ironically in reply. You won't distribute more coal, and if I want to buy some myself, you won't help me, so is it really possible for a person with heart problems to "take better care" of himself? Not only did you stop the coal, but you simply ignored our request not to turn off the electricity (it's shut off at midnight every day). Some nights I feel so awful (of course, not every night) that I would like to get up to take some medicine, but I can't see well enough to find anything. I don't think it would be an exaggeration to say that you don't seem to care whether I live or die!

I've said everything I have to say more than once, but it's just ignored. There is absolutely nothing more I can do. My ill health is now common knowledge and needs no further explanation; besides, when others just turn away, there's no use for me to say anything more.

Now that Political Instructor Zhang has returned, everyone is getting along pretty well and most of the cadres are fine too. I should also be considerate of your reputation for there's no need for me to harp over trivialities. But now that I am absolutely unable to stand it any longer and I have no other recourse, I am forced to bring this matter to your attention. What else can I do?

I am enclosing letters for the ministers of justice and public security. Please pass them on.

Wei Jingsheng

January 9, 1987

To the Ministers of Justice and Public Security:

Recently my health has taken a serious turn for the worse. I have chest pains and shortness of breath, and it was clear from the electrocardiogram I was given that my heart rate is too fast. I am currently in a myocardiac phase and there is a possibility that I could have a myocardial infarction at any time. If you want to know more details on this, please make inquiries at the Tanggemu Hospital.

In keeping with the humanist spirit of contemporary law, someone with a serious medical condition like mine should be allowed release on medical parole, since being held like this in prison could be life-threatening. But in view of the current upsurge in the tide toward democracy in our country as well as the recent student demonstrations and other matters not to your liking, you are probably unwilling to release your control over me and will refuse to allow implementation of a pertinent regulation in our nation's law. You've grown accustomed to handling matters in light of political needs rather than according to the law. Taking this into account, then, please consider transferring me to a place with a lower altitude and a warmer climate. The altitude here is three thousand meters above sea level and the climate is very cold. It's generally acknowledged that such an environment is not suitable for someone with heart problems. My recent bouts of illness have all been closely related to the climate.

Wei Jingsheng

July 6, 1987

Dear Deng Xiaoping:

You might not be able to remember a person you wronged, but it isn't easy for me to forget the one who wronged me. Our situations are very different—you are at the top of a billion people and I am at the very bottom—but life isn't easy for either of us. It's just that I am not the one making your life difficult, while you're the one making it hard for me. Therefore, when things start looking up for you, you might still on occasion remember a person you once wronged. But if my days get better, then perhaps I won't have time to remember all of the people who once wronged me. For the number of people you have wronged and who have wronged me are many.

Even if this letter does manage to make it into your hands, it will most likely have passed through many inspections along the way. All these readers probably had to cover their mouths and stifle their laughter: What a madman! An emperor and a prisoner—how can the two even speak to one another! But that's not actually the case.

Your Excellency Deng, you hold supreme powers, but after eight years of "reform" the results are inflation and an upsurge in popular dissatisfaction; you're cut off from the people and deserted by your followers; you have troubles at home and abroad; and you're so confused and unsure that you're "groping for stones to cross the river." Moreover, there are signs that you haven't made it to the other side yet and are still pacing back and forth along your old path. "Emperor of emperors" and "chairman of the Central Advisory Committee"—such titles do you little good, and the honey-laden words of flattery from abroad don't give you much comfort either! I don't think that your weak points include being taken in by flattery anyway, otherwise you would have an easier conscience by now. Your weakness is that you have great ambition, but you're untalented and small-minded. You certainly wouldn't be happy to hear me say that you're like Yuan Shao in *The Three Kingdoms*, and perhaps your attendants will see to it that you never have to read these words at all. But such a person doesn't really cause much harm to others either and few people would aspire to be ambitious, untalented, as well as small-minded. Being small-minded but without ambition, like a farmer or a craftsperson, presents no great obstacle either; at worst people might just look down on you. To have ambition but little talent is also not that harmful. The first and last emperors of the Han dynasty and the founding emperors of the Tang and Song dynasties were all ambitious and lacked talent, yet they managed to accomplish great things nevertheless.

It is the people who possesses all three of these qualities (one positive, two negative), however, who have never come to any good. Not only is this bad for the individual himself, but it's even worse for the people and society, especially for those who possess little power. On this basis, I no longer place any great hope in the future of China before your death. This isn't because your plans for reform don't have their reason, and it isn't because China is without the social and material conditions for rapid development, but it's because you, a man well into his eighties, are unable to overcome your greatest weaknesses and continue to persecute those who try to put a check on you. It's already too late and, from the look of things, this situation is irreversible. If you feel happy living your days this way, then you're not wise enough to go down in history as either a great sage leader or an infamous despot, but you'll probably end up as one or the other anyway. You couldn't end up mediocre even if you wanted to, I know you're at least up to that level. But which one to choose? Of course you would like to go down in glory, not infamy. But things often depend on your actions, not your choice. Even having good intentions or putting on a good show won't guarantee that your future will turn out as you like!

But Wei What's-His-Name's days are not easy either. I've passed eight years in this prison-within-a-prison. As a result, I've managed to contract a nervous condition, coronary heart disease, stomach problems, and chronic arthritis; I don't know what's going on in the outside world or how my family is. I'm confused and unsure too, but I don't know what stones to grope or even what river to cross, and besides, from all indications there isn't even hope of there being a riverbank on the other side or an old road for me to pace back and forth on. "Human rights pioneer" and "champion of democracy"—such titles do me little good, and the attacks and smears being flung by those "anti-democracy, anti-reform heroes" don't give me much comfort either. My weak points don't include the self-comforting spirit of an Ah Q, nor do they include the self-condemning spirit of a "capitalist-roader" like yourself, otherwise I'd be able to set my mind at ease a bit more.

My weakness is that I lack great ambitions, but I am not entirely without talent, and I may in fact not be as small-minded as I should be. I don't have just one positive point, nor only two negative ones—but then again, nobody aspires to be this way either. With no ambition, but a few talents, I'm not one of those who can learn to shamelessly flatter others, jockey for position, or undertake other such trivial maneuvers. I often incur the jealousy of others and yet I'm unable to perform the tricks that might improve my situation.

Whether in prison or out, I will always face endless troubles. If back in 1979 I had been a bit more small-minded and not waited at home for your police to come, but had hidden away instead in a place where you couldn't find me or even run away abroad, I don't think it would have been particularly good for you or, indirectly, for the country, but it wouldn't necessarily have been bad for me! Why should I act on behalf of others and the country? It seems that this too is an incurable weakness that is extremely easy for people like yourself to exploit. Just as Mao Zedong was able to take advantage of your "capitalist-roader spirit."

Of course, my optimism had something to do with it as well. It made me believe that you were actually moving toward reform and democracy and that you would show at least a bit of conscience, since I thought you would remember how you yourself suffered when you were once persecuted! But this was my biggest mistake. Admittedly, you Party elders have fought for democracy and freedom ever since your youth, but it has been for yourselves alone; once power came into your hands, you didn't plan to give the people the right to freedom and democracy. Your perspective is not much different from that of an emperor or king, of a Duvalier or Marcos. When others suffer even worse persecution than you ever did, you feel confident that you are justified in taking actions that are "proper and necessary."

During the fascist dictatorship under Mao Zedong, many of you were accused of unwarranted charges. How did you feel then? Did not Mao Zedong and Jiang Qing consider their actions to be "proper and necessary" as well? This is no different from when you feel you have "proper and necessary" grounds to use unwarranted charges to blatantly slander and persecute others. Must we wait until after Deng Xiaoping's death to clear away another "Gang of X" and for another Hu So-and-So to redress mishandled and mistaken cases? Sometimes history too is ambitious but lacking in talent and must pace back and forth along the old road before crossing to the other side of the river.

Of course, just as you yourselves boast, things are no longer the same as they once were. As political prisoners in the past, you generally enjoyed special treatment in prison. If I had been treated in such a way from the beginning, I wouldn't be in my present condition. In passing, please let me remind you: the medical checkup carried out in your prison hospital in late 1979 proves that my health was excellent at the time—there's a record of it in your files. But my current state of health is much worse than most of yours when you were released from prison. If I remember correctly, most of you were either rehabilitated or released on "medical parole." This includes Peng Zhen, Bo Yibo, Wang Guangmei, the late Ding Ling, and many others. Why, then, when I am so ill, is it only appropriate for me to receive "treatment" in prison? I guess this is just another example of how things are different today from the time of the Gang of Four!

Is it possible for one to "recuperate" in prison? What a joke! A few of you probably heard this illogical sort of reasoning before as well! How did you feel then? But now you seem to think it is very reasonable. Not only am I denied the special treatment that you once had, but even if I received it, there would be no way for me to "recuperate" in prison. My health is so poor that I need a great deal of sleep. Actually, all outsiders who come to the Qinghai highlands need more sleep—this is medical fact, not something I made up. I've been saying this for years, but it's ignored and I still can't sleep well. It's extremely cold here in this region and people in poor health have even greater trouble bearing it. I've been wasting ink writing about the lack of coal every year since I've been in Qinghai, but the problem still persists. I won't even bother raising any other matters again. My health continues to deteriorate at about the same rate that the inflation caused by your reforms grows.

I'm complaining and being somewhat disrespectful and you're probably grumbling about how this Wei What's-His-Name is always criticizing the reforms, and so on and so on. But this is just a habit of mine; I don't pose any real threat. For a long time now I've been learning to be more small-minded and to keep my mouth shut and stay out of national affairs or other people's business. After all, what I do to help others might be bad for me! Why should I harm myself for the sake of others? If you really change, or just pretend to, for better or for worse, it's no concern of mine, I'll stay out of it. I ask only that you actually keep the promises you have made many times and show more respect for human rights. Now that my condition is serious, I should be permitted to recuperate in more suitable conditions in accordance with the law—that is, I should be released on medical parole. As for a review of my case and a dismissal of the mistaken verdict against me, I'm still asking for this, but I've given up hope!

Wei Jingsheng

August 24, 1987

Dear Lingling, Taotao, and Shanshan:

Hello!

I received the map and the thirty books and magazines you mailed in late July.

It's been very dry here lately and the weather has turned warm. It's even warmer than when you were here, so my health has been pretty good and there's no need for you to worry for now. The Parker pen you gave me when you were here is very good, but I don't have any extra cartridges. Taotao, if you come in September, see if you can bring some cartridges for me. My old aversion for ball-point pens has now turned into a real love for them.

Shanshan's tape of Liu Wenzheng is very good. From his accent it sounds like he's from Shanghai. Many of his and Deng Lijun's songs are not just common popular songs, but are relatively sophisticated; you might say they are a large school in the new development of music in China—it's traditional Chinese music taken to a new level. I don't know if a modern-day Confucian listening to it would be so moved as to "lose his taste for meat," though! For me, anyway, listening to it makes meat taste even better—it's just too bad I don't have more of it! The two Deng Lijun tapes are monotone street-peddler bootlegs and the quality isn't very good. I've heard that original recordings of Deng Lijun are selling for several hundred yuan on the black market, which just goes to show that even the black market has recognized how sophisticated her talent is! I wonder when she and Liu Wenzheng will be able to come back to mainland China to give a few concerts. I'm told that Liu Wenzheng has a lot of other good songs too. They say the song "Falalala, It's Raining" is a big hit, but I haven't heard it myself. I've just heard other people singing it. I bet a tape of their best songs that feature their individual styles would be really popular. The way things are done commercially now is really disappointing. The big companies aren't any better than the street peddlers, and the quality of tapes has really declined.

I've already sent another appeal to the Supreme People's Court and cited several laws the way Lingling told me to. If you can find another lawyer in Beijing, maybe it might work. I guess we should make every effort to keep this dead horse alive, but I don't think it will be of much use. Not only are there no "upright magistrates or impartial officials" in the court (otherwise they would have taken up such an obviously misjudged case long ago), but even if there were, they would never go against the wishes of the "emperor." I wrote the appeal as a reminder, that's all.

There's a plug for an electric adaptor on my tape recorder; please ask Xiaoyi to look for one for me or else a set of rechargeable batteries. Taotao can bring them if he comes this fall, otherwise mail them. Rechargeable batteries are good because even when the electricity is shut off, I can still listen to the recorder.

Your older brother,
Jingsheng

February 11, 1988

Dear Taotao, Lingling, and Shanshan:

A few days ago in the *People's Daily*, I saw that Uncle Liang's paintings were exhibited very successfully in Taiwan. According to the caption, "the paintings were obtained through someone in direct contact with the relatives." I'm guessing that Little Ying and her husband were probably the ones who organized it! The moment her husband sets foot in Beijing, he'll be considered a "Taiwanese compatriot," won't he? How ridiculous! All a Chinese person has to do is not be a citizen of China and he can enjoy "VIP Chinese" status, just one step below foreigners. But Chinese in China have the fewest rights, and are often treated more like pigs and dogs. What the hell is the meaning of that?

Relations between the Communist and the Nationalist Parties have improved somewhat lately. This is a crucial condition for all sorts of development in mainland China as good relations with Taiwan are more crucial than relations with any foreign country. China's most despicable weakness since the beginning of this century has been to look down on the role its own people will play in the future of the nation and to always place foreigners a notch or more higher than Chinese. The Qing dynasty did this, the Nationalists did this; and the Communist Party is no exception. It's just as Lu Xun once said: "Whether foreigners are considered royalty or devils, they are never just regular people." This unnatural attitude is like treating them as "aliens from outer space" who can never be the same as us. Yet the truth is, from many of the artistic works coming out of Taiwan (novels, videos, etc.), you can see that Taiwan is in many ways more Chinese than mainland China, and the Taiwanese psychology more closely resembles the old "quintessential Chinese"—a Beijinger. Regarding them as "foreigners" who must be engaged diplomatically is ridiculous and shameful, and hopelessly stupid. I believe that Chinese people from Taiwan and Hong Kong should be treated more as equal compatriots than as "special compatriots." This will make them more willing to accept that China's concerns, whether good or bad, are their concerns as well, and that they are not outsiders. But, of course, this will have to wait for "political system reform" in the true sense. For if you can't treat the citizens of your own nation equally, then how will you be able to treat others as equals?

Once relations between mainland China and Taiwan actually improve, we'll be able to go to the province of Taiwan and do some "sightseeing" for ourselves. Not only is the scenery good over there, but there are many aspects of social and economic life that mainland China can learn from. What's more, things over there are still "Chinese style"; more so than in the "half British, half

Chinese" or "Chinese and Western mixture" of Hong Kong. I think Taiwan must be a lot like Shanghai was before the Liberation when it was considered the "First Metropolis of the Orient," surpassing even Tokyo and Hong Kong.

Jingsheng

April 10, 1988

Dear Shanshan:

Hello!

I received your New Year's card and calendar and wrote you back once, but was unable to send the letter out. I also wrote to Lingling at the end of March and sent along a copy of the appeal to the Supreme People's Court that I wrote last August for the lawyers to use. I sent it registered mail, so if you receive it, please write and let me know; you should also write if you haven't received it yet, so I can look into it.

When you get this letter, please tell Papa that he doesn't need to come to Qinghai. You all know what the climate is like here and if by any chance he were to fall ill here, there would be no place for him to receive proper medical treatment, so why not save everybody from this worry? It would be better if he took the money he is saving for the trip and sent it to me so that I can buy some things to eat. Wouldn't that be a better way for him to show his good intentions? Why should he have to come all this way?

The industrial development in Papa's hometown is still lagging behind even though it is a land of ample resources. It's not yet as wealthy or as rich as the Sunan or Wenzhou areas. From a geographic point of view, the conditions are extremely good for industrial and commercial development there: the best science and technology university in the country is located nearby; sideline agricultural income is high and therefore capital accumulation should be easier than in other areas; it borders on the Yangtze River and that makes it a "coastline region" in a sense because some of the best ports are there, including one of the largest on the Yangtze. Its basic resources far surpass many "ocean coastline districts" and, in addition, the people there have a long history of commerce and trade. When I was visiting there years ago, I learned that the local farmers traveled to trade as far away as Jiangxi, Hunan, and Hubei provinces in their little boats. There is also a coal mine nearby, and a railroad runs through the county, and so on. Few places in the whole country enjoy such favorable conditions and no one but the local officials are to blame if industry and commerce doesn't develop there.

I often think that when I get out of prison, I might go to our ancestral home and get into business because the conditions there guarantee that I can do at least as well as all those "rural entrepreneurs" of Sunan and Wenzhou. Anhui province has led the nation several times in modern history, showing that Anhui natives are pretty "modernized" in their thinking, and this, of course, is the best condition for success. But maybe the officials in Anhui are not as open-minded, otherwise the province would never have fallen behind over the past years.

If they don't want me in Anhui, though, I think I could also go to Mama's ancestral home in Ye county in Shandong province. It's one of the richest areas in the country and has been famous since ancient times. The inventor of the kite, Lu Ban, the inventor of the rocket (whose name I forget), and a famous Ming general are all well-known products of the area. Xu Fu, who is said to have traveled east to Japan along with three thousand young male and female followers, was also from this area. Whether the Japanese today are really, as legend has it, all descendants of his followers or not is pretty debatable. But it is true that, in general, people from the area do look a lot like Japanese, as they are on average not very tall and are good at fishing and seamanship!

Many ancient texts mention the whaling industry in this area and the whale-oil lamps found in Qin Shihuang's tomb were produced here as well. But in recent times the region has gone downhill and not been able to keep pace in the age of industry and information. The people from this area, however, are hardworking and skilled and they've got brains too, and an extremely large number of them have settled and started businesses in other areas of the country and abroad. It ranks third, behind Canton and Fujian, in the number of overseas Chinese who trace their roots from the region. Most of the people in Beijing who work in the grain and silk industries are originally from the area too.

As you can see, the region has a lot of potential for industrial development. The "iceberg transport project" I invented was originally intended as a way of solving Qingdao's water problems. There are abundant resources available at the Institute of Oceanology at Qingdao, which is another good reason why I might go there. Also, I could try out a lot of my ideas on marine cultivation in Ye county. I figure that I might be able to help the old family "take off" economically. I may be overestimating my abilities, but I'll only find out by trying. Who knows, Qingdao has been developing so quickly these past few years and gotten so big for its britches that they might not even let a guy like me in! After wasting away in prison for over a decade, my thinking will be so behind that I might not want to go to Qingdao and be called a "country bumpkin"!

But, no matter what, I don't want to stay in Beijing. Beijing isn't a good place; the thinking is too conservative and there isn't much future for development there. Actually, you might have more of a future if you moved to Qingdao yourself. The light textile industry is very advanced and there are many places you could put your design talents to work and leave behind the lack of creativity found in Beijing. Now that splash-ink-style paintings are all the rage, why not go to Qingdao and make a splash yourself? Xiaoyi could also get away from the bureaucratic chaos of the capital. Foreign trade is flourishing in the Shandong peninsula, so it might be better for him to do a little developing there instead of teaching. Someday you and I can collaborate on some splash-ink-style paintings and we'll leave those French artists in the dust. When it comes to imagistic art, we Chinese have a much deeper tradition than the West does, so don't go around like a fox eating sour grapes and cursing others for their "decadent" styles, since when it comes to decadence, we're more decadent than all the rest! There are places all over the country, like "Tiger Head Mountain," "Elephant Trunk Hill," "Dragon Head Rock," and so on, that are more or less all like splash-ink-style paintings, for when we say for fun that they "look like" something, it's just an exercise of the imagination. You might still call them natural formations, but in fact they are all artistic creations of the human imagination and no longer products of nature. Others have to expend some energy to push a few buttons to create decadent art, while we don't even have to lift a finger and can decadently create a huge pile of art by just opening our mouths. So how can you still have the face to curse others for being decadent?

But whether this type of high abstract imagistic art is accepted or not means nothing. There used to be a lot of Lake Tai rock formations in Beijing parks that had names like "Fairy Girl" or the "Eight Great Immortals," but after Liberation, the soldiers barracked there felt that they had no artistic value and were little more than "strangely shaped rocks." It's a question of imagination and appreciation. Anyway, all of what is considered "cultural appreciation" is, as the saying goes, just a matter of "take it or leave it." Regardless of whether you want to make it in the art market overseas or here at home, if you want to be accepted, you need to build a reputation.

I feel that, for some backward reason, our country's artistic circles don't do enough to promote art produced by our own people. They've essentially buried the true value of Chinese artists. You yourself are an example. When Little Ying wanted to put together an exhibition of your work, why didn't you do it? Pure stupidity. Not only should you have done it, but you should have had no qualms whatsoever about promoting your own art; as long as it is worthy, then promote it to the skies. Some "critics" might say this or that about your work now, but once you become "world renowned," they'll immediately change their tune—it's happened many times in the history of art. The critical community in China is so blurry-eyed, their thinking so conservative and so lacking in good taste, that it's already a common practice among young artists to "export first, import back later." This situation is not only prevalent in our own country, but many of the great schools of art and artists in the history of Western art have gone through the same thing; it's a regular pattern. Raphael, Da Vinci, Rembrandt, Picasso, Beethoven, Xu Beihong, and many others, all had a strong national quality to their work, but yet only achieved initial acceptance abroad. Some of them, in fact, were only acknowledged abroad during their lifetimes and never gained acceptance by the artistic community in their own countries until after their deaths.

This all goes to show that what I'm saying is true everywhere. It also proves the universal truth that art has no borders. The policy of confining the development of Chinese art to "nationalistic styles and national art" is really a terrible crime and actually stifles our national art and culture. As an artist yourself, you should pay no attention to national borders and freely go about finding any place you can to make your mark and to promote your own art wherever it is appreciated. You should cast aside your small-time modesty and let Little Ying or someone else help you show off your talents. Otherwise, you'll end up as nothing more than a technician. Don't trouble yourself over idle talk or gossip. After all, didn't the famed calligrapher Fan Zeng once also practice "export first, import back later" too? Didn't the painter Xu Beihong do the same? Did they lose face for this? If you listen to those peasant-minded critics, then nothing other than sweet potatoes and corn is of any real value, and, of course, they couldn't even begin to fathom how a "fake painting of sunflowers" could sell for thirty million yuan! If we left it to them, there would be no art at all. The success of the movie *Red Sorghum* proves that Chinese artistic abilities are very high; it's just that Chinese artists continue to look down on themselves too much. The most important quality for modern Chinese artists to possess is arrogance—they must dare to recognize their own worth and ignore those critics who look down on them; this is the only chance they have of gaining artistic recognition.

The "Winter Plum" verse of a poem I wrote in 1982 was meant to encourage you in your artistic endeavors. I'll copy it out here for you:

> *A tiny bud appears in the cold,*
> *A blossom finally dispels all worries.*
> *Geniuses praise the beauty of your character,*
> *Writers laud your elegant gesture.*
> *Delicate and shy, waiting until winter to bloom,*
> *Proud and stalwart, even when spring begs you.*
> *Brilliant purples and reds, yet not at a favorable time,*
> *A solitary flower enjoying its own fragrance.*

Right now you need to adopt this attitude of not caring whether others admire you or not, but, like the lone plum blossom appreciating its own fragrance, you must have confidence in your art. Artists cannot be any less brave than soldiers, and since you've even been in the army before, that's all the more reason you should have plenty of courage. In your own development strategy, you too should follow Zhao Ziyang's economic tactic of "full speed ahead, two heads outward." In other words, you should take advantage of the opportunity for an exhibition abroad by contacting Little Ying and Little Cui, and letting them build you up with praise in advance. Your other head should be trying your best to free yourself from some of your design work so that you can produce more paintings. You ought to reduce that eight-hour workday to an absolute minimum and expand your other time to a maximum. If necessary, you can even hire someone to help you complete your drafting work and separate your artistic life from your "rice bowl." This is the secret to many an artist's success. You must remember to use your brain and do your utmost to pour all of your thoughts and ideas into your art. Second-rate artists rely solely on the efforts of their hands, while top-level and master artists rely only on their brains.

When you come this summer, bring along your paintings and let me be your first "critic"!

Your brother,
Jingsheng

Tanggemu Farm, Qinghai

June 3, 1988

Dear Deng Xiaoping:

Did you receive the previous letters I wrote you? I am writing today because there is truly no longer any way for me to go on here. If you won't allow me to be released on medical parole, then please at least arrange a quieter place for me to stay. A person need not be so malicious; your past misfortunes and present difficulties were

Wei Jingsheng at Tanggemu *laogai*, a reform-through-labor prison camp in
Qinghai province, 1985. *(Collection of Shanshan Wei-Blank)*

The four siblings in Beijing, around 1957.
(Left to right) Taotao, Shanshan,
Wei Jingsheng, and Lingling.
(Collection of Shanshan Wei-Blank)

Wei Jingsheng (far right) while serving in
the People's Liberation Army, 1972.
(Collection of Shanshan Wei-Blank)

Wei (seated on the right) in the PLA in Shaanxi province, 1972.
(Collection of Shanshan Wei-Blank)

Postering at Democracy Wall, Beijing, March 1979. *(AP)*

Democracy Wall demonstrators (left to right) Liu Qing, Cai Song, Mang Ke,
and Lü Pu in October 1979, shortly before being detained. Liu Qing
subsequently served ten years in prison.
(Collection of Liu Qing)

Police arresting activists at Democracy Wall for selling printed transcripts of Wei's trial as throngs of prospective buyers look on. November 1979. *(AP)*

Wei Jingsheng reading his defense statement during his first trial, October 15, 1979. *(Marie Holzman/MPA)*

Wei and one of his rabbits at Tanggemu, during a family visit in 1985. This was one of the rare occasions on which he was allowed outside his cell.
(Collection of Shanshan Wei-Blank)

Wei and his sister Wei Shanshan, with the prison in the background.
(Collection of Shanshan Wei-Blank)

A family visit at the labor camp in the summer of 1985. Ling, Shanshan, Wei Jingsheng, Wei's niece, and Xiaotao.
(Collection of Shanshan Wei-Blank)

Wei Jingsheng's father,
Wei Zilin, and his sister Ling
await Wei Jingsheng's arrival
after his release from prison,
September 14, 1993.
(Manuel Ceneta/AFP)

Wei speaking with reporters
one week after his release,
September 20, 1993.
*(Reuters/Dennis Owen/
Archive Photos)*

Tiananmen Square student leader
Wang Dan going to visit Wei following his 1993 release. In November
1996, Wang Dan was sentenced
to eleven years for subversion
and is currently in prison.
(Manuel Ceneta/AFP)

Ding Zilin (left), whose son
was killed in the Beijing
Massacre following the
Tiananmen Square
demonstrations in 1989,
became an outspoken
victim's-rights activist.
(Marie Holzman/MPA)

Wei with his assistant
and companion Tong Yi
shortly before they were
both detained in the
spring of 1994.
(Reuters/Archive Photos)

Wei in front of Democracy
Wall—now entirely stripped
of posters—in early 1994.
(Adrian Bradshaw)

Demonstrators in Hong Kong demanding Wei's release after his second
trial and conviction in 1995. *(Thomas Cheng/AFP)*

Wei Jingsheng, Beijing, January 1994.
(Marie Holzman/MPA)

not brought about by me, so why must you continue trampling on a person after having already knocked him to the ground?

I have coronary heart disease and other ailments and according to the law I should be released for medical treatment—I have detailed all of this for you in previous letters and won't repeat it here. If you don't believe me, you can send someone to inquire at the Qinghai Tanggemu Hospital or the Beijing Public Security Hospital. Anyway, this one letter isn't very important among the voluminous number of official documents you are inundated with. You may despise me and refuse to release me on medical parole, but you must at least allow a person to survive in prison. Or are you trying to emulate the days of Mao Zedong?

The noise pollution in the prison I am currently living in has already reached an intolerable level. With the first light of day, the loudspeakers and the screeching and banging of the electric saw next door go on unceasingly. Not only has the high-pitched noise exceeded the legal limit of sixty decibels, but it exceeds the "harmful to human spirit" level of eighty decibels, and I estimate from the way the floor shakes that it reaches a hundred decibels at times. When you were under house arrest, you too experienced the loneliness and loss of spirit that being held captive can cause, so just try to imagine what the addition of intense noise can do. How do you expect a person to go on?

In Xining recently there was a case of accidental injury to a teacher that is precisely another example of this. If the local authorities had followed the law and put a stop to the noise coming out of the school's loudspeakers, the two young workers would have never used those homemade hunting guns to shoot at the loud-speakers and would never have injured the teacher. I'm afraid it's impossible for the workers to avoid trial, but what of the local authorities, who are the actual cause of this case? Of course, people will just simply say: "There is no legal alternative." But this just illustrates once again how those in power shirk their responsibilities and manipulate the law, and is not an indication that the law itself is flawed.

Why are things this way? There are, of course, many different reasons, but the most important one is that you as the "first in command" have set an example of manipulating the law since your first day in power. As Confucius said, "If you cannot rectify yourself, it is difficult to rectify others." From the ignorant outlook of all dictators like yourself (including the majority of communists after Marx), the law is not a regulation that protects the freedom of every member of society, but is merely a "legal weapon" that anyone in power can wield against his enemies. A weapon! But, of course, it's a weapon used only to punish others and not on yourselves, this is very clear. Under the guidance of this dictatorial "basic principle" your attempt to build a so-called "socialist legal system" is nothing more than a lie deliberately fabricated to fool the people. You have absolutely no intention of implementing such a system, but simply wish to use it as a "weapon." I'm afraid that the enthusiastic planners of "rule of law" like yourself will have a hard time not going down in history as "swindlers and two-faced."

The first time the world became aware of the way you manipulated the law was when you used your "legal weapon" to throw me in prison. This glorious demonstration not only provided many officials who violate the law and discipline with an example to follow, but it established a sound foundation for your own ill repute. It's difficult to wipe away facts with lies and political might. I forget what famous philosopher said these wise words, but I do know that they have been proven true again and again. Even if you nail my coffin shut, do you really think you can clear your record?

For such a "magnanimous" personality like yours, however, your reputation and the success or failure of government in your wake is of little importance. Most important is to enjoy the present and the power and grandeur of dictatorial authority. This is the "basic principle" that people like yourself dream of and then do anything to hold on to. For this, even when jokes like "classless class struggle" are made, it doesn't matter, because the power to "do whatever one wishes" is certainly no joke. If you have it, then you have everything, this is your "ism."

In order for a country as large, as poor, and with as many troubles as China not to fall behind the rest of the world, domestic unity is without question of the utmost importance. If you can manage to find peace and reconciliation with your old archenemy, the Nationalist Party, then why can't you reconcile with the young democratic activists inside China? As you adopt peaceful tactics toward the rest of the world, you should make more peace and less oppression in your own country. As you open up to foreign businessmen, you should also open up to the businesspeople and democratic activists inside your own country. Otherwise, isn't it unreasonable to believe that people will have faith in your actions? This reconciliation and openness should also include releasing me, since your abuse of public power for personal vengeance has already kept me behind bars for ten years and now I am very ill. If you don't release me, then you should at least allow me out on medical parole. I'm waiting for you to see things more clearly.

Wei Jingsheng

Wei's next letter marks the anniversary of the May 4, 1919, student demonstrations in Beijing protesting Chinese government territorial concessions after World War I. Seventy years later, the students of Beijing poured into Tiananmen Square again, only this time their protests were recorded by journalists and news cameras from around the world. When Wei wrote this letter, he could have known only a few details about the demonstrations taking place thousands of miles from his prison cell, and he certainly did not know the role Li Peng would play in the brutal crackdown a month later.

May 4, 1989

Dear Li Peng:

When you've finished reading this letter, please pass it on to Zhao Ziyang and Deng Xiaoping.

It's been another eventful spring. There have been many such springs since May Fourth 1919, all of which have had their consequences. From a global perspective, the fervent hopes of the masses always come to fruition. It might be sooner or later, and it might take on a variety of forms, but a strong outburst of public will of the kind we are now witnessing is never left unfinished. Whatever the outcome, it depends on how those in power handle the situation.

In China, our traditional mentality and thinking about "benevolent dictators" has frequently led to great tragedy. Not only have those in power ended up being swept into the garbage heap of history, but the blood of the ordinary people has flowed like rivers. They've had to pay a painful price, particularly those outstanding persons among them who should have become pillars of society, but who instead ended up being dragged out by the dictators and trampled underfoot, turning into crumbled ruins amid heaps of rubble. It will take decades for our country and our people to recover from this great loss. That is why for the past century the hardworking, intelligent, and brave people of our nation have been going continuously downhill.

But the responsibility for this does not lie with the people. The people not only have the right to choose between good and better, they also have the right to choose between bad and worse. This is a right that they cannot and should not be deprived of. Despotic rulers have often thought that by using laws and other measures, they have effectively deprived the people of their right to determine the course of history. But recent events have shown time and again that this choice remains the right of the people. No one can deny them their right to choose the course of history because this right is not something bestowed upon them by an individual; instead, all other rights and powers are derived from it. Emperors and ministers in ancient times all know the universal truth that "he who wins the people's hearts, wins all under Heaven; he who loses the people's hearts, loses all under Heaven."

Right now people are facing a choice between two evils: Either we allow the country to fall into chaos for twenty or thirty years before returning to general order, or we continue on with this kind of dictatorship exacerbated by corruption and incompetence, until it finally ends in utter destruction. The people have chosen the former. Suffering is always better than complete extinction. In addition, this still gives the ruling circles plenty of room to make their own choice. That is to say, there is still ample possibility that some of those in power will work with the people to overcome hardships and avoid chaos. But this will require the ruling powers themselves to undergo a painful reform and in order to comply with the wishes of the people, they must steel themselves against those who try to dissuade them. In other words, you can choose a quick but painful reform like Robespierre, or else you can go on dragging your feet, finally delaying yourselves and delaying the country and ending up like Czar Nicholas II. This is the range of choices that you have. Don't fantasize about using juvenile tricks such as threats or bribes to divide, demoralize, and repress others in order to overcome your own difficulties. Even if you survive this time, you won't necessarily the next, and each time will come more quickly and ferociously.

Wouldn't it be a huge mistake for you to wait until the point where you no longer have the chance to tidy things up or to make a choice about your actions? You should be rejoicing that the people and the students have enough sense and restraint to give you the opportunity to choose this time, but you shouldn't think that you will be so lucky the next. And you must take special care not to submit to the will of Deng Xiaoping and his minions. Deng Xiaoping is growing senile and he has always been headstrong by nature; all his lackeys just feed off of him, none of them help him. They're no better than the in-laws and eunuchs that surrounded emperors in ancient times and only brought harm on the country and the emperor. When a new government comes into power, they will use the same flattering and toadying for favor to greet the new leaders and devour the new emperor. If Deng Xiaoping weren't already so senile, he would do well to think a bit about how "Little Bottle," as he is called, has in the past decade gone from being the focus of support to being smashed to pieces as he is today. This is no symbolic gesture to be laughed at, but a model lesson taken from the pages of political history. If Mr. Little Bottle still had some of his old shrewdness left, he would have recognized by now who has harmed him, and who has helped or tried to help him in the past. At present, the students and "those bearded intellectuals backing the students" are still trying to help you. Their demonstrations and petitions are expressions of respect for you. (This also includes the old Tibetans who demonstrate and petition.) Please remember, if they didn't respect you, they would not be petitioning you, but would be using bullets to force you to accept their choice, for they have this right as well. And don't forget also that there are limits to how many soldiers and policemen you can buy off with petty favors, since most of them have roots among the people as well.

Below I would like to offer several concrete suggestions:

1. Satisfy all of the people's needs and desires and take great strides to implement a democratic government as quickly as possible. Anyone who "leads" in advocating the postponement of political reform, or is hostile to democracy, or complains that reform measures are too "ahead of their time" should be removed from office immediately. This is the chief goal and the foremost demand of the current mass movement. Their demands haven't "gone too far" in the least bit. Such demands are a basic right of the people and no one can deprive them of it, so what do you mean by "going too far"? What exactly is "too far"? Think about that, and please remember that the people's rights come before all else, and this includes the Constitution and the law if either runs counter to the rights of the people. Playing such childish tricks is petty and stupid. In general, there is no democratic country in the world that had better conditions in the areas of education, ideology, politics, social fabric, economics, and the news media for taking the first steps toward democracy than can be found in present-day China. What, then, is meant by these ideas being "too ahead of their time"? Those who say such things are members of the dictatorial faction, and their so-called "neo-authoritarianism" is just another name for Nazi-fascism. There's nothing to be discussed or investigated with them; they should be thoroughly eliminated.

2. Establish a democratic government as the fundamental condition for wiping out corruption. Without it, all the measures for "clean politics" put together amount to little more than zero, that is, if they don't actually have a negative effect. Dictatorial government is a breeding ground for corruption. Buying off the small number of bureaucrats in the upper ranks and avoiding their supervision is not difficult to do, but buying off the people and avoiding their supervision is an almost impossible thing to do. Corruption must be wiped out on a credible basis and not merely on trust in the conscience of your Communist Party. Your "measures to quell popular anger" make it even less possible to deceive oneself and others with your good intentions and fine-sounding

promises. Officials are people too and don't wish to offend others; therefore only democracy can guarantee freedom from corruption. In a democracy, if you are corrupt you offend great numbers of people. Therefore democracy is the most powerful tool against corruption; it is more iron than an iron fist.

3. In order to gain the people's trust and facilitate public participation in government, you must immediately drop all restrictions on the press and emulate examples of freedom of the press found in democracies everywhere. The rights to freedom of expression, publication, assembly, and association are all guaranteed in the Constitution. It is not true that there is "no law to refer to." These are the basic rights of the people, and a government in which the people have entrusted their rights has no authority to abolish these rights; if it does, it is a usurper, and this is the very definition of fascism. The Beijing municipal government's "Ten Articles on Demonstrations" and all other regulations attempting to deny the basic rights and freedoms of the people are unconstitutional. They are fascist measures taken to usurp the rights of the people and should be abolished immediately.

4. Deal harshly with officials who have taken positions of extreme conservatism during each of the student and mass movements (that is, all of the real, not the "ordered," revolutionary mass movements since 1978) and have carried out suppression of the masses. Those soldiers and police who have directly ordered or carried out killings or beatings of the masses should be punished according to military law as an offering of apology to the people. Even without looking at it from a military or legal standpoint, it is clear to anyone that these soldiers and police officers have committed all kinds of outrages. The situations in Lhasa and Beijing have been exacerbated by their violation of law and discipline. If they are not punished, then there is no true rule of law. If they are allowed to go about stirring up trouble everywhere, the nation will be unable to continue.

5. In the present period before a system of public participation in government can be set up immediately, expand the scope of dialogue with the students and all facets of society and directly

involve the public in order to assure that political and economic policies are appropriate. This is not dialogue of the type Yuan Mu so jovially called "casual chatting," neither is it the "lectures" He Dongchang is so used to giving, but a more primary form of direct public involvement in politics. This is serious political activity, not just "shooting the breeze." Yuan Mu said it wasn't negotiation, but he was wrong. This was most certainly a method of negotiation. It may have been informal, yet it had wide repercussions. It was a method of mutually acquainting oneself with each other's views and positions and trying to persuade each other and come to a mutual understanding. This is negotiation. You officials have an instinctive arrogance that keeps you from looking upon others as equals, as if for you to sit down with others at the negotiating table somehow lowers your status. Now is the time for you to toss aside these big-boss airs; you yourselves didn't always hold such positions of privilege either. You should adopt a more realistic attitude and accept that people from all levels of society and from different groups and political forces have negotiating status equal to that of the government. You should behave this way not only toward students, intellectuals, workers, and democratic parties, but to representatives of the Dalai Lama and Taiwan as well. Negotiation and activities surrounding negotiation should be carried out in order to solve real problems and should not be like the arguments of maids and servants haggling over positions in the old novel *Dream of the Red Chamber*.

If you don't acknowledge people equally or don't even acknowledge their existence, then who the hell, may I ask, are you planning to negotiate with? You don't allow others to state preconditions, yet you expect everyone to accept your conditions and your unconditional leadership without discussion. I'm afraid this is the most unreasonable precondition of all; it basically means that you have no intention of negotiating. I don't know what bastards gave Deng Xiaoping this lousy idea of postponing and thereby intensifying this urgent domestic problem that could basically have been solved quite easily, but they should be shot.

Negotiations acknowledge the existence and equal standing of the other party. It is a reality that our one country has two governments (three if you count the government-in-exile of the Dalai Lama). Even if you don't acknowledge this, the fact remains true. If you take steps toward unity with the small government of the Republic of China on Taiwan and prevail upon the government-in-exile of the Dalai Lama to return and work together toward the great task of national rejuvenation, it would be an extremely important move toward political unity and social stability. It would be very important for overcoming domestic political and economic difficulties and would have even greater benefits for national defense and foreign diplomacy. If you don't unite with all of the people and political forces in the country, your slogan "stability and unity" is nothing more than another label for dictatorship. And don't fantasize that in negotiations the other side will always give in to you, for you must also learn to give in to others; compromise is an important political skill. In politics, the one thing that cannot be wavered from and must be upheld at all costs is the interest of the country and the people, and not some "Four Cardinal Principles." If you want to uphold these additional principles, you're free to do so, just as others are free to oppose them. But in upholding them, you must not deprive others and the people of their equal rights.

6. In view of the fact that the forces of conservatism and reactionary opposition are still very powerful within the highest power structures, it may be very difficult to make great strides toward democracy and reform. But the fate of the country and the people are all at stake. In addition to relying firmly on the support of the people, you can also make some compromises with the conservative forces on matters not related to fundamental principles. For example, if continuing to hold me will satisfy certain people, then don't hesitate to postpone resolution of my case. And, if you can, use my continued imprisonment to exchange for concrete implementation of other basic rights of the people. Even if such an exchange would only mean the realization of freedom of the press, or the protection of the rights to freedom of expression and publication, as long as it will help you to escape great turmoil, then I would sit in prison for a few more years without a word of complaint; in fact, I would feel extremely honored to do so.

In short, the question of what direction and route should be taken can't be left murky. Otherwise, your fate will be even less assured than that of Deng Xiaoping. You must realize, Deng Xiaoping's current troubles are not the result of a few mistakes made recently, but are ten years' worth of mistakes that have accumulated into one great big one. He brought ruin upon himself. I hope you can take the fates of those before you as a warning and not follow the same disastrous path.

Wei Jingsheng
Solitary confinement, Tanggemu Farm

In the early morning hours of June 4, 1989, People's Liberation Army troops opened fire on unarmed pro-democracy demonstrators, killing and wounding hundreds near Tiananmen Square and in other areas of Beijing. Wei Jingsheng's outrage over the June Fourth, 1989, Beijing Massacre is evident in the following letter in which he accuses Deng Xiaoping of staging a military "coup" by overthrowing then Premier Zhao Ziyang, who showed sympathy for the student movement.

June 15, 1989

Dear Deng Xiaoping:

So, now that you've successfully carried out a military coup to deal with a group of unarmed and politically inexperienced students and citizens, how do you feel? If the impression I got from the brief scenes I saw on television is correct, you are not quite as relaxed and self-congratulatory as Li Peng. Your head is a bit clearer than I had originally thought and you're not so muddled that you're blind with success; you can still understand the heavy political price you've paid by initiating this bloody coup. That's more appropriate behavior for an old statesman like yourself, so I'm not too disappointed. But other than this, everything else you've accomplished can be described as nothing less than complete chaos.

Going down in infamy for carrying out a military coup doesn't sound too good to you, does it? Even the likes of Yuan Shikai and

Duan Qirui had trouble accepting such a terrible reputation. I've heard that their grandchildren and descendants are still trying in vain to clear their names. Being so advanced in age, who would want to leave an "inheritance" like this to his descendants? And who would want to leave such a bad mark on his own reputation? An evil reputation can only be brought on oneself—nobody else can help another gain such "glory," except perhaps one's own subordinates. I've long known that you are precisely the kind of idiot to do something foolish like this, just as you've long known that I am precisely the kind of idiot who will remain stubborn to the end and take blows with his head up. We know each other well; probably better than anyone can imagine. It's just that we have an intimate mutual disgust that probably also exceeds anyone's imagination. The forest is so vast that it contains every variety of bird, even a pair like us; the "Eighth" Great Wonder of the world!

Several years ago I told you that you were small-minded and lacking in vision. And now, not only have you managed to miss an extremely good opportunity to stand together with the people; what's more, after finding that it's difficult to get off a tiger's back once you're on it, you just kept going. You refused to give in, so in the end you not only damaged your reputation, but you also harmed your own initiatives and turned yourself into a person who will go down in history as a laughingstock. It's nearly impossible to reverse course now that you've already used the fresh blood of students and soldiers to mark a path for reactionary forces to find their way in. Once you let them start turning the clock back, they are capable of kicking even you out of their way. After having been shown the entryway, they can proceed in by themselves—what need have they for an old master like yourself? In other words, not everyone can be a politician, but anyone who can breathe can get by as a dictator; it basically doesn't matter whether his name is Deng or something else. The toadying parasites who live off of dictators prefer nothing better than an obedient emperor; they don't care who it is. Once an emperor distances himself from the people, he becomes the plaything of such parasites, and even talented emperors such as Emperors Yangdi and Xuanzong of the Sui and Tang dynasties were no exceptions. Your case offers rich material for my historical studies. Actually, Confucius figured this game out long ago, but he "only stated it and didn't act on it," therefore he merely warned rulers to "surround yourself with gentlemen, distance yourself from petty men." Unfortunately, people don't take this profound teaching to heart and the same tragedy repeats itself again and again in all times and in all countries, without exception. What a shame!

But the high you must be feeling from your latest "victory" (?!) together with the lavish praise of your lackeys probably makes it impossible for you to even see that there is any problem. It may be several years before you can look back and see that the setbacks all started from now. I'm afraid, however, by that time it will be too late and there will be no chance whatsoever left for recovery. So now I am going to offer three strategies (one good, one mediocre, and one bad) for you to consider. These are for you, my old friend, to contemplate as well as for the record. In the future, when we are both dead, these will be looked upon as my offering to history so that no one can curse me for standing by while my country was in crisis and watching the tragedy unfold. For then I would not only be unable to face the people who raised me and the teachers and parents who sustained me, but I could not face you who have bestowed so much honor upon me. I wouldn't be what I am today without you. You can take these words however you like; it's up to you.

THE MOST DESIRABLE STRATEGY: MOVE FORWARD, CUT OFF YOUR RETREAT, PROMOTE DEMOCRACY, AND SAFEGUARD FREEDOM

You old men love to talk about carrying on the "cause of the pioneering Party martyrs," and so on, yet you need to clarify for yourselves exactly what sort of cause these martyrs died for. Did they die so that a few people could act as they please and commit all kinds of outrages, foster corruption, and use tanks and planes to suppress the people? No matter how many propaganda videos you make, this will always remain true. People's minds are not controlled by propaganda organs and "public opinion guides" for their lack of credibility limits their effectiveness. "Public opinion guides" that are not trusted actually have the exact opposite effect from what was intended. If you tell me that the early martyrs spilled their blood for the recent triumph of greed and tyranny, then was not their blood spilled in vain? To deny this is an absolute and shameless lie. The martyrs who died to found the People's Republic of China made it clear that they were willing to stand up and sacrifice themselves for the democracy, freedom, and happiness of the people. If it were only for the dictatorship of a small minority of people or for corrupt officials even more savage and cruel than the evil and despotic landlords who once oppressed them, then no one would have been willing to sacrifice their lives in vain.

Who betrayed these martyrs? Their former comrades who changed once they got in power? Or the old officials who get a headache every time they hear the words "democracy" and "freedom," and who call the common people "ruffians" or "social miscellanies"? Forgetting how they themselves were once cursed by the opposition, these degenerate old revolutionaries now stand in place of their former enemies and curse their own people. They've sold their souls to the enemy in a thorough betrayal.

Who, then, has inherited the will of the martyrs and pushed forward the cause they pioneered? It is "our sons and brothers" who since the 1970s have been once again raising the great banner of "democracy, freedom, and science" first flown by the founding martyrs and who are as fearless of sticking out their necks and spilling their blood as their forebears. They are no different than you once were: Although they are inexperienced, blood flows hot in their veins; although they are unarmed, they enjoy the trust and support of the masses. You, of all people, ought to know what your fate will be if you oppose them. Temporary success is merely a postponement of the inevitable. Like Xiang Yu, who after hundreds of battles and victories still had to admit defeat and say "farewell my concubine." As he put it, "It's the will of Heaven, not that I can't fight." And this will of heaven is nothing other than the people's will. To defy popular feeling and oppose the "cause" of history, even when your soldiers are victorious in every battle, is futile. You should know; you yourself are a perfect example. After all, how did you gain prestige in the late 1970s? Was it because your contributions surpassed those made by Mao Zedong or Liu Shaoqi? Of course not. It was because slogans about democracy, freedom, and human rights were pouring from your lips at the time, making it look as if your only concern was for the happiness and rights of the people. That is why you became their spiritual leader, and it is the only reason why so many hot-blooded young people risked their lives in the face of police clubs, jail sentences, and even execution in order to push you back into power. But as you ascended the throne, step by step you gradually betrayed yourself, and now by ordering tanks onto Tiananmen Square you have fallen to even lower depths than the Gang of Four. Your power may be great now, but I'm afraid that you will come to an even worse end than they did. After all, you didn't imitate just anybody, but deliberately modeled yourself after those "third world" military dictators. Yet you must bear in mind that this is China, not Haiti or Panama; without the support of the people, a military dictatorship will never last for more than a few days.

It is still not too late to trade in the butcher's knife for the robes of a Buddha. The Chinese people are unsurpassed in their political savviness and they will, for the most part, be willing to take the whole situation into account. You need only to return once again to the side of the people and the majority of them will let bygones be bygones. You have done quite a few good things in the past decade, so if you now make the morally correct choice in order to save the Chinese people from tragedy, the people will forgive you for your past mistakes. If you wait until people pressure you to reform yourself like the Gang of Four did, then it will be too little too late. Do it sooner rather than later, because once you've gone past this village, you'll find no other place to rest.

Your actions over the past two months have already pushed the cart back downhill and unleashed an enormous reactionary inertia, so it will require an equally enormous effort to brake the cart and start it moving upward again. Such strength can come only from the people and the only leaders capable of uniting the spirits of people from all over the country and all walks of life are the students who demonstrated on Tiananmen Square these past few days. Relying on that worthless bunch of toadying parasites around you will only cause you to further lose the trust of the people with each passing day. At this critical moment the people trust only "the backbone of

China"—those who risked arrest and execution on behalf of the people. The parasites who sway with the wind as easily as grass growing on top of a wall have always been despised by the people, especially in China. Therefore, if you want to harness this forward momentum, you must learn better how to utilize people: "Surround yourself with gentlemen, distance yourself from petty men." First, you must get rid of all of those subordinates and officials who are hated by the people; second, you must use any means necessary (including some that may have no precedent and break entirely with convention) to enlist the help of the mass leaders, many of whom have already been placed on wanted lists, including those "bearded intellectuals behind the scenes." Use them to fill the spots left vacant when dismissing those petty persons. They might not have the experience and obedience of your longtime officials, but by enlisting them you also enlist the trust of the people. Whoever takes hold of them takes hold of the future of China; whatever you do, don't drive them into deeper waters.

You know a few things about alternative measures for governing the country, and there are experts and a great many comrades who will help you if you don't. A few mistakes won't be life-threatening. Only major matters of principle concerning the protection of national unity cannot be ignored for even an instant. You may have taken the wrong drug now, but the illness is not yet terminal and there is an antidote. Relations with the students, intellectuals, workers, and peasants have not yet reached the point of life and death; it's just that it will take some time to return them to health. Put an immediate stop to the arrests of students and citizens, and you might be able to get them to cooperate with the government. Put an immediate stop on purging the ranks of the media and allow all the broadcasting agencies to reappear in more acceptable forms by weeding out those unpopular ones on the basis of quality. Restore the people's trust in the government and boost government credibility. Only by acting in such a way can you turn the tide back in your favor and recover gradually.

It isn't at all easy to quit smoking or stop drinking, and kicking a drug habit is even harder. So, if you want to carry out this strategy, in addition to destroying your weapons, cutting off all means of retreat and making a determined effort, you will also need the assistance of those who can help push you along forward. They can help you fight to the end and keep you from relapsing and following the same old road taken in the 1960s. This is your only chance for success. According to the estimation of a country bumpkin like myself, who is restricted in vision and shallow-minded, Zhao Ziyang, who courageously resigned in the face of a major issue of right and wrong following Hu Yaobang's death, might actually turn out to be your helper in this. No matter what, he would always be better than that slovenly good-for-nothing Li Peng.

THE MEDIOCRE STRATEGY: PUT UP A SMOKESCREEN, USE LI PENG AS A SCAPEGOAT, SLOW DOWN DEMOCRATIZATION, AND ALLOW THE ECONOMY TO STAGNATE

With the suppression of this mass movement, it's fair to say that you have completely lost the support of the people. Only a fool would believe your high-sounding rhetoric and lies! I don't think your stupidity has regressed from the level it was in 1978 all the way back to what it was in 1968! From the brief glimpses of you I've seen on television I feel it has not; that is to say, in your heart you know what a great mistake you have made. But with your stubborn personality (let me note in passing that although most people who have such unyielding personalities end up being great heroes, most despotic dictators are also this personality type), it appears you would rather die than admit that you were wrong. In your heart, you know well that without complete social harmony, your initiatives toward democracy and reform will immediately fall through and you yourself will turn into a failed joke in the tide of socialist reform. This too is a consequence you would no doubt rather die than face. Therefore, if you don't want to take great strides toward reform and step up democratization, then you can only find a scapegoat to divert the focus of people's displeasure and give them someone to vent their dissatisfaction on. This way, you can then go on deceptively with your so-called "reforms," and at the same time you'll have ample reason to check any regression. This is another commonly used *realpolitik* tactic, but it is also the approach taken by small-time bureaucrats who can think of no better alternative. In the end, however, the successes usually don't outweigh the failures.

Although you might manage to shake free from the hands of fate, you will still have destroyed the harmony inside the government and society. There will be no way for you to regain credibility and it will be difficult to inspire the motivation needed for social development. Your reforms will slow down due to urban unrest and degeneration and this will lead to economic stagnation.

The outcome of adopting this mediocre strategy might not be ideal, but it is a method that will prevent the complete breakdown of unity and it may stop any further regression. Brother Li Peng might have to suffer a bit, though. Comrade Zhao Ziyang resigned in order to show that he had nothing to do with this bloody coup, so the only plump scapegoat around is Brother Li.

THE LEAST DESIRABLE STRATEGY: MISJUDGE THE SITUATION, BE INDECISIVE AND HEADSTRONG, LEAD THE COUNTRY INTO CHAOS

Judging merely from your recent television appearances and your past behavior, I can guess that you are not stupid. But even if I had something more reliable to base my judgment on, I would still be doing no more than venturing a guess. According to what I can gather from the media, it appears that you are as headstrong as Jiang Qing once was, sticking obstinately to your own course, even if it means insisting coal is white or dumplings are black. You are this type of personality and if you want to reverse black and white, there are many others like you in the Communist Party who are willing to help you, whatever the color. In fact, you are doing this right now as you quell the so-called "rebellion." But who is "rebelling"? Any ordinary person can see that if the army had not entered the city, there would be no "rebellion." Before their arrival, social order in the city was extremely good. As for the students on Tiananmen Square, no matter how you look at the situation, there is no way you can say that they were stirring up "turmoil" since the square is a public place and every citizen has the right to carry out political activities in public places. It isn't your personal property and there is no admission charged to enter the square, so what right do you have to prohibit others from carrying out political activities there? Of course, occupying a public space for a prolonged period of time is not a normal occurrence, but who is at fault for bringing this about? Wasn't it all of you corrupt traitors who incited public indignation by refusing to engage in dialogue with the masses? Who is to blame for the blood spilled in June? Was it the students and masses who went to the army barracks and initiated violence? No, it was the army that drove into the city and carried out an armed suppression of the students and masses and provoked their indignation. Only then did both sides turn to violent methods. This is called provoke first and fabricate a justification for it later. When the people's emotions are aroused, anything can happen. Responsibility for this does not lie with the students and masses because they are not responsible for protecting social order and safety. A responsible government would accept full responsibility for the violent clash it created. I'm sorry to tell you, but this amounts to just common sense in modern and ancient times, in China and elsewhere. Such thoroughly unreasonable reasons as you've come up with are no longer easy for most people to accept. Even in times past people did not readily accept them, but they were forced to suppress their rage. The result of forcibly using lies and false evidence in the media to support such a complete lack of reason is to bring chaos to the country's thinking and decrease the government's credibility. This is the cause of utter turmoil.

True "social upheaval" begins with confused thinking, and confused thinking stems from unreasonable behavior on the part of those in power. The sum total of over twenty-five hundred years of political experience has proven this to be true in China and abroad, and that is why Confucius said that only by "selfish devotion to propriety" can "humanity attain benevolence." You were unable to transform your own selfish desires and anger into "selfish devotion"; instead, you used tanks and machine guns to massacre the people and chase down and arrest students. The word "benevolence" never came into play. The moment the army troops entered the city, things suddenly turned hostile and all trust was lost. It was unwise of you to accept as truth the rumors fabricated by your own henchmen that turned right into wrong and harmed people. For, if benevolence, righteousness, intelligence, and trust are all similarly abandoned, what kind of future can your government possibly have? Your seditious lies will result in nothing less than utter chaos.

If there is a "reason" for you to use army troops to intervene in politics and massacre ordinary citizens, then anyone else can find the same reason; if it is legal for you to make up reasons after you have done something, then others can do exactly the same; if you can play with the "rule of law" in the palm of your hand, then others can do the same. It doesn't take any schooling to accomplish this; it's something any walking and breathing human being can do. But what then? While you're still alive, you will be able to maintain and control your great power, but the Empress Dowager Cixi was even more powerful than you, and in the end you'll die just as she did! You've already set a precedent of using the military to decide political questions, so once you are dead, what Communist Party official will rely solely on his mouth and pen, and swear off the use of tanks, machine guns, and large artillery? As the old saying goes: "When confronted by a soldier, even a successful scholar can't rely on reason." How will you instruct the leaders to manage the country from now on? How will you deal with the hoodlums who make up the so-called "people's army," but who eat the people's food and use guns purchased by the people to kill the people? The disaster you are leading China toward might even surpass that brought on by Yuan Shikai or the Empress Dowager Cixi. If you refuse to adopt one of the first two strategies I have described above, you will be unable to overturn the evil precedent you have set and then this final strategy I have described to you will be your only option.

From what I can tell, you still have control of your senses, and that is why I am willing to say these things to you. I just hope I am not mistaken.

Wei Jingsheng
Tanggemu Farm, Qinghai

Late in the summer of 1989, Wei Jingsheng was transferred from Qinghai to Nanpu New Life Salt Works, a laogai *prison near the city of Tangshan in Hebei province on the Bohai Gulf about two hundred miles east of Beijing.*

November 3, 1989

Dear Deng Xiaoping:

I've written to you so many times now that I'm probably beginning to get on your nerves and you're wondering, "Why can't this guy just sit in prison quietly?" This appears to be a real problem, but it is not entirely my fault. I am very capable of staying quiet, but if people don't allow me to be, then I can also be very *un*quiet. This makes me no different from most people in our country. When we are living in times of relative peace and tranquillity, we are the quietest people on earth; but if we are oppressed beyond reason, then, as the history books show, we can be the most *un*quiet, and the "most imbued with revolutionary zeal" of peoples. My endless letters and constant badgering are in the tradition of "oppressive government drives the people to rebel."

Before and after leaving Qinghai, I was always hearing, "You are being transferred to Hebei purely out of our concern for your ill health." At the time, I wondered, "Since when has Deng Xiaoping learned to treat others with such generosity? Is it possible that, nearing death, his actions are becoming kinder, as when a bird nears death, its cry becomes mournful? Is it possible that some loyal servants and worthy ministers have appeared at the old man's side to assist him and there is hope for national reconciliation and unity? Or has some other inexplicable, unknown great event occurred?" Even an optimistic old fool like myself was thrown for a loop for several days.

But now I understand clearly. You, old sir, are still "remarkably healthy" (as they say on the news) and you're every bit the "Sichuan pepper" hot for a fight that you've always been. You haven't allowed tolerance to "spiritually pollute" you. I myself know all too well that all of your efforts to arouse people are little more than smokescreens to cover for some short-term ulterior goal; anyone taken in is a fool.

Just consider how I was "cared for" all the way here to Hebei province and from this small clue the whole picture becomes clear. The climate in Qinghai is very cold and quite dangerous for a person suffering from coronary heart disease or arthritis. But although the winters there may be cold and there is a lack of oxygen, the leaders at all levels in the Qinghai *laogai* were very concerned over this situation. They always asked whether we were cold and tried to make sure we had enough coal and a stove to use. They solved the heating problem, or at least did the best they could under prevailing conditions. But it's exactly the opposite here, where there is only an unrefined brick stove placed in the next room with a flue extended into my cell. They do this, I am told, because they fear I might poison myself with the fumes. In Qinghai, I burned a local low-grade coal and never gassed myself, so why when I get here do I receive this special "loving care"? This is a coastal region and it is windy in both spring and winter and always damp and cold, so if I continue to be cared for in this fashion, I'm afraid I won't make it. I already had a small taste of what's to come recently when I got so cold that all my many ill- nesses began acting up again. There is hardly a place on my body that doesn't have some problem, yet I am still prohibited from using an electric blanket, so even if I want to rely on my own efforts to get by, I can't.

The conditions for recuperating in Qinghai were far inferior to those provided here at the Nanpu Salt Works, since there was nothing in Qinghai other than a single, nearly bankrupt farm "hos- pital." But in Qinghai, everyone from the hospital chief to the doc- tors was very conscientious. As long as the hospital had a certain medicine I needed, they would do their best to give it to me, and they kept close tabs on my condition. I was surprised to find that the coronary heart disease, which I was most concerned about, did not worsen in Qinghai, nor did my arthritis, sinusitis, and intestinal problems recur. I managed to withstand the harsh climate of low temperatures and a lack of oxygen and go on living to see today. There is no lack of oxygen here, but in the few months since my arrival, I have not taken any medicine, nor has a doctor come to examine me; I eat cold rice and drink unboiled water; I can't sleep well or take a shower, and my body is so filthy that I'm nearly breaking out in sores. My sinusitis is so bad that I have a splitting headache, and my joints are so swollen that I can't move my legs and feet properly; abdominal pain and diarrhea bother me all day long, my heart gives me trouble every three to five hours, and even with plenty of oxygen I often find I am short of breath. As you can see, I am no better off than if you sent me back to the Tanggemu Farm in Qinghai. There may not be much oxygen there, but there is a bit more humanism. The farm may be losing money, but you can at least earn some humaneness there. Perhaps it is precisely for these reasons that the *laogai* system in Qinghai is not considered as "advanced" as the one here in Hebei!

You, sir, have always hated hearing my "presumptuous nonsense," so I should try not to get you angry and risk taking years off your life! Below, however, I would like to discuss some of the "presumptuous nonsense" of your former subordinates. You're old, but you can still help straighten them out and, by doing so, avoid taking years off the life of the nation.

Recently, from the Central Committee to the villages, from the newspapers to the television, you can hear the enlightening phrases "We are not afraid of isolation, we are not afraid of pressure, no one has the right to interfere with our internal affairs." How impressively you've assumed this bullying posture and given people the impression that you've decided "Since I've started, I'm going to carry it to the end," and that you're alone in single-mindedly clinging obstinately to your course. It doesn't matter whether the country or the people live or die; you're ready to risk everything to forge ahead.

But this is not at all a clever or appropriate thing to do, and it is far from responsible. If you were a real hero of the Chinese people, then when you suffered in the hands of the Gang of Four, long before achieving your present success, you would have stood up to them. Even when his ribs were broken in a criticize-and-denounce meeting, Peng Dehuai refused to bow, and I too would rather sit in jail than do something against my conscience. This is the only way to come even close to being a hero! A person in a dictatorial position can never become a hero by playing with the fate of the country and the people. How can you, by wresting all power in your hands and taking sole control of the economy and the people's livelihood, pose as a hero? Power and position gained in this manner won't make you a hero. I am merely risking my own neck, but you are playing with the fate of the country and the people. Is this not completely irresponsible? Is this the way to become a hero? Or just a scheming tyrant?

Regardless of whether you are a hero or a tyrant, if you possessed the national strength of the United States or the Soviet Union, and were as influential and resourceful, perhaps you could flaunt it for a short time, because our country and people still have a bit of "forbearance" left in them! But our country is poor and our people impoverished; there are domestic troubles and problems abroad; new conflicts, intricate and complex, piled upon old ones. How many more storms and floods do you think our country can weather? You've lived to eighty-five and broken just about even; you've had more than your share of glory and fortune, adventures, and irritations, but in the end there is nothing for you to complain about. Of course you don't fear that the country falls into chaos, and of course you don't fear whether the ordinary people are suffering from poverty and starvation. But I do fear these things, and the majority of humane and good people fear them as well, and the ordinary people fear them the most. They are the greatest fears the people have.

There isn't a person alive who is not afraid of being isolated. In our daily lives we might come across a few bullies who like to boast, "What am I afraid of? I don't need to please anybody. I can fend for myself and don't need anything from anybody." But if you really isolated such a person, he too would be afraid because he knows that he isn't some kind of mighty tiger that can roam about on his own, but is rooted in society and relies on it for his very existence. There's no way around it; after all his high-sounding talk, he must still try to make good with others, and he'll have to expend even more energy now and not dare to complain that he suffered before, for he must be willing to humble himself for a time and possibly never regain his old standing among others. But he has only himself to blame for offending his old friends and must warn his sons and grandsons to take this as a lesson.

Then there are also those who, like stones in an outhouse, hard and rank, remain firm in their lone-tiger ways and eventually end up being ostracized from society. They never come to any good and drag their tired wives and children along, being cursed and swallowing their tears. Society finds many ways to rid itself of such dregs; there are no set rules, but being made to face thousands of condemning fingers pointed at you is to perish without losing blood! It is no wonder, then, that people interfere with your internal affairs, for when you act in such a way, who can you blame but yourself? Who would let you go on abusing your parents or beating and cursing your wife and refusing to listen to reason? After urging and prodding, you still don't listen, and insist, "My domestic affairs are no business of yours." But once public indignation is provoked, it is no longer just your own affair. The most effective means of maintaining public order are not legal or ethical codes, but mutual understanding and a common sense of social and cultural values; this is even more pertinent for international society. Democracy, freedom, and human rights for all people have long been values commonly held by modern society; the defense of human rights and the promotion of democracy has never been an "internal affair." Just as you and your own forebears have said, it is "the foremost task of human progress." Those who have been ostracized for disregarding this task in the past were all emperors, monarchs, or fascists, and in recent times we have the racist regime of South Africa. And now, Deng Xiaoping, you too will be counted among their ranks if you go on trying to rival their reputations for inhumaneness. This is absolutely inconceivable!

The country's internal affairs resemble those of a family. Even if you have the strongest arm in your family and are a strict head of the household, you still can't look on your wife and children as less than human. Nowadays, people have already grown dissatisfied with your old-style patriarchal attitude, and you would do well to learn to adapt to others and reform your methods and attitude in running your household. Arguing and fighting all day long, cursing this and beating that, is certainly not good for a family; it will not thrive in any respect. Sooner or later the masses will oppose you and your followers will desert you; you'll have to close up shop. As a patriarch, you don't know how to treat others with tolerance, but instead force everyone to admit that everything you do or say is right; even when you call a deer a horse or say that coal is white. Your family will never be at peace.

Are your children the ones who destroyed stability and unity? Obviously not. They are mature and experienced and have their own ideas, which is nothing less than a sign of their future potential. You, with your old-fashioned patriarchal ways, in fact are the one who has upset stability and unity. A modern patriarch who stubbornly adheres to his unalterable governing style and has even found people to take over after him is the greatest tragedy for a family, for it will certainly fall into rapid decline, no matter how illustrious it once was. I'm afraid that we Chinese have seen this happen all too many times!

Let me recommend a model family to you for your reference. This is a bit "immodest" of me, as it is actually my own family. Except for me, all the children in my family have formed their own families, but we still stick together "like brothers and sisters," and none of the many storms we have faced has shaken our unity—you yourself should be well aware of just how serious some of the storms we have faced were. Contrary to everyone's expectations, we are not the peaceful, traditional "model family" that, with the exception of one renegade, keeps its eyes lowered and nods in agreement with everything. We often argue and are quite raucous; when several of us get together there are always differences of opinion; none of us would just echo the other's viewpoint or be coerced by another. Even I, being the great filial son that I am, have been known to talk back, and on occasion have even had to leave the family to cool off for a night or two. Can such a person still be considered a filial son? Can a family like this still unite to weather all manner of severe storms? The answer is: Absolutely yes. The key to this is to be concerned for, but never force others; to argue with, but not pressure others; to persist in your opinions, but also be tolerant of others. In this way, not only are your internal affairs stable and unified, but your external relations are very good as well, and you make many friends. Everyone in my family is extremely popular in all of his or her activities and circles, and no one is ever considered a weak or indifferent member of a group. We all like to debate and poke our noses in other people's business. My family is much stronger than yours, so don't you think it's worth taking a look at it?

It's time to make a fresh start. Your family's internal and external affairs are encountering all kinds of problems that are completely due to your old-style patriarchal manner. You ask of others things that you yourself refuse to do. You prohibit others from interfering in your internal affairs, but you persist in having the absolute authority to interfere in the affairs of the ordinary people—in other words, you meddle in their human rights. I don't think contemporary society will accept such behavior quietly. Furthermore, when people censure, denounce, or advise you, or even curtail their relations with you, they are doing so out of concern for your family. They've yet to resort to legal or more forceful means to do so. What personal internal affairs of yours are they actually interfering in?

As you leaders like to say again and again, there is no such thing as absolute freedom. In the same way, no ruler has absolute freedom in managing his so-called "internal affairs." When a situation has developed to a certain point, not only does everyone have the authority to concern themselves with the "internal affairs" of others, but when things get more serious, they also have the right to interfere in your affairs whether you have invited them to or not. There are precedents for this everywhere. Examples from the annals of Confucius might be too far removed to be relevant, but then, the Germans never invited the Americans, Soviets, British, and French to interfere with the "internal affairs" of their Nazi fascism, and the South Africans who proclaimed that they had the "authority to represent everyone" never asked anyone to interfere in their racist "internal affairs," did they? When, under brutal oppression, a nation's citizens are helpless to safeguard their own internal affairs, including both the rights of individuals and society as a whole, the international community has the right to support, aid, and protect them in any way necessary. Isn't this a pet phrase that you yourselves often have on the tip of your tongues? And isn't this also the legal and moral basis for the United Nations' peace-keeping efforts? And are not peacekeeping efforts the most obvious form of "interfering in internal affairs"? There are many other forms of interference that you cannot avoid even by relying on your purchase of a voting seat in the United Nations. "Don't interfere in internal affairs" is hardly an immutable, universal truth passed down since ancient times. It is only a bilateral contract made with prerequisite conditions that both parties understand and agree upon. If you can understand and accept the racism of South Africa, then there's no harm in declaring that you will never interfere in their internal affairs. This, then, is your internal affair, and no one can force or pressure you as long as you are not afraid that the poison of racism might spread to your own family. Poison and disease has, after all, never paid much attention to the concept of geographic borders.

Let me also point out in passing that South Africa once had quite a few "friends" who understood them as well. But after having managed to benefit from these "friendly relations," under preconditions that were more harmful than beneficial to South Africa, those countries all ran over to the more radical camp calling for the imposition of strict sanctions on South Africa. Only Britain, the United States, and other countries that South Africa had often accused of interfering in its internal affairs are still working hard and persistently for the peaceful and stable transition to social and political reform there; they are still taking responsibility for the nation of South Africa and its people. Who, then, are your real friends? Should you spend money on those sly dogs who hang around your feet just for the scraps you throw them? Is the panting and pawing of these dogs helping you, or hurting you? It's pretty easy to see which. Of course, no two situations are ever exactly alike, but it's interesting to note that their basic principle is always the same, and they aren't problems that "guiding public opinion" can solve.

I wish you good health! I hope that you will go on living so that one day we can finally meet. Up until now I haven't had the chance to greet my dear old friend and have a heart-to-heart chat with him! Please don't disappoint me. An old person like yourself should really take an early retirement and let the younger generation look after things. Otherwise, I don't know whether I will have the opportunity to meet with my old friend or not. Take care of yourself.

Wei Jingsheng
Nanpu Salt Works

December 11, 1989

Dear Deng Xiaoping and Members of the Judiciary:

I would like to thank you all for transferring me from Qinghai to Hebei out of consideration for my health, but after more than four months of trying to get accustomed to the place, I have discovered that Qinghai is far better than here, and this is no place for my recuperation. Aside from the climate, which I have no control over, the other conditions, including food, clothing, accommodations, medical care, hygiene, study, and so on, are far inferior to those at Tanggemu Farm in Qinghai. These problems are, of course, mainly due to the fact that you and I are trying to accomplish different things, and that leaves little room for discussion or improvement. Even without mentioning the long-term effects, these past four months have been very difficult for me and my health is beginning to take a turn for the worse. I don't want to imagine what might happen if I go on like this for long.

As for the conditions for studying here, this place is very close to Beijing and can't be considered a remote region, so one would assume that the kinds of books and news available should be far superior to those found in Qinghai. But in reality the exact opposite appears to be the case. Overall, my impression is that this place is even more isolated than Qinghai. A decade after the start of reforms and openness in China, I seem to have been transported back to the days when class struggle still reigned. The main characteristic of that era was the belief that the more the people knew, the more they would resist, and so ignorance was considered the foundation for revolutionary victory.

As for living standards, the food here doesn't even compare to that in the Qinghai or Beijing prisons, and if I want to buy myself a few extra things to supplement my diet, I am strictly prohibited. Even things that in no way interfere with prison order or management are not allowed. My goal is not to make trouble, not to do anything wrong, and not to think too much about my situation, but to just try to eat well, sleep well, and stay healthy, so I'll be able to walk out of prison alive. Unfortunately, as long as people in prison are not considered human beings, they will not only lose the freedom their sentences legally determined they should, but they will also lose their right to lead a basic existence. In here, you become like a head of livestock: If you're allowed to live, you barely live; you must live as you're told; and if you get sick and die, you can only blame yourself for not being strong enough, because nobody will take responsibility for your weakness. Actually, one wouldn't even treat livestock like this; we're cared for more like the animals on a state-run farm or like slaves would be, and not allowed the right to even human subsistence.

As for medical care and hygiene here, it's been several months since I last bathed. It's not that they don't have the provisions for bathing here, it's just that they don't have them here for me. Whatever the reason, I can't shower and can only wash with cold water on the hottest days in the summer. Of course, I can't complain that this is inhumane because there are many humans who never wash at all. Tibetans, or the Han Chinese peoples of some regions in the Northwest, either never bathe or only take dry baths. They don't go to the doctor either, but still they are entered as "living conditions very good" on United Nations census forms, because, after all, "Aren't they still alive?" And other than those among them that do lose their lives, as the guards tell me, "They might even be healthier than you!"

There are doctors here, and naturally I went to see them when I got sick. But when I did so, I discovered that the doctors here (with the exception of the dentist) are very different from those in other places where they try to find your illness in order to cure it. Here, the doctors merely try to find whether you have irrefutable evidence to prove that you are not "faking an illness"—they are police doctors worthy of the name. And then, Deng Xiaoping, there is also your ruling that "release on medical parole is prohibited." So if a doctor dares to diagnose an illness that should be treated outside, he might be suspected of "using the law to oppose the leadership of the Party." Must I drop dead suddenly like Hu Yaobang before I can receive a "final diagnosis" of heart disease? Even if you have destroyed all the evidence, I still have my illness, and I will go on asking you to allow me to be released for medical treatment in accordance with the law. If you really need proof, then you should arrange for me to be examined and treated in a large hospital with the proper equipment and expertise that is outside of the public security system (Beijing Fuwai Hospital, for example), and not just by a few semi-qualified, amateur doctors making hasty diagnoses.

It's frequently the case that preserving the "face" of important figures is more important than the lives of lowly ordinary people, so there may be some who would be appalled if I were released for medical treatment. If so, I have heard that a transfer back to Tanggemu Farm in Qinghai is "a possibility," therefore my second request is to be transferred back to Qinghai, where the living conditions are somewhat better. Even though the high altitude is very dangerous for my heart disease, I'll take it as the lesser of two evils.

Wei Jingsheng
Nanpu Salt Works

September 5, 1990

Dear Jiang Zemin:

Although you looked fatter on television recently than you did when you were in Shanghai, I can guess that this is only an indication of your cook's talents and not because you are having an easy time of things. Those who transfer to Beijing from elsewhere don't usually have it easy because they don't have a foothold in the local network of official connections. Nominally, you are the most senior leader in the country, but you're still forced to say only the words of others—I've yet to hear your own voice once. Squeezed in on both sides, things don't always turn out as you had hoped, and even an outsider like myself feels uncomfortable on your behalf. I would offer to lend you a hand, but my abilities fall short of my desires. Fortunately, our ancestors taught us that a gentleman can give words of advice to others, so I would like to offer some opinions to you now; whether you listen to them or not is up to you. As the old saying goes: "Nearest the emperor, nearest the gallows." I hope you will take heed of the warnings of Hu Yaobang and Zhao Ziyang, whose overturned carts are not far ahead of your own.

My observations are limited, so they may be mistaken, but it appears to me that you are neither a wise chancellor like Zhou Enlai nor a crafty old scoundrel who bends with every gust of wind (although I used to think you were). You have a daring personality, so you have the potential to be either a hero or a scheming traitor. But you have been in office for over a year now, and still you have achieved nothing. Doesn't this show that you're having a hard time? As far as your position, naturally, you are in a worse situation than any of your predecessors. As for personnel, you don't have the authority of those longtime local officials who have many subordinates and can create insurmountable obstacles for you. In terms of influence, you are also no match for the reactionary "home-going legions" who do nothing but persecute other people. Although such people were faring poorly a few years ago, they're getting bolder ever since Deng Xiaoping's foolish use of the military last year helped to give them a boost. But they've gotten a bit wiser this time and will no longer be taken in by "reform" and other such nonsense, and will grab for power any way they can. A decade of "reform" has taught them that for people like themselves who are good for nothing in other respects, grabbing power and persecuting others is the only reliable way of protecting their interests. Reforms may be well and good, but having seen that after reforms they fared far worse than most people, they inevitably came out strongly against them. If you try to act as their leader, I am afraid you are doomed to fail, because they already have a leader. After experiencing ten years of reform, they won't readily place their trust in an "outsider" like you, even if you are the general secretary. You fall way back in the ranks, as you have never held great prestige within the Party. I doubt whether being the executioner who suppressed the Shanghai students will do much to boost your reputation among the people either.

Our country is riddled with thousands of gaping wounds, and many abandoned projects are waiting to be taken up again. I can only offer my views on a few major ones.

The economy is always the number one problem facing our country because it is so poor! The first thing any poor person must know if he wants to get rich is: Do not offend the rich. The second is: Do not incur additional debts. And the third: Be benevolent in the pursuit of riches. Otherwise, any good fortune he gains will not last for long. Only after adhering to these three points can one begin to talk about other issues. Furthermore, whether a country is rich or poor, it must safeguard national economic interests in its dealings with foreign countries. At present, your "anti-isolation" diplomacy, which you consider so successful, has offended the rich by reducing China's trade revenues, while burdening the country with several new debts. Of course, if the diplomacy you consider successful only serves to free you from the isolation in which you have been kept since you butchered the people, then the ordinary people will not consider it a success. They will see it as using their hard-earned money to pay the price of butchery and enslavement. Such diplomacy fails both the country and the people. For a poor country and its people, a successful diplomacy is one that seeks to win interests for the country and its people while promoting economic development instead of surrendering interests and submitting itself to other countries. The diplomacy you consider "successful" certainly does not meet these criteria or achieve your goals and is beneficial only for a handful of leaders who butchered the people.

You should learn from the Japanese in handling foreign affairs. The Japanese gave top priority to the task of making their country rich and turned their embassies into "trade agencies." This might seem ridiculous to a rich country, but it is a necessity for a poor one, and should be imitated at least to a certain extent. Namely, we should reduce by half or more the number of military and cultural attachés, as well as other embassy staff engaged in subversive political activities, and double and redouble those involved in commercial activities. We should improve the working conditions for those staff members gathering information on foreign trade and promote normalized foreign trade (as long as it is profitable) without dumping goods at low prices just to earn foreign exchange. By placing too much value on obtaining foreign exchange, you old bumpkins, who know nothing about economics, have given the Chinese people the message that "Chinese currency is worthless." This is a root cause of the "worship of foreign things" that also includes the special stores in China that give preferences to foreigners. You dictatorial leaders yourselves have been the first to deprive the Chinese people of their dignity. You should develop a new outlook on foreign trade. Foreign trade is just like any another form of trade; making money, not simply "earning foreign exchange," should be its objective. Goods that make a profit on the domestic market should, therefore, be offered there first.

Next is commerce. If commodities are not allowed to flow freely, production is adversely affected. All of us have learned this during the recent period of "sluggishness," but the government still did not take appropriate measures, or actually did things that defeated their efforts. If you go on supporting the mismanaged commercial enterprises that monopolize the market and keep shoddy goods in stock for long periods, the economy will remain chaotic and troubled and will become more difficult to revive even if the current sluggishness is overcome. Of course, it is the people's purses and the state treasury that will suffer the greatest losses, but what will you gain from it? Stability? Your idea of stability is that you can avoid mistakes by doing nothing. But what the people need is money, not this kind of stability. To enliven commerce, you must treat state and privately run enterprises equally. You should support enterprises that are managed well, eliminate those that are mismanaged, and reorganize those that should be reorganized. The people want to buy goods; they don't care whether they are produced by state or private enterprises.

Ours is a large but poor country. Public works are a great burden on the government and the construction of highways, bridges, and ports still falls far short of demand. The government's resources have never been ample, but instead of using them to do what should be done, the government has entered into competition with the people for profits. As a result, we've not only lost the chicken but the eggs are broken as well—what should have been done wasn't, and now the resources for doing them are gone too. Apart from building public works, the government should support urban development. (This can be contracted and subcontracted.) Why are urban lands leased to foreigners? If the land was to be contracted out for business use, priority should have been given to Chinese people. Why should foreigners always take precedence over Chinese? Only in the colonies of Hong Kong and Macao do Chinese and foreigners stand equally before the law. No wonder foreigners flock to China while the Chinese rush to go abroad. We do not treat ourselves like people!

So much for now! More next time.

Wei Jingsheng

September 20, 1990

Dear Lingling and Taotao:

The Asian Games are about to open, so the traffic is probably heavy. Please be careful on your way here to visit me. In addition to the things I asked for last time, please bring a watch, a calculator, and a tape recorder. The watch Xiaoyi gave me has stopped completely. Also, the television English program is moving pretty quickly now and the textbook says you should use a tape recorder to help review the lessons. The earlier lessons were easier and I could keep up without taping them, but from now on I don't think I'll be able to. A small, good-quality one would be the best, as the television sound itself is so distorted that if the tape recorder is no good I won't be able to understand the recording at all. Bring along two extension cords as well and bring back the electric pot you took home last time. The quality of the one they gave out here is so bad that the controls and wire burned out after just half a year. I fixed it well enough to use for a while, but I don't know when it will be totally done for.

If domestic goods are all of this quality, no wonder there are overstocks and people worship foreign goods. The quality of domestic products is so bad sometimes that it can really get in the way of things, and there's no way a difference in price can make up for that. For example, if this electric pot were used by somebody with no electrical know-how, he could blow out the electricity. And then there are the cars used on the high plains in Qinghai. Quite a few people have frozen to death after a breakdown in the middle of nowhere. We spent a freezing night stranded on Bird Island once and we were lucky it was only September. It's worth it to spend four or five times the price to buy a reliable foreign product because in matters of life and death, there's no way to be "patriotic." The examples are so numerous that the worship of foreign goods has lowered the relative value of Chinese goods and currency. This is precisely why even though China's scientific level is not that low and shortcomings are being made up for every day, the per capita output is still very low. It is a rule of pure economics that the market determines value and this is something that Taotao and his "science and technology national revitalizationists" should understand. It's also something that the "production-oriented socialist" bureaucrats don't get. Judging from history, once this trend is under way, its very difficult to reverse. For example, around the turn of the century, Japan was well known for producing low-quality goods, and now, even more than half a century later, although Japan is famous for its high-quality, low-priced goods, the Japanese still crave foreign products.

I predict that the next bout of inflation will start after the Asian Games. It shouldn't get as severe as last year, but you might still take care to save some money and stock up on goods, especially household goods. If Shanshan had left for West Germany two years sooner, she might have cut her travel costs by a third. Maybe then she and Xiaoyi could have gone together. They can't live apart as they do now for long. Taotao, when you see Xiaoyi, ask him when he's going. Hamburg is a famous old commercial and academic city; it's a good place for Xiaoyi to go to study business. From the information I've gleaned from watching television, Hamburg is a relatively conservative and mild-tempered place, and I'm sure it's safer than southern Germany, and definitely more so than southern

Europe. I don't know what Shanshan's situation is. Write her and tell her to write to me. And tell her to give my regards to Little Ying and her husband. I still don't even know what this man's name is or what kind of person he is. I only know that Little Ying married a "Taiwanese gentleman." Tell Shanshan to write and let me know how Little Ying is doing and ask her to send some Deng Lijun and Liu Wenzheng tapes. I really like their singing styles. And she can send along some classical German orchestral and violin music as well; isn't Germany, after all, the "homeland" of music? I hear that the German language is somewhere between English and Russian, and that Esperanto, the "world language" that nobody actually speaks, and that was "created" by a Polish man, has elements of both German and Russian. Who knows, maybe he even threw in some Ukrainian to boot?!

I'll stop babbling here! I hope you can visit before the Mid-Autumn Festival. Please bring my winter clothing and a heavy blanket as well. Tell Papa not to buy anything else for me. If he drinks less and takes care of his health, that's better than anything. Taotao, you should drink less too. Say hello to Fanfan and Weiwei for me! My regards to everyone!

Your brother,
Jingsheng

December 31, 1990

Dear Jiang Zemin and Li Peng:

This is the time of year when people receive large numbers of New Year's cards, yet I doubt you will get many cards like this one. But since it will probably be spring before it reaches your hands, I doubt it will affect your holiday mood or appetite.

Today is already the seventieth day of my hunger strike, which I believe I wrote you about before. Whether or not you have the intention of resolving this situation, when confronted with matters of life and death or people who might not be completely irrelevant, regardless of how high and mighty your position might be, you should still offer them a word of response! It doesn't matter how you choose to do it.

With all my illnesses, it's very difficult for me to go on like this. If I still don't receive a few words from you in response, I can only assume that you have thought this problem over long ago and don't have any intention of solving it. If that's the case, then I too have no reason to go on with my suffering.

Wei Jingsheng
Nanpu Salt Works

January 28, 1991

Dear Taotao and Lingling:

I've been waiting for you to come visit and bring me some winter clothing. Why haven't you come yet? I'm hoping that you'll come soon and that when you do, you'll bring me some warm clothing and the cigarette lighter, pen, books, and so on that I asked you for last year. I've been told that the few letters I've written you over the past six months were all sent out; I wrote you everything I need in them, so there's no need for me to repeat it here. Please don't forget the tape recorder. The television English program is moving quickly now and the lessons are very in-depth. It's really difficult for me to study without the aid of a tape recorder. I can't get a solid grasp of the lessons and there's no way for me to pronounce things accurately at all, so please don't forget to bring it.

I'll leave other matters for when I talk to you face-to-face! That is, if you come soon.

Say hello to everybody!

Your older brother,
Jingsheng
Nanpu Salt Works

NOTE: On February 9, 1991, Lingling and Taotao came to visit on their way back from a trip to Tianjin. They told me that they had not received any of my letters since their visit the previous summer.

June 15, 1991

Dear Jiang Zemin and Li Peng:

Human rights have become a popular topic of conversation lately and even the Party line on the issue seems to have softened somewhat. It has declared that it intends to "study human rights theories and questions in order to deal with the peaceful evolution of hostile forces," and so on. These very words prove that the basic theories of the Communist Party as they currently exist do not cover the issue of human rights, and that people are no more than tools for production and struggle within its theoretical framework. Tools, naturally, do not have any rights. All they have is the "right" to be submissive and to be used. When "peaceful evolution of hostile forces" comes into the picture and the tools are no longer as docile and useful, then it becomes necessary to find out what to do to make them docile once again. At least, this is the stand and attitude revealed in your Party's newspaper. As for the many proclamations you have made during international diplomatic occasions, based on experience and your Party's own views, they cannot be taken at face value.

You may consider my views to be the futile and worthless thoughts of a heretic. After all, I am a former tool whom you now regard as no longer docile, and a leading dissident who has been falsely branded as part of the "human rights vanguard." But I have never been incited or instigated by "human rights diplomacy employed by hostile countries or hostile forces" and have not been influenced by theories of modern human rights in the West. The only information on human rights that I have access to comes from your Party's own publications. One thing I do know for sure, however, is that your Party unyieldingly holds the same view of human rights that the Nazis did, which helps to explain why you gnash your teeth at the mere mention of human rights and are so eager to get rid of them.

The Tibet problem (since the founding of the People's Republic), for example, did not stem from the "ambitions of imperialist forces" and human rights diplomacy. It is true that serious human rights problems, and even racial discrimination, have occurred in that region during the past forty years and imperialist aggression did indeed take place (several decades ago), but this all happened before human rights diplomacy came onto the scene. The imperialists had left India long before, and besides, what ambitions would they have for Tibet, a region which they had never even colonized in the first place? The root causes of the problems in Tibet are all internal and lie particularly in the theories and practices of your party. Do not call the crow black, when you yourself are blacker. Neither the existence of South African racists, nor the Ku Klux Klan, nor feudal serfdom in old Tibet gives you the right to ignore human rights, or proves that you have a good human rights record.

But what is the use of saying all this nonsense anyway? Let us take a serious look at human rights theories and practices, how they stand in relation to socialism, and in particular why Marxist societies often turn out to be political structures that do not respect human rights. These questions are matters of primary importance for modern China. They may seem very far removed from us, but actually they are very close to home; they might appear as merely abstract concepts, but they are, in fact, very concrete. The lack of human rights is the principal cause for many of the concrete problems confronting Chinese society. Human rights are also a problem about which fallacies and confusion abound. It will take concerted efforts by all to clarify these human rights theories and activities. I can only talk on the basis of some of the precise information gleaned from your Party publications, so my lack of thoroughness is inevitable.

FALLACY ONE: *Human rights are the internal affairs of a country, and foreign governments and organizations have no right to interfere.*

Internal affairs are matters decided on by the government of each country. If human rights issues are the internal affairs of a country and the government decides not to respect human rights, do human rights simply cease to exist as a problem? Rights that a government does not recognize as human rights naturally cannot be considered human rights issues. In other words, they become merely questions of internal legislation and jurisdiction, and problems not stipulated by the law are problems that do not exist. Your Party obviously adheres to such logic, which also happens to be the sort of thinking upheld by Hitler, the South African racists, and ancient Chinese emperors. According to such logic, it is both legal and reasonable to ignore and infringe upon human rights, and democratic revolutions, socialist revolutions, and revolutions for national independence in various countries are thereby all considered illegal and unreasonable.

FALLACY TWO: There are different standards of human rights. Different standards apply to different countries, nations, cultural traditions, and social systems, and people should be content with the human rights standards stipulated in the laws of their country.

If such a theory were tenable, then all human rights conditions would be reasonable and there would be no such thing as "human rights problems." What, then, is the use of talking about "international cooperation on human rights," "condemning so-and-so for gross human rights violations," "resolutely imposing sanctions against so-and-so's apartheid," and such? Yours is a sovereign state, but so are other states; your human rights standards are "stipulated by law and represent the will of the government," but is this not also true of other countries? In your country, you say, human rights conditions are the consequences of "cultural traditions, the social system, and historical changes." Did you think that in other countries they just fell out of the sky? Your "internal affairs" will bear no interference, but do you think other countries welcome your interference in their "internal affairs"? All this goes to show that the "theory of different standards" does not hold water because you have no way of proving that your laws and policies are of a reasonable standard while those of others are not. In order to prove that yours are reasonable, you would have to cite more objective standards.

We can also see that, although the safeguarding of human rights and basic freedoms depends on legislation and policy enforcement on the part of sovereign states, human rights themselves have objective standards that cannot be modified by legislation and cannot be changed by the will of the government. "Human rights issues" pertain to how a government protects and respects the rights of its individual citizens, not how reasonable the government is in its actions. These "issues" have to do with how to protect the relatively weak rights of individuals under the relatively strong organs of power. They are common objective standards which apply to all governments and all individuals and no one is entitled to special standards. Like objective existence and objective laws, they are objective truths. That was why Rousseau called them "natural rights."

These "natural rights" are not "protected by heaven" as your bootlicking hack propagandists try to argue, but are "rights with which every person is born." They are things that we fight for as a matter of course and we don't need to be taught by "hostile countries and hostile forces" to do so. They are the natural laws and rights of life—just like eating or having sex. In other words, they are instinctive and that is why they are called "natural." It is abominable sophistry to try to argue that people can do without food because there are some people who have nothing to eat; or that people can do without sex because there are widows and bachelors around. It is similarly abominable to argue that people do not need human rights because they are able to adapt to an animal-like existence or because there are people who consciously act in a servile manner; or that there is no such thing as objective human rights standards simply because dictatorial slave societies still exist.

It is precisely because human rights are independent of the will of the government, and even independent of the will of all mankind, that people fight for the realization and expansion of human rights as a natural and unprovoked matter of course. They gradually come to the realization that the more widespread and reliable the protection of human rights is, the more their own human rights are protected. Just as man's understanding of objective truths and objective laws is a gradual process, man's understanding and comprehension of human rights is a gradual process. Just as man's grasp and utilization of objective laws is a progressive process, man's protection of the theory and practice of human rights is a progressive process. Thus, it is a plausible excuse to say that our theories and practices in this regard are still backward and that human rights conditions differ in different countries and nations under different cultural conditions and social systems.

However, the presence of different conditions and views cannot be taken as an excuse to violate and disregard human rights or to demonstrate that laws enacted by individuals can override objective truths or to argue that laws that violate human rights are justified. Any doctrine that preaches the supremacy of law is just another form of fascism. To them, the law is not the servant of the people's will or the embodiment of objective truths, but quite the other way around: The people and truths become the servants of the absolute law and its enforcing agents. Not only the people but also objective truths become subordinate to the ruler's will as expressed in the name of the law and the state.

Chinese people as a whole find the fascist soil of this "doctrine of the supremacy of law" quite unacceptable. Most Chinese people judge whether a person is right or wrong based on whether or not he or she abides by the law. However, they also look at whether or not the law protects and serves the people in judging whether the law is right. They take particular care in judging the law enforcement agents. There is no place for the "doctrine of the supremacy of the law." When there is a conflict between the people and the law, they favor putting the people first.

This may sound like the "human rights theory" handed down since the time of Rousseau, but it is also the essence of the humanistic, or democratic, tradition found in traditional Chinese culture. This tradition has been deeply rooted in people's hearts for over two thousand years and there is no way it can be pushed aside for the feudal or prefeudal ideology of the "doctrine of the supremacy of law." What is really important now is not so much counteracting the effects of this doctrine as finding out how political and administrative organs can be made to show more respect and provide more protection for human rights. This is in keeping with the wishes of the times and of the people and will save your Party and you yourselves from being wiped out. In the face of the crushing tide of history, one must go along with it or perish. This is true at all times and in all countries.

FALLACY THREE: *It is permissible to discuss the issue of human rights and carry out international cooperation on human rights, but it is an "abnormal phenomenon" to preach specific values, ideologies, and models.*

The difference between a democratic system that respects and protects human rights and basic freedoms and a totalitarian system that does not lies in their different "social models." It also lies in a difference in ideologies—the theories on the basis of which social models are established and exist. There is also a difference in values—the basis for these ideologies.

The values of Hitler and all totalitarian rulers can only produce fascism, or "national socialism," an ideology that takes away or suppresses individual rights and freedoms in the name of the state or the society. A social system established on the basis of such an ideology can only be a Nazi or totalitarian social model. Whether or not a system respects and protects human rights is what basically distinguishes the values of democracy and freedom from those of totalitarianism and enslavement.

If people are allowed to "discuss human rights and carry out international cooperation on human rights," they will naturally try to interfere with, stop, and change those systems or institutions that do not respect and protect human rights. Opposition to, and sanctions against, South African apartheid, for instance, is large-scale "international cooperation on human rights." If, in this exercise, people are not allowed to promote values based on the basic human right of equality for all, or to rely on the ideology of "democracy based on individuals" in trying to promote a social model of "democracy and freedom," and can speak only "within the limits prescribed by law," can this cooperation on human rights be effective? It is nothing more than a fig leaf covering the ugly features of the anti–human rights social model of enslavement; it is merely a clever trick to oppose social progress.

FALLACY FOUR: *It is permissible to discuss and even protect human rights, but no international pressure will be tolerated. Emancipation of human rights under a dictatorship can only come about through the dictatorship's "own choice."*

Without exception, any social model based on dictatorship and enslavement that does not respect human rights is held together by force and defiance of reason. However, if it is reasonable and can accept reasonable exchanges, it can become a democratic social model that respects human rights. It is only under this precondition that inadequate protection of human rights can be rectified and remedied through discussion and cooperation. Even then, the governments of these countries may not take the initiative to make major moves to improve their human rights conditions unless they are subjected to pressures from within and without. The civil rights movement that took place in the United States not long ago is an obvious case in point.

A social model that must be held together by deception and violence can only give rise to a society of enslavement where human rights are not respected. The most obvious trait of such regimes is that they only recognize authority based on violence and strength (the threat of violence), but do not recognize rights that should be respected and protected. Their maxim is that political power grows out of the barrel of a gun; in other words, if you win a country on horseback, you must rule it on horseback. It is brute force rather than the people's will that constitutes the cornerstone of these regimes. Such is the essence of dictatorship.

Under the circumstances, there are only two ways to bring about change: Either use violence to counter violence and topple the government through revolution, or force it to change gradually, that is, to reform, through the exertion of pressure from within and without, but mainly from without. Of the two, reform seems more desirable because it is less destructive. Although it implies greater difficulty and complexity, it ensures a more stable and predictable situation. It will also be socially, politically, economically, and culturally less damaging to the country itself and countries with related interests. One way to minimize losses and setbacks for all sides is for countries with related interests to exert pressure and help bring about internal progress and reform. If other countries are not allowed to exert pressure, and the forces of reform are left to fight the bloody and powerful apparatus of violence alone, they will be left with only one choice: violent revolution entailing numerous setbacks, huge losses, and an uncertain future.

If I remember an official statement by your Party correctly, the fascist regimes of Hitler and Mussolini owed their expansion to the fact that the international community "did not exert any pressure or intervene in their internal affairs." Your Party called this a "policy of appeasement" in various official documents and said that "the stupid imperialist governments and profit-seeking bourgeoisie" were partly to blame for the outbreak of World War II, which I think is a correct historical conclusion. But why are you taking an opposite stance now? The reason is not difficult to see! It is because you have identified your values, ideology, and social model with Hitler and present-day South Africa.

FALLACY FIVE: *"We have managed to feed and meet the subsistence needs of over one billion people" and "this is the greatest human right."*

If feeding the people and keeping them from starving or freezing to death constitutes the greatest respect for human rights, then consider the feudal lords and slave owners. The fact that slaves and serfs were kept from starving or freezing to death could prove that the slave owners had protected "the greatest human right" as you have done. The Nazi concentration camps were also responsible for feeding the Jews and other "inferior races" in captivity and keeping them from starving or freezing to death. Following this reasoning, are not the survivors of the Holocaust, like the ordinary Chinese people who survived numerous brutal and barbaric movements and "mistakes" by the Communist Party, proof that Nazi racism was one of "the greatest human rights" doctrines? If this is in fact your concept of human rights, then it is an anti–human rights concept similar to that held by the slave owners and Nazis and is something that goes against a perception of value that respects the dignity and rights of every individual.

Is this the concept of human rights held under communism and its manifestation in Marxism? In my opinion, no Marxist since the time of Marx would openly admit that it is. With the exception of a small number of foolish pigs who've left their sties and do not really know what they are talking about, the majority of genuine or self-proclaimed Marxists would, either sincerely or out of their

need to hide, deny that they believe in an anti–human rights concept that goes against the interests of mankind. The thing is, not
only Marxism but every ideology that advocates "reliance on violence and all means both fair or foul" when the "interests of all
mankind or of all the people within a certain scope" are at stake,
turns a blind eye to human beings and believes in doctrines
that go against human rights and values. Nazism, fascism, anar-
chism, and all brands of modern terrorism have basic principles
that go against human rights incorporated in their theories and
practices.

You claim that "we have managed to feed one billion people"
when it is actually you who are living off the labor of the people,
and you claim that "we have met their subsistence needs" when it
is the people who have solved the problem of food and clothing
themselves through their own wisdom, resourcefulness, and arduous
labor under extremely difficult conditions that have been com-
pounded by exploitation and oppression carried out by Party ruffians and bureaucrats. Doesn't your rhetoric sound like that of a
slave owner? Somewhere between the anarchist slogan inviting
workers and peasants to "take back the fruits of your labor" and
the tune of the slave owner, there is "a red thread that runs through
all" and which serves as a balance and link. This thread is your
Maoist doctrines, "Once one has power, one has everything" and
"Political power grows out of the barrel of a gun," together with
Marxism and the doctrine of the supremacy of violence that
preaches the seizure and maintenance of a totalitarian regime
through violence.

At a time when China is moving from an agricultural and pas-
toral economy into the modern industrial and information age, its
traditional moral basis in "benevolence, righteousness, and propriety" has been destroyed, but it has not yet accepted "human
rights, freedom, and equality" as the moral basis of the age of
industrial democracy. China's wise ideological and cultural traditions likewise have no way to accept any moral basis of "universal
fraternity and equality" as it is religious and based on superstition.
Society is thus left in a nihilist and chaotic state. By opposing tradition and making violence supreme, your doctrine of general

hatred can only add fuel to the fire and bring greater chaos and suffering to society. It is because of this that I say that the human rights issue is truly one of the basic issues in determining whether or not a country can enjoy long-lasting peace and prosperity.

FALLACY SIX: *"Looking after the interests of the majority of people is our major point of departure on the issue of human rights."*

On the surface, these words sound fine, but in fact there are often things that need to be examined beneath the surface. When talking about the rights that every person should enjoy, the claim that "the majority is the point of departure" is an act of deceptive sophistry and excuse-making. It occurs when faced with a situation which one cannot deny but in which one is unwilling to admit fault. This is because even if we talk about "gross violations of human rights," the phrase still refers to the violation of the rights belonging to every individual—in other words, the violation of an individual's internal affairs. It does not refer to a matter of contention that may or may not belong to a particular individual, and does not refer to public matters in the political, economic, or environmental domains. These are expressed by other concepts. Rather, it refers to rights that should belong to every individual. This has nothing to do with "the majority," and the majority has no right to curtail the basic right to freedom of even a small minority. Although parts of their concepts can be duplicated and may overlap, we cannot thus say that chemistry equals physics, that energy equals transport, that grain equals smelly night soil, and so on. This is the same sort of sophistry as using the majority as an excuse to confuse the issue of the human rights that belong to every individual.

Perhaps these words indicate that in our country's society, there exists a majority that enjoys rights and a small minority that does not enjoy basic rights. Who, then, is this majority, and who is the small minority? Do we need to redraw class divisions? Or are some minority nationalities going to serve as the antithesis, as was the case in the 1950s and 1960s? Regardless, juggling with terms such as "the majority" on the question of basic human rights proves that this society is an unequal one and that the Constitution and laws that talk of "all persons being equal" are nothing more than waste paper. This, then, produces a dilemma. Either the Constitution and the laws have been cleverly juggled by people so that some enjoy full rights and others enjoy fewer rights or none at all, and the surface and content of the laws and the Constitution are different or even meaningless; or else some people have usurped the rights that should belong to every person rather than to only some of the people and therefore there has been a large-scale violation of human rights. Which of the two situations do you think is the most likely? Or do both exist simultaneously?

South Africa is a country in which a small number of white people violate the rights of the majority of the people, including some white people. This certainly cannot be tolerated and it is certainly valid to openly attack such abuses. However, people of your age should remember that the Nazis and some "socialist comrades" who were not Nazis used the pretext of "the majority" to eliminate the "inferior races"—the Jews, the Tartars, and the blacks. Is it the case that because some persons constituted "the majority" in Germany, the Soviet Union, and the United States they had the right to violate the rights and freedoms of other people? Was it the case that because such violations did not violate the laws of these countries at that time, and were tolerated, supported, and implemented by the governments, that they were reasonable and should not have been denounced, since as you say, "interference in internal affairs is impermissible"? While the violation of human rights based on race and national differences is obviously a barbarous act, is not the violation of human rights within a single race or nation, based on artificial differences or even with no basis at all, even more barbarous and intolerable? If the people allow those who hold power in the people's name to violate and ignore the rights of some of the people, then at the same time they are giving them the power to violate the rights of all the people. This is especially so in a society where there are no racial or cultural differences.

FALLACY SEVEN: *Marx had a famous popular definition: "Man's nature is the sum of his social relations." Some people, on this basis, infer that as different societies have different social relations and the sums of such relations are different, there are also different human natures. Thus, the different views on and practices of human rights are suited to different types of human natures and the rationality of all of these should be fully recognized. It would be an abnormal phenomenon to have uniform requirements.*

Man is not a product of his social relations, nor indeed of any relations. He is not a robot, nor is he a product created by other people based on a pattern for man. Rather, he is a product of nature. Thus, his essential qualities are likewise a product of nature. These are "instinctive" and very basic and they constitute a human "commonality" which is inborn and possessed by all and on which all other human natures and social relations are based. Human rights and basic freedoms refer to the satisfying or realizing of this part of human nature. They are the sum of hopes and aspirations that emerge naturally and do not need to be taught.

Human rights are themselves a type of social relation. The respect and protection of human rights and basic freedoms is in itself a social institution, a social system, and a mechanism to ensure its own effectiveness. However, this refers to primary-level social relations, which emerge from man's basic nature or, put another way, are the foundation of all social relations. These are basically different from those social relations that are derived and that are stipulated or manufactured by man.

Wherever a great amount of social injustice is enshrined in law, that is to say, where the cornerstone of a legal system is social injustice maintained through violence, the social models are societies of enslavement such as slavery and fascism. These societies can be distinguished by determining the degree of human rights existing in them. We need to look at whether or not within these societies the basic freedoms and rights of a part or the majority of the people have actually been expropriated "by law." Law is people's social nature and is not the sole or most basic standard for social relations. Human rights are a more basic standard.

In order to have progressed to its present stage, Western civilization has had to safeguard outstanding elements of its culture and tradition and learn many things from the remarkable achievements of the civilizations of China and elsewhere. This has enabled it to maintain appropriate development for itself at pace with an increasingly rapid global development. Chinese civilization has begun a similar process of study and assimilation. At the present time, is it really necessary that we continue to enshrine and worship "isms" that Western civilization has already spit out?

Wei Jingsheng

February 12, 1992

Dear Jiang Zemin and Li Peng:

China's situation today has taken a turn for the better. We've already passed through the dangerous rapids in our relations with the West; the economy has left its low valley; and most importantly the "anti-liberalization, anti-peaceful evolution" spirit is weakening. Therefore, the political atmosphere and social relations in our country have hope for gradual improvement. This is the key to allowing the country and its citizens to stand up and move forward, but if this key breaks, how will the other parts function?

But let me get to my point. There are a few matters that must be resolved. My hunger strike to protest the abuse of political prisoners and to demand better treatment must come to some conclusion. Or, to put it another way, your plan to kill a chicken to scare the monkey in order to halt protests by political prisoners must also come to a conclusion. Either the fish will die or the net will tear; something must happen. If the fish dies, then that demonstrates conclusively that the "socialist legal system" of Deng, Jiang, and Li is still nothing more than the anarchy and chaos of the Mao Zedong era.

Although you've already used the tactics of mental abuse, starvation, disease, and loud noise, there are still many other ways of ending a life in the blink of an eye. I don't have enough strength left, however, so please excuse me for quitting before the game is through. It's a great pity and quite difficult to keep your honorable Party from reaching new heights in the art of punishment and keeping the great minds of your Party's experts from being utilized to their full potential. Yet it looks like any fantasy I still harbored about you has been destroyed, and I can do nothing more than end my three-month hunger strike and await the consequences as I enter the last substantial period of my confinement. From the looks of it, you can barely hold yourselves back.

Wei Jingsheng

Plagued by illness and tormented by physical and mental abuse, Wei Jingsheng wrote a series of "memorandums" in early 1992, all similar to the one below, as a way of recording the mistreatment he was receiving in prison.

February 23, 1992

A Memorandum:

Your aim in changing personnel this time is just as I thought: You suspect that the old people aren't fully carrying out your orders and don't make me suffer enough, so you've replaced them with new ones who are ignorant of my situation in order to intensify my suffering. The old one named Ma is certainly the most effective tool you have to punish me. It's my guess that this was not a low-level decision made within the brigade.

The results are obvious: I've been so tormented these days that I'm suffering from a serious sleep deficiency. The newly arrived old comrades don't know my health problems or my living habits, and the one who's been here for a while called Ma deliberately organizes them to stay up at night. Even though the old men themselves suffer from all this, they have to keep making noise, by coughing, going in and out of the door, moving the tables and chairs about, or something like that. They must make just enough noise to disturb my sleep. And if this weren't enough, Ma uses his familiarity with my habits to deliberately make even louder noises that cause my heart to skip a beat. I can't keep silent about this, but no one (especially the police guards) wants to listen. And that guy Ma manages to sow even more discord among us and makes my relationship with the people who work here increasingly tense. He then twists this tense relationship so that everyone singles me out for attack. His plan is carefully thought out and he can be very effective with little effort. So I decided right away: This time around, there is no way I am going to go along happily with all of your tricks.

I am recording the facts here so that I won't forget them later.

Wei Jingsheng

May 1, 1992

Dear Prison Authorities:

I was wondering whether the tape recorder, books, and other things that my sister brought for me are finished being inspected or not. I'm anxious to use them and hope that you can pass them on to me soon.

Books and magazines mean more to me than they do to you. They are not only my study tools, but necessities for my daily life. If I don't have books, television, music, and so on, my days are very hard to get through. You've never experienced the full "benefits" of the Party, so of course you wouldn't know. But human beings, after all, are not barnyard animals; they aren't just satisfied once they've had enough to eat, but have well-developed brains that get rusty if they aren't used. Without proper use, the mind can grow idle and go astray. That is why Stefan Zweig wrote *The Story of Chess*. People put to work in here for the first time have all experienced it, but they never work more than one shift every three to four days, while I am here day after day like this. You are all intellectuals, so you must understand at least a bit of this reasoning. No excuses are valid; this is in reality a form of abuse. It's like you've stolen a page from the Nazis' book. I even suspect that revenge for an old grievance has some role in it.

Use of the tape recorder, for example, isn't some new privilege I am asking for. Permission to use a tape recorder was agreed to by the judiciary while I was still in Qinghai. But when I first got here, I wasn't given electricity, then my tape recorder was confiscated. If this isn't retaliation for some old grudge, then how can it be explained? The tape player I am using now is no good—it can't record and can't even rewind a tape, so it's very inconvenient to use for studying. Furthermore, my use of a tape recorder does not constitute a threat to your work in any way. To put things slightly less politely, the truth is you have a habit of lying and going back on your word. I don't keep a record in a little book in order to settle accounts later and I am even less able to use a wiretap to gather evidence, so what are you all so afraid of? Of course, I know you are not the type of people who would do such things, but then who is making the decisions? What hatred do those people feel toward me that makes them treat me so harshly? I am at an absolute loss to understand and don't know if even you know the reasons why or not.

My younger brother and sisters always follow the rules and can even remember the regulations of several years ago quite clearly. That is why I asked them to buy a tape recorder that does not have a radio in it to be used for the sole purpose of my own study and enjoyment. I never guessed this would be such a problem and that you would be so unpredictable, issuing orders only to change them again. How is a person supposed to communicate with you? Confucius said: "A gentleman is always calm and composed; a petty man is often in distress." I very much hope that we can be open and aboveboard like gentlemen, coexisting in peace and not scheming and plotting behind each other's backs like petty men stirring up antagonisms. Ever since my arrival here I have been straightforward and sought you out to discuss any problem, but what have you done in return? No wonder all those backstabbers who foment conflict are in such stable positions here, for doesn't it show that their superiors are doing the same? I have never been able to understand what good it does you (or your superiors) to intensify unnecessary conflicts. Doesn't it tire you out? I think it is a lot more reasonable for you and the others to coexist in peace by being honest and avoiding friction.

I hope you will give me my books and tape recorder very soon. I am waiting to use them!

Wei Jingsheng

October 5, 1992

Dear Deng Xiaoping:

The propaganda campaign you have launched shows that you are not only dissatisfied with your handpicked successor, but also concerned about the affairs of Tibet that are under your personal care. Therefore, your lackies have hastily worked out a white paper called "Tibet—Its Sovereignty and Human Rights" to cover up their incompetence and ignorance, which is your incompetence and ignorance as well. They continue to use old lies and distortions to deceive you and many other Chinese people in order to maintain their position and power.

As a result, when all of these people wake up from their dreams, Tibet will no longer be part of China. The domino effect will reach far beyond the 1.2 million square kilometers of Tibet and you will be laughed at and condemned by history. In order to improve the situation and solve the Tibet question, the first thing to do is understand what the problems are. Merely listening to the soothing lies of your subordinates will not help you understand the reality of the problem, let alone resolve it.

I myself know only a small amount about Tibetan history, but I still believe that I am more clear-minded on it than you and your people. Therefore, I venture to write this letter to you and hope that you will create an academic atmosphere of free expression, so that people of knowledge can express more of their insights on this issue and explore the problems involved. This is the only way to avoid losing your last chance to settle the issue and repeating the situation of the former Soviet Union or Yugoslavia.

The Tibet issue is a difficult one because of its uniqueness and the vagueness of the issue of sovereignty. As a matter of fact, existing international law provides little help in finding a solution, since many parts of it are mutually contradictory, and thus it cannot be invoked in making judgments on the more complicated matters in today's world. Overemphasis on outdated and nonbinding international law will not in any way help find a solution to the problem we face today.

For instance, in reality, Canada and Australia enjoy total independence and sovereignty. Yet it would be ridiculous if we defined them as Britain's colonies or even Britain's territories by arguing that the head of state of these two countries is the queen of England and their top government officials must be approved of by the queen. In solving problems, people should face reality and not try to find "evidence and facts" only from the history books. The Tibet issue is a more special and complicated case than those mentioned above. The union between Tibet and China (beginning in both the Qing dynasty and the Republic of China) took such a unique form that it is not understood by many scholars. The authors of the white paper are even worse than other scholars, however, and their arguments have failed to clarify the facts.

Tibet's special status was that although Tibet did not lose its sovereignty it was never a completely independent country. It was not independent, but it was not a colony either. It was not taking care of all its affairs as an independent sovereign country, but at the same time it was not ruled as a province of China by the Amban, the official appointed to Tibet by the Qing dynasty court. The fact is that Tibet had total autonomy over its domestic affairs while being part of the Qing court with regard to foreign affairs. It is because of such arrangements that many Chinese and foreigners who don't know all the facts consider Tibet a province of the Chinese Empire. Hardly any similar cases exist that demonstrate a union of this kind.

From a legal point of view, it is somewhat similar to the United Kingdom or the European Community or the future European Union. The people identify themselves with the unified entity (United Kingdom, Europe, or China) while simultaneously identifying themselves with their respective independent countries. The unity is voluntary and the countries concerned reserve the right to break away from it. In the case of the United Kingdom, the unity of kingdoms led to the unity of sovereignty. In the case of Europe, democratic unity on an equal basis has led to a unity of sovereign countries. And in the case of Tibet and China, the actual unity of sovereignty was caused by the mutual participation of the supreme authorities. The unions of Europe and China are not the same from a legal point of view.

In accordance with agreement and customary practice, the Qing court and its successors sent troops to Tibet only at the request of the Dalai Lama. These troops would return to Sichuan or Qinghai province immediately after finishing their tasks as requested by the Dalai Lama. There was no permanent army in Tibet sent by the Qing court. There were only some forces assigned to protect the Qing Amban to Tibet that were stationed in designated barracks in Lhasa. The Qing court was partly responsible for the external and military affairs of Tibet and was in charge of the security of Tibet and the suppression of rebellions on an irregular basis.

The religious force led by the Dalai Lama was entrusted with the important task of maintaining the national unity of the Qing court. The Dalai Lama performed the role of the supreme spiritual leader of the national religion of the Qing dynasty. He was not like the "imperial teachers" of ancient times, but was the supreme spiritual leader of the national religion and enjoyed a popularity even surpassing that of the emperor in three-quarters of the Qing territory (Tibet, Xinjiang, Qinghai, Gansu, Sichuan, Yunnan, part of Burma, Inner and Outer Mongolia, provinces in the Northeast, and part of the Russian Far East). The main reason that the first emperor of the Qing dynasty made Lamaism the national religion was that he realized "in order to rule the various areas of Mongolia, it is necessary to unite Lamaism."

Lamaism became the main force uniting the nation during a period when China controlled the largest territory in history (larger even than the Soviet Union). The Qing court, in turn, with its military force and huge financial support, helped the Dalai Lama to maintain his supreme position and power as well as sovereignty over much more territory than at present. The word "tremendous" is hardly adequate to describe the benefit each side obtained from this union. The union was therefore stable and long-lasting. The legal status of the two sides was equal, though real power was not. The appointment of a minister to Tibet and the sending of a large amount of supplies to Tibet were methods employed to maintain the equilibrium of relations between the two sides. Otherwise, the influence of the Tibetan religious leader would have surpassed that of the Qing emperor at the expense of the equilibrium and equality of the two sides.

It is true that relations between the Qing court and Tibet underwent a lot of changes over the years, but this basic pattern was maintained until the late years of the Qing dynasty and relations between the two sides remained stable. It was for this reason that Tibet did not break away from China like Korea, Vietnam, Laos, Burma, and Mongolia. Tibet stood firmly on the Chinese side even when British troops occupied Lhasa. The main reason for all this was that a voluntary union based on common interests was in accord with the basic laws of humanity—namely, the principle that "the people's interests reign supreme."

For over a hundred years, from the late Qing dynasty to the Republic of China, China failed to fulfill its commitment to security in Tibet because of the weakness of China itself, yet the government of the Dalai Lama continued to respect the treaties between the two sides and did not do anything to jeopardize the sovereign union. Should Tibet have attempted to "split," it could have easily done so, as Outer Mongolia did, given the internal turmoil in China and the fact that foreign powers encouraged Tibet to claim independence. The white paper says that nobody ever recognized Tibet as an independent country. This is not true. During the period when Britain ruled India, especially at the time of the Simla Convention, a seat was reserved for Tibet as an independent country. The attempt to make the independence of Tibet a fait accompli was not successful only because the government of the Dalai Lama declined to do so. The protest lodged by the representative of the weak Chinese government did not carry as much weight as it was later said to have done.

At a time when the then Chinese government had failed to fulfill its obligations for a long period of time and large areas of Tibet were occupied by or affiliated with foreign countries, the position of the Dalai Lama's government was even greater. It was during this period that relations between China and Tibet became estranged. First, China was becoming a modern society in which the influence of religion was declining. Religion was no longer as important as it had been during the Yuan, Ming, and early Qing dynasties, although its influence should not be disregarded completely. Second, China had become so weak that it could hardly afford to take care of its western neighbor and Tibet had already learned to defend itself. The military assistance from China was no longer a necessity and could no longer be relied upon. Third, the close trade relations between Tibet and China were gradually being undermined by commodities from Britain and India. Fourth, the Han culture had lost its appeal to the cultures of the neighboring countries and regions and its attraction to the neighboring peoples had weakened.

In this process, the extent of estrangement between the two peoples was larger than that between the governments, and the mental estrangement was, in other respects, even greater. In the minds of the Tibetans, deceitfulness (mostly brought on by people in your home province of Sichuan and by Muslims in northwest China) had replaced the image of the Chinese as allies and defenders. In the minds of the Chinese, who considered themselves as being enlightened, Tibetans became backward and ignorant, "half human, half beast," rather than subjects of the living Buddha. Although this mutual discrimination and distrust did not cause an immediate split, it laid the foundations for future retaliations and a possible split. The orchestrator of this tragedy is no other than you, Deng Xiaoping.

As early as the 1940s, the rulers of Tibet initiated the discussion of social reform in Tibet. What they wanted was a social system like that in Britain or India and moderate reforms based on religious values. In accordance with convention established over several thousand years, they wanted to carry out the reform by themselves. They did not like the idea of being reformed by foreigners or a foreignerlike Han people (the Nationalist Party managed to respect this tradition, so that relations between the Nationalists and Tibet were more harmonious), nor did they like the revolution to fight landlords, distribute land, and kill class enemies. This was not only true of the ruling class, but of the entire society. The chanting that "liberated serfs look forward to the coming of the Communist Party" is but a slogan in your propaganda. It in no way represents the true feeling of the serfs at that time. You can go and ask your old subordinates Ya Hanzhang and Phuntsog Wanggyal to tell you about the real "great achievements" of the Communists in inciting the Tibetan serfs and you will realize that I am not being biased.

In fact, in most countries, such as Germany and Russia, the toughest obstacle to the liberation of serfs came from the serfs themselves. It was because of this shared social will and the practices of the Chinese Communist Party that the Tibetan government did not oppose allying with the Nationalists but firmly refused to let the Communists enter Tibet and expelled the Tibetan Communist Party led by Phuntsog Wanggyal, using the excuse of expelling the Chinese. These diplomatic methods clearly show that Tibet at that time exercised total sovereignty (in both foreign affairs and national defense). The expulsion of the Sichuan army and the Tibetan Communist Party via India was arranged through diplomatic channels.

During that period, the Chinese Communist Party was at the height of its powers. Like all other communist parties, it had little respect for sovereignty and national self-determination. Meanwhile, India, which had just gained independence from British rule, could hardly afford to help Tibet in its struggle against the Communist Party. Therefore, the effort to oppose the entry of the Communists into Tibet ended in failure. Moreover, the ignorance of the young Dalai Lama and the corruption of the Tibetan bureaucracy were the major factors aiding the smooth occupation of Lhasa by Communist troops. Deng Xiaoping, the decision you and Mao Zedong made to liberate Tibet peacefully should be deemed a correct policy, but since it was an agreement reached under the pressure of a heavy military presence, according to international law, it must therefore be rendered invalid. However, if this policy had been implemented seriously, the government of the Dalai Lama might have accepted it and the sovereign unity of China and Tibet may have continued and the international community would have accepted the fait accompli.

If this had been the case, Tibet would not have become such a headache for China. The Tibetans are a trustworthy people and are not good at playing tricks. Unfortunately, the leaders of the Communist Party, Mao Zedong and yourself included, became bigheaded with the "victory" in the Korean War and the economic recovery. At the same time, when you carried out the Great Leap Forward and ultra-leftist policies in the mainland, you also began to implement leftist policies in Tibet by deciding to accelerate democratic reform there. In doing so, you had in fact torn up the "Agreement on the Peaceful Liberation of Tibet." This caused

anger among Tibetans of all walks of life and a popular war broke
out against the leftist policies of the Communist Party under the
banner of fighting against outsiders and foreign religion. The Chinese government considered this a rebellion.

During the war and for a long period afterward, the mutual discrimination and contempt between the Tibetans and the Chinese
added to the hatred that caused the killing of innocent people by
the army and the torture of people by officials. The estrangement
between the peoples deepened and the Tibetan struggle for independence escalated. To talk about sovereignty under these circumstances would only give people the false impression that the
Communist Party ever even considered the issue. The situation
and pattern of confrontation between the two sides was just like
that between the colonial powers and the colonies in the old days.
It was also like the situation in present-day Yugoslavia.

Let's have a look at two recent examples in the world—one positive, the other negative. One is Yugoslavia. Like you in the Chinese
government, Yugoslavia would not recognize other peoples' right to
national self-determination and even resorted to armed force to prevent other peoples from gaining such rights. As a result, it has not
achieved its goal, but planted tremendous hatred that it will be
paying for a long time. The other example is Russia. It has
respected the right to self-determination and autonomy of other
nationalities and managed to keep together the Commonwealth of
Independent States and leave some room for possible unity in the
future. What's more, the customary mutual trust and good feeling
has remained intact. The differences between these two examples
will become more evident. Serbia was in a much better position
than Russia. In the past, Russia had done a lot more than Serbia
in fomenting grievances among other nationalities, but the differences in how such questions have been handled have resulted
in different consequences. Other conditions remaining the same,
the largest difference is that Russia has abided by the law governing human society and respected the right of other nations to
self-determination and autonomy. Therefore, factors in favor of
unity have been able to play a role.

In modern human society, the trend toward unity is stronger
than the trend toward division. Overemphasizing sovereignty and

the administrative authority of one nationality over the other is detrimental to unity. The societies that have already divided or are in the process of division are those that have placed undue stress on the limitless administrative power of one nation over other nations. The toughest obstacle facing the societies that have already achieved unity or are in the process of achieving it is also the overemphasis on sovereignty. The advantage of unity is obvious, but the arguments against unity are also strong. Why should people put emphasis only on the arguments against unity? Can you find a case which shows that unity can be maintained only by the use of high-pressure tactics? Even if you can find one, it must be because the time for division has not come yet.

You have been shouting about anti-colonialism and national independence for decades when, in fact, you do not understand what either of them really is. Like all of your other slogans, you employ them only as a convenient tool and do not really want to understand them or genuinely believe in them. This is precisely the source of your "leftist" sickness.

The relationship between China and Tibet could be much better than those within the former Soviet Union and Yugoslavia. Up until 1949, China had never oppressed Tibet, nor had it forced Tibet to be a vassal state. The two sides achieved sovereign unity voluntarily. Even today, the chances of unity between China and Tibet are much better than within the former Soviet Union or the European Community. In the early days of his forced exile, the Dalai Lama did not demand independence, nor is he demanding it today. This shows that a very good chance of unity still exists. However, you have adhered to old ideas and policies and continued to trust old bureaucracy. What you are doing is pushing Tibet toward division. China has already lost nearly half of the territory it had during the Qing dynasty. Should this continue, later generations will have to make a living by exporting labor, and revitalizing the Chinese nation will be impossible.

There is much to be done to eliminate the evil consequences of the suppression and killings of the last forty years and to put the China-Tibet relationship back on the track of normal development. The three pressing tasks are as follows.

First, mutual hatred and discrimination between the Han people and the Tibetans must be rooted out, especially erroneous ideas in the minds of the Han people about the Tibetans. Due to the propaganda of the last forty years, cadres in Tibet (and in other areas too) have developed a deep-rooted prejudice against Tibetans, which in turn has deepened the hate among the Tibetans against the Han. The real situation in this regard is beyond your imagination and it is not at all as your people have told you.

Let me give you a few examples to help you understand the seriousness of the situation. First, my parents never knew any Tibetans and had never studied Tibet. Whatever they knew about Tibet was what the Communist Party had told them. In their minds, Tibetans were half human and half beast, so it was only natural that when I planned to marry a Tibetan woman, they expressed the strongest opposition and they even threatened to sever all ties with me. Only later, when they got to know the woman, did they change their thinking. However, the woman's parents would not tolerate in-laws like my parents and I never did become the son-in-law of this Tibetan family.

Now the second example. When I was imprisoned in a Tibetan area in Qinghai, I overheard many conversations that showed me the contempt the Han cadres have toward Tibetans. They look down on everything that has to do with Tibet. For instance, although Tibetan dogs are famous, Han cadres would rather raise dogs brought from the heartland. They laughed at me when I told them how good Tibetan dogs were. They were only convinced of what I said when a television program said that foreigners would pay a lot of money for a Tibetan dog. In another instance, they would not believe that Tibetan butter was similar to the butter in a Western restaurant. How could it be possible that "old Tibetans" eat the same food as foreigners? Yet another example: Though yak meat is delicious to eat, the Han cadres in Tibet say things like, "As there is nothing else to eat, we'll have to buy some yak meat." When a Tibetan doctor learned that I enjoyed yak meat and wanted him to buy some Tibetan butter for me, he was so surprised at first that he assumed I was one of his own people.

These examples illustrate what the Communist cadres think of Tibetans and how they treat them. It is even worse than the way white people in the United States have discriminated against the Indians. Frankly speaking, you yourselves hold such discriminatory attitudes against the Tibetans, and this is expressed in all the relevant documents, statements, and other propaganda materials. This has deepened the estrangement between the Han people and the Tibetans and could eventually lead to division.

It will be extremely difficult to heal the wounds caused by forty years of grievances. However, efforts should be made every day to this end. Cadres at various levels who do not respect ethnic minorities should be replaced. At the same time, all ethnic minorities should be treated equally without special preferences, because special preferences imply that certain people are being treated as outsiders. Han chauvinism should be eliminated from all the publications. Over the last forty years, people have tended to view narrow nationalism and national chauvinism as patriotism. People always think of the Tang Princess Wencheng who married a Tibetan king as the Chinese "savior" who civilized Tibet. This is too much and it is not in accord with history. The labor camp I was sent to in Qinghai was located where the Tibetan army defeated the hundred thousand Chinese troops led by General Xue Rengui. As a result of this battle, Princess Wencheng was married to Tibet to make peace; however, none of the cadres in that region knew this story. They all believed that the Tibetans had been "enlightened" by the Chinese princess. Also, believing that they had been sent to Tibet to help reclaim the barren land where Tibetans had lived for generations, they acted and talked just like colonialists. It is your one-sided propaganda that has resulted in this national discrimination against the Tibetans. This kind of mentality must be changed, while at the same time the kind of exaggeration and deceit demonstrated by the authors of the white paper must be eliminated.

The second pressing task is that the government should speed up the development of the market economy in Tibet and establish closer economic ties between the heartland areas and the Tibetan market. In the last century, British and Indian commodities have been increasingly available on the Tibetan market. In the last forty years or so, the Tibetan market has suffered great damage. The so-called "socialist planned prices" fixed for Tibet's mineral resources and livestock, which resemble nothing more than colonialist exploitation, have caused tremendous losses for the Tibetan economy. Your aid could in no way make up for these losses. Furthermore, most of the aid you have given has been used to support the mechanisms of suppression or the scientific research being conducted there by Han people. This includes funds for government offices of various levels, hospitals and hotels for the Hans, military facilities, observatories, and geothermal power plants, which are not what the Tibetan economy really needs.

No matter what excuses you give the Tibetan people, they are not as stupid as you think. They know that you are not sincere in helping them, so they will not trust you. Decision makers should consider Tibet as part of their own homeland and put the financial assistance to proper use so it truly helps the economic development of Tibet in the most efficient way. The various economic barriers and "managed prices" should be eliminated; Tibetan commodities should have easier access to the heartland market and be given preferential prices. Efforts should be made in other areas too in order to improve economic and trade relations between Tibet and other areas of China. This is most important in consolidating Tibet-Han relations.

Third, the Chinese government should abolish its policy of detaining Tibetan religious leaders as hostages. Both religious and nonreligious Tibetans have a strong aversion to this policy, and this is a clear violation of human rights. The Chinese government must eliminate the mentality of the so-called "great Han Empire" and sit down at the negotiating table with the Dalai Lama. He is concerned about your sincerity, because you failed to win his trust in the past. Therefore, you should let him choose the place for negotiations, and he should be allowed to return to Lhasa if he wants to do so. All these are reasonable basic conditions; there is nothing here that is not understandable. There is no reason why you should fail to agree to all this. Now even the appointment of the Dalai Lama's negotiating aides has to be approved by the Chinese government. Isn't this really too much? To postpone the negotiations with these excuses is an indication that your people have no confidence in themselves. They are afraid that all their nonsense will be fully revealed should negotiations begin in earnest. The chances of Tibet remaining a part of China will improve if negotiations start, and therefore negotiations should start with no preconditions. It would be desirable to invite the Dalai Lama to return to Lhasa, and it would be much better than letting him be surrounded by self-serving careerists. In fact, the Dalai Lama should realize that without an alliance with the Han people, he will have to rely on ambitious Indians who are no better than the Han people. Sikkim, Bhutan, and Nepal are good examples for a future independent Tibet.

If we can do a better job, why should the Tibetans bring suffering on themselves by breaking away from the unity that has already existed for several centuries? The trend of the modern world is toward eventual unity. The advantages of unity outweigh its disadvantages. Judging from what the Dalai Lama has done in recent years, I believe he understands better than I do about the real issue. The Dalai Lama has his own difficulties. We should not press him too hard or he will run into the arms of others.

Wei Jingsheng

By January 1993, when Wei Jingsheng wrote this final letter from prison, he was beginning to feel the effects of mounting international pressure on China to improve its human rights record. His living conditions had improved somewhat and he was taken on short trips to Beijing and other cities to observe the benefits of the economic reforms. The videotape of a trip to the city of Tangshan that Wei refers to in this letter was released to the foreign press in March 1993 as proof that he was healthy and well treated. On September 14, 1993, Wei was released on parole after serving all but six months of his fifteen-year sentence.

January 16, 1993

Dear Jiang Zemin and the Judiciary:

Your people recently took me on a cursory tour of Beijing and Tangshan. The changes are enormous. They made an old Beijinger like myself feel like a tourist—a stranger in his own hometown. I doubt, though, if I would note such a great contrast if I hadn't been sitting in prison for more than a decade. I hope that when you are relieved of your position and return to Shanghai you too will notice so many changes, for then the people in your hometown will be very fortunate indeed.

This further demonstrates the successful efforts the reform faction in your Party have made, proving that it was the right path to take, and so on and so on with other words of praise that have all been repeated ad infinitum by the trumpets of your blaring propaganda machines. Coming out of your mouth or my own, they just sound vulgar, so I'll pass. But it is worth asking how best to maintain the current momentum of economic reconstruction and whether it is possible for your Party to pursue the present reform and development while relying only on the independent initiative of its reform faction without tapping into the powerful support for reform that exists in all layers of society. These two issues are actually one. Even old peasants aren't fooled by the saying "I'm the hero, I'll take care of everything," so why do you fantasize that you are some kind of "Mao Zedong junior"? It's not that none of you is as good as Mao, but that the days when the people could be so easily hoodwinked have long since gone, never to return. But you still aren't ready to recognize this fact, and seem to cling to an unrealistic fantasy about becoming "Mao Zedong junior." Your guiding principle—"be conservative in politics; economic reforms will solve everything"—is a clear revelation of your ignorance of reality. As a result, you overlook many extremely important matters, occupying yourself instead with patching up tattered political sails that are clearly rotted beyond repair, and fantasizing that the miracle of the all-powerful economy will guide you to the shores of paradise: communism.

If you argue that at the start of the reforms it was necessary to act deaf and dumb to the point of playing the fool in order to coddle the strong feelings of the anti-reform forces, that is an easily understandable tactical maneuver. But nowadays, after the disappointments of the fierce trials of the late eighties and the great retrogressive tide of the early nineties; and after managing not only to overcome the retrogressive tide, but to ride a new wave of progress, you won't fool anyone any longer by dodging the truth. If you are caught up by the destructive forces of either tide as the Soviet Union was, or if you ride on a later tide to counter the retrogressive tide, even if you drown, you'll still go down in infamy. This is really an epoch when people choose history and history chooses people. But people like you and me, who history has already tossed to the crest of the waves, can only choose between wiseness and stupidity, survival and destruction. And does not our nation face a similar predicament?

My trip back to a "state-run bookstore" was really quite eye-opening. The superficial changes that have taken place in cultural arenas stand out in clear contrast to the towering buildings and skyscrapers. Aside from the fourteen years you've kept me in prison, I've always been a loyal bookstore customer. There is a vast difference in the variety of books and magazines available today as compared with during the Cultural Revolution. That was a special period when your Party took anti-humanist thoughts to the extreme and culture naturally became a primary target. Now, a decade after "bringing order to chaos," culture should be thriving and developing to a level surpassing that before the setback. But this is where my simple hypothesis was mistaken. Fortunately I didn't publish this flawed theory and make the wrong impression. In quantity and quality, academic and general-interest books have only regained the level present before the Cultural Revolution and no further.

The chaotic management and the apparent lack of any cultural understanding in the bookstore made this reader feel quite amiss. The books were so disorganized that it was almost funny to find them arranged according to the most basic standard of "fancy cover versus plain cover." It was enough to leave an old book stall regular like myself as dazed as a country bumpkin. Readers can't find their books and books can't find their readers; and there's no clue which direction to look in. Even someone like myself, who didn't have any great expectation of getting hold of the best and was willing to settle for second best, and who was even aided immediately by a very enthusiastic book clerk (perhaps the fact that I was being videotaped increased his enthusiasm), still went away empty-handed. I was so disappointed that I couldn't help but ponder as Deng Xiaoping has pointed out, that "the greatest short-coming of the reforms is in education" and that culture is in decline more deeply.

I have always advocated that we must learn from the outstanding accomplishments of all humanity in order to remold modern Chinese culture. I first raised this point in 1978 and from the news-papers I can see that you are raising the same point now as well. This goes to show that your own decisions are gradually getting more sensible. If people only learn from others without developing their own national culture, they will never be able to push their society and economy into the advanced ranks; they'll always be looking at others' rear ends and eating the dust they kick up. The precondition for all development is the modernization of the people—this is what I said fourteen years ago and recent history has demonstrated it again and again.

The rebuilding of Japan, Germany, Russia, and other countries has been accomplished by basing long-term economic and social development on making great strides in cultural education; through this they have risen swiftly as wealthy and powerful countries. Referring to the indemnity paid to Japan after the Sino-Japanese War, the Japanese emperor declared that "one of every two hundred silver coins should be used for education"; Prussia used every victory in the economy and on the battlefield to boost "national education"; and during the difficult years fol-lowing the October Revolution, Russia paid great attention to culture and education. Everyone knows the story of how Lenin gave the food that others gave him to the children, but it is also true that when people were going hungry, he still approved of food rations for the scientists to feed the dogs they were using in their experiments. Only by abandoning the small-minded Party view for foresight and sagacity did these few nations promote cul-ture and education at an unusually quick pace and thereby create an enduring stimulant to social and economic development. Although they didn't state so explicitly, these countries certainly understood and put into practice my reasoning: The modernization of the people is the prerequisite for all modernization, and without the modernization of the people, all modernization is nothing more than empty talk.

But what have all our "great leaders" been up to instead? They've been plucking food from children's mouths to carry out a cleanup of culture; and they've taken the money they've exploited from the children and culture to spare no effort in supporting tens of thousands of Party bureaucrats. They'd rather build tall skyscrapers and purchase fancy limousines than worry about the quality of books or allow the book and culture markets to really open up. Your tenures in office will soon be up and all the Party bureaucrats will soon be old and gone. But what is the future of the Chinese people? Has anyone given a thought to them?

Enough—I shouldn't complain on and on and overdo it. I shouldn't waste too much paper voicing my disappointments, for your world outlook isn't changed that easily. I should calmly discuss a few real problems and see if I can avoid offending your "old peasant" mentality and come to some compromise.

Let me first discuss an understanding of the question of "intellectual property rights." When we were visiting the Tangshan Earthquake Memorial Museum we were told not to videotape. Several of the people in charge told us with embarrassment that many of the photographs on display were not their own and they were afraid of provoking a copyright suit, so they had no alternative but to inconvenience us. Let me explain first that I myself didn't care about the video; it wasn't being filmed for me anyway and since I still don't know if I'll ever even see the video, what would I care? I just went along with the people making it. But I could tell from this incident that there were already many suits of this kind being raised and it was seriously hindering the dissemination of culture.

The original intention of the copyright and patent system was to enhance the dissemination of knowledge and skills by protecting intellectual property rights. But now precisely the opposite has occurred. Where is the problem? An inaccurate understanding of intellectual property rights still exists. For example, the photographs in the Memorial Museum have already been published and are not classified materials. Inclusion of

such photographs in a video is not considered plagiarism or anything of the sort. This is completely different from reproducing
the original for profit; and even if they did reproduce the origi-
nals, it wasn't for commercial purposes and shouldn't be prohibited. Besides, even if it were for commercial purposes, the suit
should be between the filmmaker and the photographer. When
the city gates catch fire, why should the fish in the moats suffer?
Memorial halls and museums are nonprofit organizations and
they shouldn't be dragged into such suits, for this can really
hinder the dissemination of knowledge. From this example you
can infer the incorrect thinking and ignorance of so many people
who own intellectual property rights. Having your work shown in
a memorial hall or a museum should be an honor, why be so calculating and petty minded! In addition, places like the Tangshan
Earthquake Memorial Museum ought to be free public facilities
and should be supported by the government or foundations and
not rely on profits from ticket sales.

Bookstores, on the other hand, should be commercialized completely. There has never been a better way of managing published
materials than through commercial management, unless of course
you give them away for free! So we should just accept the reality
and allow the publication of printed matter to get on the commercial track. The problem today isn't the left or the right, it's both
sides.

Bookstores in China are all too conservative and don't trust their
managers. They hold on tightly to the old Party routine and
methods for disseminating cultural knowledge. They're often
managed by old Party officials who don't care much for reading
themselves and don't even like books. They are satisfied with
just displaying *Cadre Essentials* and allowing their bookstores
to completely lose their role as intermediaries in disseminating
knowledge. That's why you often see scholars in the newspapers
complaining that nobody publishes books and readers often complaining that they can't find high-quality books. Is it still possible
to find bookstores like Sanlian Books that are run by intellectuals
and disseminate new ideas and knowledge quickly? But this is precisely your goal; you've learned from your own political experiences that if you want to maintain a dictatorship, you must first

dictate thinking. Widespread cultural ignorance is the basic foundation for dictatorship.

Teachers today not only have a low social status (they are the "third world" in cultural and intellectual circles), but their living situations are not stable, hence your "relaxation policy" that allows schools themselves to "generate income." As a result, a number of excellent teachers have left, other teachers can no longer put all their energy into teaching, and even more have no skill at all in "generating income." The burden therefore falls on the students. Once the door has been opened, it's too easy to find ways of extracting money. If there aren't just a couple of "blackened hearts" raising the stakes, then it's a whole lair of hungry lions with their mouths agape. I hear that some elementary school students must pay ten thousand yuan to enter a school. What even relatively well-off household can afford that? My brother and his wife, for example, both engineers, had to rely on relatives from abroad to put their daughter in school. This must be nearly the worst system in the world! And what about the majority of ordinary families who live below this well-off level? Who knows how many potential Edisons and Madame Curies are stifled in this way every year? Can a servile people that cares only for bowing and scraping in obedience and does not cherish its Newtons and Einsteins ever be a nation with a boundless future and potential?

The bureaucracy should be reduced. In particular the bureaucracy that sponges off the education system should be ruthlessly cut and the money saved used to greatly increase the salaries and welfare of teachers. At the same time, it should be strictly forbidden to seek profits from the children. Children are not adults; they should not have to bear the weight of conflicts inherited from a former generation and they have the right to receive equal treatment. We already know that the best way to do this is for society to take collective responsibility for educating the next generation. They should be given the same if not better treatment and not be so harshly introduced to the mechanisms of competition.

I am ignorant and ill-informed and have been bothering all of you for so long now, I should take a rest. There will be opportunities to speak again. If possible, I would like to go to Shanghai and Guangdong to have a look at the open economic areas and the financial markets there. I've always felt that a well-developed finance industry is the foundation for a flourishing market economy. But I'm not sure; perhaps my habit of always finding problems in things is still unwelcome.

Wei Jingsheng

Appendix I

the

fifth

modernization:

democracy

(december 1978)

The following "big character" poster appeared on Beijing's Democracy Wall long before dawn on the morning of December 5, 1978. By boldly insisting that the government's Four Modernizations (in industry, agriculture, defense, and science) were inadequate without the addition of a fifth, democracy, the previously unknown author, Wei Jingsheng, catapulted himself into history, and prison. The document, newly translated here in full, was subsequently published in the inaugural issue of Exploration, *the unofficial journal Wei helped to edit, on January 8, 1979.*

Newspapers and television no longer assail us with deafening praise for the dictatorship of the proletariat and class struggle. This is in part because these were once the magical incantations of the now-overthrown Gang of Four. But more importantly, it's because the masses have grown absolutely sick of hearing these worn-out phrases and will never be duped by them again.

The laws of history tell us that only when the old is gone can the new take its place. Now that the old is gone, the people have been anxiously waiting to see what the new will bring; gods never betray the faithful, they thought. But what they've long awaited is none other than a grandiose promise called the Four Modernizations. Our wise leader, Chairman Hua Guofeng, along with Vice Chairman Deng Xiaoping, whom many consider even wiser and grander, have finally crushed the Gang of Four. There is now the possibility that those brave souls whose blood flowed over Tiananmen Square might have their dreams of democracy and prosperity realized.

After the arrest of the Gang of Four, the people eagerly hoped that Vice Chairman Deng Xiaoping, who might possibly "restore capitalism," would rise up again like a magnificent banner. Finally, he did regain his position in the central leadership. How excited the people felt! How inspired they were! But alas, the old political system so despised by the people remains unchanged, and the democracy and freedom they longed for has not even been mentioned. Their living conditions remain the same and "increased wages" have far from kept up with the rapid rise in prices. There was talk of "restoring capitalism" and instituting a bonus system, but after careful consideration, it was determined that such measures would simply be "invisible whips" of the type once cursed by our Marxist forefathers as "the greatest form of worker exploitation."

There are reports confirming that "deceptive policies" will no longer be implemented and that the people will no longer follow a "great helmsman." Instead, "wise leaders" will lead them to "catch up with and surpass the most advanced nations of the world" such as Britain, the United States, Japan, and Yugoslavia(!). It's no longer fashionable to take part in the revolution, a college education will take you further in the world. Cries of "class struggle" no longer need fill people's ears, the Four Modernizations will take care of everything. Of course, in order to realize this beautiful dream, we must still follow the guiding central spirit passed down from the "April Fifth Society" as well as the guidance and direction of a unified leadership

There are two ancient Chinese sayings that go: "Sketch cakes to allay your hunger" and "Think of plums to quench your thirst." People of ancient times had such wit and sarcasm, and they've even been said to have progressed since then. So now no one would ever actually consider doing such ridiculous things, would they?

Well, not only did some consider doing such things, they actually did.

For decades, the Chinese people faithfully followed the Great Helmsman while he used "Communist idealism" to sketch cakes and offered up the Great Leap Forward and the Three Red Banners as thirst-quenching plums. People tightened their belts and forged ahead undaunted. Thirty years flew by and the experience taught them one lesson: For three decades we've been acting like monkeys grabbing for the moon's reflection in a lake—no wonder we've come up empty-handed! Therefore, when Vice Chairman Deng called for "practicality," the people's enthusiasm surged forth like a rolling tide and swept him back into power. Everyone expected him to employ the maxim "Seek truth from facts" to review the past and lead the people toward a promising future.

But once again there are people warning us that Marxist–Leninist–Mao Zedong Thought is the foundation of all things, even speech; that Chairman Mao was the "great savior" of the people; and that "without the Communist Party, there would be no new China" actually means "without Chairman Mao, there would be no new China." Official notices will clear things up for anyone who refuses to believe this. There are even those who seek to remind us that Chinese people need a dictator; if he is even more dictatorial than the emperors of old, this only proves his greatness. The Chinese people don't need democracy, they say, for unless it is a "democracy under centralized leadership," it isn't worth a cent. Whether you believe it or not is up to you, but there are plenty of empty prison cells waiting for you if you don't.

But now someone has provided us with a way out: Take the Four Modernizations as your guiding principle; forge ahead with stability and unity; and bravely serve the revolution like a faithful old ox and you will reach your paradise—the prosperity of Communism and the Four Modernizations. And these kind-hearted someones have warned us that if we are confused, we must undertake a serious and thorough study of Marxist–Leninist–Mao Zedong Thought! If you're still confused, it's because you don't understand, and not understanding only reflects just how profound the theory is! Don't be disobedient or the leadership of your work unit will be uncompromising! And so on and so on.

I urge everyone to stop believing such political swindlers. When we all know that we are going to be tricked, why don't we trust ourselves instead? The Cultural Revolution has tempered us and we are no longer so ignorant. Let us investigate for ourselves what should be done!

I. WHY DEMOCRACY?

People have discussed this question for centuries. And now those who voice their opinions at Democracy Wall have carried out a thorough analysis and shown just how much better democracy is than autocracy.

"People are the masters of history." Is this fact or merely empty talk? It is both fact and empty talk. It is fact that without the effort and participation of the people there can be no history. No "great helmsman" or "wise leader" could exist, let alone any history be created. From this we can see that the slogan should be "Without the new Chinese people, there would be no new China," not "Without Chairman Mao, there would be no new China." It's understandable that Vice Chairman Deng is grateful to Chairman Mao for saving his life, but why is he so ungrateful to all of those whose "outcries" propelled him back into power? Is it reasonable for him to say to them: "You must not criticize Chairman Mao, because he saved my life"? From this we can see that phrases like "people are the masters of history" are nothing but empty talk. Such words become hollow when people are unable to choose their own destiny by majority will, or when their achievements are credited to others, or when their rights are stripped away and woven into the crowns of others. What kind of "masters" are these? It would be more appropriate to call them docile slaves. Our history books tell us that the people are the masters and creators of everything, but in reality they are more like faithful servants standing at attention and waiting to be "led" by leaders who swell like yeasted bread dough.

The people should have democracy. When they call for democracy they are demanding nothing more than that which is inherently theirs. Whoever refuses to return democracy to them is a shameless thief more despicable than any capitalist who robs the workers of the wealth earned with their own sweat and blood.

Do the people have democracy now? No! Don't the people want to be the masters of their own destiny? Of course they do! That is precisely why the Communist Party defeated the Nationalists. But what became of all their promises once victory was achieved? Once they began championing a dictatorship of the proletariat instead of a people's democratic dictatorship, even the "democracy" still enjoyed by a tenth of a millionth of the population was displaced by the individual dictatorship of the "great leader." Even Peng Dehuai was denounced for following the orders of the "great leader" and airing complaints.

A new promise was made: If a leader is great, then blind faith in him will bring greater happiness to the people than democracy. Half forced, half willingly, people have continued to believe in this promise right up until the present. But are they any happier? No. They are more miserable and more backward. Why, then, are things the way they are? This is the first question the people must consider. What should be done now? This is the second. At present, there is absolutely no need to assess the achievements and failures of Mao Zedong. When Mao himself suggested this be done, it was only out of self-defense. Instead, the people should be asking themselves whether without the dictatorship of Mao Zedong China would have fallen into its current state. Are the Chinese people stupid? Are they lazy? Do they not want to live more prosperous lives? Or are they unruly by nature? Quite the opposite. How, then, did things get the way they are? The answer is obvious: The Chinese people should not have followed the path they did. Why, then, did they follow this path? Was it because a self-glorifying dictator led them down it? The truth is, even if people had refused to follow this path, they would still have been crushed by the dictatorship. And when no one could hear any other alternative, the people felt that this was the one and only path to take. Is this not deceit? Is there any merit in this at all?

What path was taken? It's often called the "socialist road." According to the definition formulated by our Marxist forefathers, the premise of socialism is that the masses, or what is called the proletariat, are the masters of everything. But let me ask the Chinese workers and peasants: Aside from the few coins you receive each month to feed yourselves with, what are you the masters of? And what do you master? It's pitiful to say it, but the truth is, you are mastered by others, even down to your own marriages!

Socialism guarantees that the producer will receive the surplus fruits of his labor after he has fulfilled his duty to society. But is there any limit to the amount of this duty? Are you getting anything more than the meager wage necessary to sustain your productive labor? Can socialism guarantee the right of every citizen to receive an education, to make full use of his abilities, and so forth? We can observe none of these things in our daily lives. We see only "the dictatorship of the proletariat" and "a variation of Russian autocracy"—that is, Chinese-style socialist autocracy. Is this the kind of socialist road the people need? Does dictatorship, therefore, amount to the people's happiness? Is this the socialist road Marx described and the people aspired to? Obviously not. Then what is it? As ridiculous as it may sound, it actually resembles the feudal socialism referred to in *The Communist Manifesto* as feudal monarchy under a socialist cloak. It's said that the Soviet Union has been elevated to socialist imperialism from socialist feudalism. Must the Chinese people follow the same path?

People have suggested that we settle all our old accounts by blaming them all on the fascist dictatorship of feudal socialism. I completely agree with this because there is no question of right or wrong. In passing, I would like to point out that the correct name for the notorious German fascism is "national socialism." It too had an autocratic tyrant; it too ordered people to tighten their belts; and it too deceived the people with the words: "You are a great people." Most importantly, it too stamped out even the most rudimentary forms of democracy, for it fully recognized that democracy was its most formidable and irrepressible enemy. On this basis, Stalin and Hitler shook hands and signed the German-Soviet Pact whereby a socialist state and a national-socialist state toasted the partition of Poland while the peoples of both countries suffered slavery and poverty. Must we go on suffering from this kind of slavery and poverty? If not, then democracy is our only choice. In other words, if we want to modernize our economy, sciences, military, and other areas, then we must first modernize our people and our society.

II. THE FIFTH MODERNIZATION: WHAT KIND OF DEMOCRACY DO WE WANT?

I would like to ask everyone: What do we want modernization for? Many might still feel that the times depicted in *Dream of the Red Chamber* were just fine. One could do some reading, dabble in poetry, cavort with women, and be fed and clothed effortlessly. These days such a person might even go to see foreign movies as well—what a godlike existence! It's not bad to live like a god, but such a lifestyle remains irrelevant to ordinary people. They want simply to have the chance to enjoy a happy life, or at least one that is no less than what people enjoy in other countries. A prosperity that all members of society can enjoy equally will only be achieved by raising the level of social productivity. This is quite obvious, but some people have completely overlooked one important point: When social productivity increases, will the people be able to enjoy prosperous lives? The problems of allocation, distribution, and exploitation still remain.

In the decades since Liberation, people have tightened their belts and worked hard to produce a great deal of wealth. But where has it all gone? Some say it's gone to plump up small-scale autocratic regimes like Vietnam, while others say it's been used to fatten the "new bourgeois elements" like Lin Biao and Jiang Qing. Both are correct, but the bottom line is, none of it has trickled down into the hands of the working people of China. If powerful political swindlers, both big and small, have not squandered the wealth themselves, then they have given it to scoundrels in Vietnam and Albania who cherish ideals similar to their own. Shortly before his death, Mao Zedong got upset when his old lady asked him for several thousand yuan, but did anyone ever know him to feel any pain as he threw away tens of billions of yuan earned with the sweat and blood of the Chinese people? And this was all done while the Chinese people were building socialism by tightening their belts and begging on the streets for food. Why, then, can't all those people who keep running to Democracy Wall to praise Mao Zedong open their eyes and see this? Could it be that they are deliberately blind to it? If they genuinely can't see it, I would ask them all to use the time they spend writing wall posters to go over to Beijing or Yongdingmen Train Station, or to any street in the city, and ask those country folk arriving from the provinces whether begging for food is such a rare occurrence where they come from. I can also bet that they aren't that willing to give away their snow-white rice to aid "friends in the Third World"! But does their opinion matter? The sad thing is that in our people's republic all real power is in the hands of those people who live like gods and have nothing better to do after stuffing their faces than to read novels and write poetry. Are not the people completely justified in seizing power from the hands of such overlords?

What is democracy? True democracy means placing all power in the hands of the working people. Are working people unable to manage state power? Yugoslavia has taken this route and proven to us that people have no need for dictators, whether big or small; they can take care of things much better themselves.

What is true democracy? It is when the people, acting on their own will, have the right to choose representatives to manage affairs on the people's behalf and in accordance with the will and interests of the people. This alone can be called democracy. Furthermore, the people must have the power to replace these representatives at any time in order to keep them from abusing their powers to oppress the people. Is this actually possible? The citizens of Europe and the United States enjoy precisely this kind of democracy and can run people like Nixon, de Gaulle, and Tanaka out of office when they wish and can even reinstate them if they so desire. No one can interfere with their democratic rights. In China, however, if a person even comments on the "great helmsman" or the "Great Man peerless in history," Mao Zedong, who is already dead, the mighty prison gates and all kinds of unimaginable misfortunes await him. If we compare the socialist system of "centralized democracy" with the "exploiting class democracy" of capitalism, the difference is as clear as night and day.

Will the country sink into chaos and anarchy if the people achieve democracy? On the contrary, have not the scandals exposed in the newspapers recently shown that it is precisely due to an absence of democracy that the dictators, large and small, have caused chaos and anarchy? The maintenance of democratic order is an internal problem that the people themselves must solve. It is not something that the privileged overlords need concern themselves with. Besides, they are not really concerned with democracy for the people, but use this as a pretext to deny the people of their democratic rights. Of course, internal problems cannot be solved overnight but must be constantly addressed as part of a long-term process. Mistakes and shortcomings will be inevitable, but these are for us to worry about. This is infinitely better than facing abusive overlords against whom we have no means of redress. Those who worry that democracy will lead to anarchy and chaos are just like those who, following the overthrow of the Qing dynasty, worried that without an emperor, the country would fall into chaos. Their decision was to patiently suffer oppression because they feared that without the weight of oppression, their spines might completely collapse!

To such people, I would like to say, with all due respect: We want to be the masters of our own destiny. We need no gods or emperors and we don't believe in saviors of any kind. We want to be masters of our universe; we do not want to serve as mere tools of dictators with personal ambitions for carrying out modernization. We want to modernize the lives of the people. Democracy, freedom, and happiness for all are our sole objectives in carrying out modernization. Without this "Fifth Modernization," all other modernizations are nothing but a new lie.

Comrades, I appeal to you: Let us rally together under the banner of democracy. Do not be fooled again by dictators who talk of "stability and unity." Fascist totalitarianism can bring us nothing but disaster. Harbor no more illusions; democracy is our only hope. Abandon our democratic rights and we shackle ourselves again. Let us have confidence in our own strength! We are the creators of human history. Banish all self-proclaimed leaders and teachers, for they have already cheated the people of their most valuable rights for decades.

I firmly believe that production will flourish more when controlled by the people themselves because the workers will be producing for their own benefit. Life will improve because the workers' interests will be the primary goal. Society will be more just because all power will be exercised by the people as a whole through democratic means.

I don't believe that all of this will be handed to the people effortlessly by some great savior. I also refuse to believe that China will abandon the goals of democracy, freedom, and happiness because of the many difficulties it will surely encounter along the way. As long as people clearly identify their goal and realistically assess the obstacles before them, then surely they will trample any pests that might try to bar their way.

III. MARCHING TOWARD MODERNIZATION: DEMOCRACY IN PRACTICE

To achieve modernization, the Chinese people must first put democracy into practice and modernize China's social system. Democracy is not merely an inevitable stage of social development as Lenin claimed. In addition to being the result of productive forces and productive relations having developed to a certain stage, democracy is also the very condition that allows for the existence of such development to reach beyond this stage. Without democracy, society will become stagnant and economic growth will face insurmountable obstacles. Judging from history, therefore, a democratic social system is the premise and precondition for all development, or what we can also call modernization. Without this precondition, not only is further development impossible, but even preserving the level of development already attained would be very difficult. The experience of our great nation over the past three decades is the best evidence for this.

Why must human history follow a path toward development, or modernization? It is because humans need all of the tangible advantages that development can provide them. These advantages then enable them to achieve their foremost goal in the pursuit of happiness: freedom. Democracy is the greatest freedom ever known to man. Therefore, isn't it quite apparent why the goal of all recent human struggles has been democracy?

Why have all the reactionaries in modern history united under a common banner against democracy? It is because democracy gives their enemy—the common people—everything, and provides them—the oppressors—no weapons with which to oppose the people. The greatest reactionaries are always the greatest opponents of democracy. The histories of Germany, the Soviet Union, and "New China" make this very clear and show that these reactionaries are also the most formidable and dangerous enemies of social peace and prosperity. The more recent histories of these countries make it apparent that all the struggles of the people for prosperity and of society for development are ultimately directed against the enemies of democracy—the dictatorial fascists. When democracy defeats dictatorship, it always brings with it the most favorable conditions for accelerating social development. The history of the United States offers the most convincing evidence of this.

The success of any struggle by the people for happiness, peace, and prosperity is contingent upon the quest for democracy. The success of all struggles by the people against oppression and exploitation depends upon achieving democracy. Let us throw ourselves completely into the struggle for democracy! Only through democracy can the people obtain everything. All illusions of undemocratic means are hopeless. All forms of dictatorship and totalitarianism are the most immediate and dangerous enemies of the people.

Will our enemies let us implement democracy? Of course not. They will stop at nothing to hinder the progress of democracy. Deception and trickery are the most effective means they have. All dictatorial fascists tell their people: Your situation is truly the best in the entire world.

Does democracy come about naturally when society reaches a certain stage? Absolutely not. A high price is paid for every tiny victory; even coming to a recognition of this fact will cost blood and sacrifice. The enemies of democracy have always deceived their people by saying that just as democracy is inevitable, it is doomed, and, therefore, it is not worth wasting energy to fight for.

But let us look at the real history, not that fabricated by the hired hacks of the "socialist government." Every small branch or twig of true and valuable democracy is stained with the blood of martyrs and tyrants, and every step taken toward democracy has been fiercely attacked by the reactionary forces. The fact that democracy has been able to surmount such obstacles proves that it is precious to the people and that it embodies their aspirations. Therefore the democratic trend cannot be stopped. The Chinese people have never feared anything. They need only recognize the direction to be taken and the forces of tyranny will no longer be invincible.

Is the struggle for democracy what the Chinese people want? The Cultural Revolution was the first time they flexed their muscles, and all the reactionary forces trembled before them. But at that time the people had no clear direction and the force of democracy was not the main thrust of their struggle. As a result, the dictators silenced most of them through bribes, deception, division, slander, or violent suppression. At the time, people also had a blind faith in all kinds of ambitious dictators, so once again they unwittingly became the tools and sacrificial lambs of tyrants and potential tyrants.

Now, twelve years later, the people have finally recognized their goal. They see clearly the real direction of their fight and have found their true leader: the banner of democracy. The Democracy Wall at Xidan has become the first battlefield in the people's fight against the reactionary forces. The struggle will be victorious— this is already a commonly accepted belief; the people will be liberated—this slogan has already taken on new significance. There may be bloodshed and sacrifice, and people may fall prey to even more sinister plots, yet the banner of democracy will never again be obscured by the evil fog of the reactionary forces. Let us unite together under this great and true banner and march toward modernization of society for the sake of the tranquillity, happiness, rights, and freedom of all the people!

Appendix II

the
trial
of
wei
jingsheng
(october 1979)

Following is the defense statement made by Wei Jingsheng during his October 16, 1979, trial. A tape of the trial was transcribed and published in an unofficial journal, leading to the arrest of several of Wei's Democracy Wall associates, including Liu Qing. This translation was compiled and first published by SPEAHRhead.

I see as unfounded and unsubstantiated the charges in the indictment brought by the Beijing Municipal People's Procuratorate. My editing of publications and my writing of posters were both in accordance with Article 45 of the Constitution: "Citizens enjoy freedom of speech, correspondence, the press, assembly, association, procession, demonstration, and the freedom to strike, and have the right to speak out freely, air their views fully, hold great debates, and write big-character posters." Our reasons for producing our publication were simply to attempt a tentative exploration of the path along which China could achieve prosperity. We felt that this goal could be attained only by undertaking a free, unrestrained exploration based on seeking truth from facts. Our activities, motivated by the principles I have just mentioned, are described as counterrevolutionary by the Public Security Department and the Procuratorate. We cannot accept such a description. I shall now go on to express substantiated views on each of the charges listed in the indictment.

THE FIRST CHARGE

The indictment states that I provided foreigners with national military information and committed the crime of counterrevolution. If my memory serves me correctly, the new penal code and the old "Act of the People's Republic of China for the Punishment of Counterrevolution" read alike: Providing military information to *the enemy* constitutes the crime of treason. Yet, in the eyes of the public prosecutor, my discussions with English and French foreign correspondents are seen as treasonable acts. Is this not as good as describing the English and French journalists as the enemy? I would like to draw the attention of the prosecution to the fact that when Party Chairman Hua Guofeng met with journalists from four

Western European nations, he quite clearly addressed the correspondents from each nation as "my friend."

The Constitution stipulates that it is the duty of all citizens to "keep national secrets." Yet here, where the wording of the Constitution is quite explicit on this aspect of the citizens' duties, the indictment uses the vague term "military intelligence." It is common knowledge that a lot of what passes for military intelligence or information is obtainable by an analysis of what is stated in the public media of any nation's newspapers, radio and television news reports, etc. It is clear, then, that the term "military information" or "intelligence" is an overgeneralized concept. Since it is the duty of all citizens to keep national secrets, this presupposes that the citizens know in the first place what the secrets are they are supposed to keep. That is to say, this secret must be recognizable from the outset as a piece of classified information. It must be clearly indicated or marked down as a national or military secret. Only then do the citizens have the duty to maintain its secrecy. Never once in the period that followed the outbreak of the Sino-Vietnamese War did I come into contact with anything whatsoever marked as a classified secret. Thus, there is no question of my furnishing anyone with anything that can be described as secret by the terms of the legal definition.

When I chatted with reporters and foreign diplomats from friendly nations, it was difficult for me not to mention various aspects of our country's domestic situation. I saw such discussion with these reporters and diplomats as a means of promoting friendship and understanding between us and the peoples of their countries—a way of promoting the basis of mutual support among working people of all nations. Once the Sino-Vietnamese War broke out, it became a major issue of common concern to both the people of our own nation and those in foreign countries. Thus, inevitably, I couldn't help discussing this aspect of the national situation in my talks with foreign journalists and diplomats during this period.

Whether or not the news I mentioned in my conversations with foreigners was news that the government preferred not to divulge I had no means of knowing. Since I am just an ordinary citizen, my sources of information remain the grapevine and rumor, not official government documents. Whether or not my information might have happened to coincide quite fortuitously with points of information marked as classified secrets in government documents I likewise have no means of telling, because I have never set eyes on any classified documents. But the news I discussed could not have had any harmful effect on the frontline situation. That was something which I considered before I said anything. As far as my mention of the name of the commander-in-chief at the front: Who ever heard of a victory being lost because the commander-in-chief's name was revealed? Conversely, who ever heard of a defeat being suffered simply because the enemy knew the name of one's commander-in-chief? No cases of either kind exist, so in what way can my mention of his name have had an adverse effect on the frontline situation? Such a theory just doesn't hold water.

Naturally, the public prosecutor may state that, according to established custom and practice in our nation, this may be considered a national secret. When the Gang of Four was still in power and a policy of isolation held sway, anything that appealed to the authorities became a national secret, and just to say a few words to a foreigner could, if the powers wished, be construed as having illicit relations with a foreign country. Does the public prosecutor want all citizens to abide by the established practices of the Gang of Four era? Or does he just want them to adhere to the law? In this respect the Department of Public Security has already spoken, when it said I must abide by the rules and regulations governing the maintenance of official secrets. I do not know what these rules and regulations are. I only know that they themselves are a secret; and, because they are not publicly promulgated for ordinary citizens to abide by, they can only be considered an internal regulation. The ordinary citizen, therefore, may be obliged to abide by the Constitution and the law, but he is under no obligation to abide by internal regulations about which he knows nothing.

To sum up: First, I had no intention of betraying the motherland. Second, I supplied the enemy with nothing at all. Third, I gave my friends no official secrets, either national or military. Thus the prosecution's accusation that I committed treason is unfounded. If the prosecution considers the content of my discussions with foreigners as something the government would rather I had not mentioned, and if I made a mistake by doing so, I am perfectly willing to accept that. Moreover, in response to the government's reasonable demands hereafter, I will maintain secrecy about matters the government feels should be kept secret because this is the duty of every citizen. But, in turn, I trust the government will be able to be more explicit in its stipulation of the actual scope of those secrets it expects its citizens to maintain, and not leave them in a state of perplexed bewilderment. The customary practices of the Gang of Four are no longer relevant. Preventing Chinese nationals from having friendly relations with the nationals of other countries will only further confuse the administration of justice and adversely affect the nation and its people.

THE SECOND CHARGE

The indictment states that I carried out counterrevolutionary propaganda and agitation, and it describes my essays—"The Fifth Modernization: Democracy" etc.—as reactionary. Likewise our publication *Exploration* is referred to as reactionary. In view of this, we must first make it clear what is meant by such terms as "revolutionary" and "counterrevolutionary."

As a result of the influence of many years of cultural autocracy, and the obscurantist policy of keeping the people in a state of blind ignorance during the Gang of Four era, there are still people who feel that "revolutionary" means doing things in exact accordance with the will of the leadership currently in power, and to run counter to this will is "counterrevolutionary." I cannot agree with such a vulgar debasement of the concept of revolution. The term "revolutionary" entails following a course of action whereby one moves with the current of historical development and strives to remove all that is old and conservative and that is blocking and impeding the onward flow of history. Revolution is the struggle of new phenomena against old. To attach the label of perpetual revolution to the will and ambition of those currently in power is tantamount to stifling all diversity of thought. "Power is truth" is a vulgarization of the concept of revolution. It served as one of the most effective tools with which the Gang of Four suppressed revolution and the people for more than twenty years.

Now allow me to turn to the term "counterrevolutionary" and its valid and proper frame of reference. Strictly speaking, "counterrevolutionary" is a political concept applied to a given problem at a certain historical moment. In the realm of politics there is no such thing as an immutable concept, and at different historical periods, because the revolutionary trends or currents are different, each conception of the word "counterrevolutionary" differs, as indeed do the phenomena to which the term is applied. If one particular conception of the term (valid for one particular period) is made the norm, the result can only be the arbitrary attaching of labels to the wrong people. Due to limited levels of understanding among the populace, even in times of revolution there arise a number of conflicting interpretations of this one word "counterrevolutionary." To use this term as an immutable political concept for assessing the guilt of those charged with crimes is like using willow branches blowing in the breeze to guess one's height. This is the reason behind the great number of injustices, wrongs, and misjudged cases that have arisen in this country over the past thirty years. It is also one of the reasons why the Gang of Four was able to gain power in the very face of popular resentment. The inevitable result of using current political concepts as legal norms or standards is to invite deception by such terms as "counterrevolutionary."

Next we come to the connection between my articles and the present revolutionary current. The present historical current is a democratic one that flows against the fascist dictatorship of the feudal past. At this stage in the development of Chinese society, the population is confronted with the following problem: Without reform of the social system, without eradication of the social origins of dictatorial fascist autocracy, and without a thorough implementation of democracy and guarantees on the people's democratic rights, Chinese society will be unable to advance and socialist modernization of the country will be impossible. Thus democracy is this revolutionary current of the present day, and those autocratic conservatives who stand in opposition to it are the real counterrevolutionaries of the day.

The central argument of my articles, including "The Fifth Modernization," is that without democracy there will be no Four Modernizations; without the "fifth" modernization, or democracy, any talk of modernization will remain an empty lie. How does such an argument constitute counterrevolution? Surely it is those very people who oppose democracy who should be included in the counterrevolutionary category? Naturally I do not claim that the grounds of my argument and its thesis are always perfectly correct. They too must await the ultimate test of historical practice and should undergo criticism from every quarter. Only in this way can they be made more accurate. But even if the grounds of my argument and the underlying thesis are not completely accurate, this in no way impairs the revolutionary nature of my central point, which is clear in its argument.

THE THIRD CHARGE

The indictment states that I slandered Marxist–Leninist–Mao Zedong Thought by calling it an even more brilliant piece of quackery than any of the old itinerant pox-doctors' panaceas and poultices. My understanding of the term "slander" is that it refers to a person being groundlessly charged with a crime he has not committed. The manufacture of poultices and panaceas is no crime. By quoting me out of context and giving a garbled version of what I said, the prosecutor can hardly be said to have made a case for slander.

The Marxism I attacked in my essays is in no way the Marxism of more than a hundred or so years ago, but rather the form of Marxism favored by that school of political swindlers such as Lin Biao and the Gang of Four. I recognize nothing in this world as constantly immutable, nor any theory as absolutely correct. All ideological theory is relative, for within its existing context it contains elements of relative truth and, conversely, elements of relative absurdity. At one given time and in one given situation it may be a relatively accurate theory, whereas at another given time and situation it can be relatively preposterous. In the face of certain data it may be a correct theory, while in the face of different data it may appear incorrect or even absurd. Certain theories in themselves share at one and the same time the possibility of being correct and the possibility of being absurd. Marxism is in no way an exception. Marxism, in over a hundred years of development, has been successively transformed into a number of divergent schools—Kautskyism, Leninism, Trotskyism, Stalinism, Maoism, Eurocommunism, etc. While these different theories all abide by the basic tenets of Marxism, or do so in part, they have also carried out partial modifications and revisions of Marxism as a system. Thus, though they are called Marxist, none of them is the original Marxist system. To a considerable extent the theoretical core of original Marxism is in part centered around a description of a perfect society, an idealistic state that is by no means unique in its conception to Marxism alone. For such a society was a widespread aspiration, shared by the working classes and intellectuals of Europe who were alike in their desire for liberty and equality, public ownership of property, and social justice. The method Marxism advocated for the achievement of this ideal society was the fusing of common democracy with a dictatorship in which power had been centralized. It is this fusion that is the most striking characteristic of the Marxist tenets.

Following a hundred years of actual practice, those governments that have emerged from this method of dictatorship, where power has been concentrated—such as those of the Soviet Union, Vietnam, and China before the smashing of the Gang of Four— have without exception deteriorated into fascist regimes, where a small leading faction imposes its autocracy over the large mass of ordinary laboring people. Moreover, the fascist dictators, in whose grasp the government has come to rest, have long since ceased to use the dictatorship of the proletariat as a tool of implementing the old ideals of communism itself. Precisely the opposite is the case. For without exception these rulers have used the ideals of communism to reinforce the so-called dictatorship of the proletariat so that it may function as a tool for the benefit of those in power.

Thus, Marxism's fate is common to that of several religions. After the second or third generation of transmission, its revolutionary substance is quietly removed, while its doctrinal ideals are partially taken over by the rulers to be used as an excuse to enslave the people, and as a tool to deceive and fool them. By this stage, the nature of its teachings has also undergone a basic change, in that the ideals become, respectively, the excuse and tool of enslavement and deception. Thus, the nature of the teachings has been fundamentally changed. We call the practice of using ideals to mislead and enslave people "idealism," while others may call it blind faith. The feudal fascist dictatorship of the Gang of Four represented the culmination of such a development. When such forms of fascism make use of fine and glorious ideals to instill blind faith in some modern superstition so that the people may be the easier cheated and deceived, is this not a modern form of charlatanism? Is it not an even more brilliant piece of quackery than any of the old itinerant pox-doctors' panaceas and poultices?

Here I should point out that it was by basing my studies on the course of the historical development of Marxism that I reached these conclusions, and that any possible inaccuracies can be resolved by further theoretical inquiry. Though I welcome anyone's criticism of these conclusions of mine, regardless of their accuracy, according to the principle of the freedoms of discussion and publication, it does not constitute a crime to promote tentative theoretical inquiry and exchange such ideological conclusions with others. We should always adopt a critical approach to ideological theory, whether of the past or present. As this is the Marxist approach to pursuing studies, why can't we treat Marxism critically as well? Those who forbid the critical treatment of Marxism are engaged in the very process of transforming Marxism into a religious faith. Any person has the right to believe and adhere to the theories he holds to be correct, but he should not use legally binding stipulations to impose on others the theories he has faith in; otherwise he is interfering with the liberties of his fellow men.

THE FOURTH CHARGE

The indictment claims that, by flaunting the banner of so-called free speech for democracy and human rights, I incited the overthrow of the socialist system and the political power of the dictatorship of the proletariat. First of all, allow me to point out that there is nothing whatsoever "so-called" about free speech. On the contrary, it is stipulated by the Constitution as a right to be enjoyed by all citizens. The public prosecutor's choice of such a term in discussing rights granted citizens by the Constitution not only shows his prejudice when thinking on such matters, but further illustrates that he has forgotten his responsibility to protect the democratic rights of his fellow citizens. He turns the democratic rights of the citizens of this country into an object of ridicule.

I feel there is no need for me to refute item by item the public prosecutor's method of quoting me. I would merely like to point out his carelessness and his negligence. In the indictment there appear the following words: "a system of feudal monarchism in the guise of socialism." Was not the Gang of Four's fascist dictatorship simply feudal monarchism in the guise of socialism? Again there appears this expression of mine, "we do not want to serve as tools of dictators with personal ambitions for carrying out modernization," which was followed in my original by, "we want to modernize the lives of the people." Don't tell me the prosecutor wants to carry out the ambitions of dictators but does not want to modernize the lives of the people? I don't think the prosecutor can be like that. I am also unwilling to believe that the prosecutor would forbid criticism of the Gang of Four's feudal fascism. Why do I quote these illustrations as evidence? I do not desire to make improper comments. I merely know that those remarks of the prosecutor in no way illustrate that I wanted to overthrow the government and the socialist system, nor do they illustrate that I was harming the democratic cause.

In the course of publishing our magazine *Exploration*, we never once joined up with any conspiratorial organization, nor did we ever take part in the activities of any violent organization. *Exploration* was on sale to the public as a publication designed to explore and probe theoretical problems; never did it make the overthrow of political power its aim, nor could it ever have been engaged in activities aimed at overthrow of the government. It saw itself as a part of the democratic cause, and could never have acted to harm that cause. For those people who ask us if we were ever prepared to participate in armed struggle or carry out actions aimed at the overthrow of the government, I have supplied a precise answer: I do not recognize armed struggle as an indispensable means to foster democratic government. Instead, I recognize legitimate propaganda and the democratic movement as the primary and indispensable means to foster democratic government. Overthrowing the government is not the same thing as establishing a democratic government. Only when it has been understood by the majority of people will democratic government gradually come into being through reform of the old political system. This viewpoint was one of the basic aims of our publication. Yang Guang, Lu Lin, Zhao Nan, and Liu Qing can all bear witness to this fact. They have all heard what I have to say on this subject.

The public prosecutor's accusation that I wanted to overthrow the socialist system is even more at odds with the facts. The prosecutor claims to have examined my essays, so he should have noticed the section entitled "Socialism and Democracy" within the article "The Fifth Modernization—A Continuation." On the many occasions that the prosecutor talked with me, I also mentioned this same question, so he cannot say he does not know. Of course, the prosecutor's interpretation of a socialist system may differ enormously from my own conception of that system. I recognize that in reality the socialist system may take many different forms and not fit one stereotype. In the light of their most obvious distinction, I would classify socialist systems into two large categories. The first is the Soviet-style of dictatorial socialism, with its chief characteristic of having power concentrated in the hands of the minority in authority. The second category is democratic socialism, with the power reinvested in the whole people and organized on a democratic basis. The majority of people in our nation all wish for the implementation of this kind of socialism. The aim of our exploratory inquiry was to find a way of attaining such a socialist system. I took part in the democratic movement precisely because I sought the implementation of this form of democratic socialism in our country.

I believe that without carrying out social reform, without a true establishment of popular democratic power, and without a democratic system of government to act as a guarantee, then the modernization of our nation's economy is unattainable. A democratic system of government is the prerequisite for our country's total modernization. This was the idea behind the title of my article

"The Fifth Modernization: Democracy" and it was the central idea expounded upon within that essay. Perhaps the members of the office of the Procuratorate do not agree with my theory, but their disagreement with my theories does not brand me as someone wanting to overthrow the socialist system.

THE FIFTH CHARGE

There is no need for me to refute item by item in the list of charges in the indictment those places where the prosecution quotes me out of context. I would only like to point out two things. First, the Constitution grants citizens the right to criticize their leaders, because these leaders are human beings and not gods. It is only through the people's criticism and supervision that those leaders will make fewer mistakes, and only in this way that the people will avoid the misfortune of having their lords and masters ride roughshod over them. Then, and only then, will the people be able to breathe freely. Second, if we wish to carry out the reform of our nation's socialist system, we must base this on the entire population using the methods of criticism and discussion to identify the defects in the present system; otherwise reforms cannot be successfully carried out. It is the people's prerogative, when faced with unreasonable individuals and unacceptable matters, to make criticism. Indeed, it is also their unshirkable duty to do so, and this is a sovereign right with which no individual or government organization has a right to interfere.

Criticism may not always be pretty or pleasant to hear, nor can it always be completely accurate. If one insists on hearing pleasant criticism only and demands its absolute accuracy on pain of punishment, this is as good as forbidding criticism and banning reforms altogether. In such a situation one might just as well deify the leadership outright. Surely we are not expected to retread that old path of blind faith in the leadership as advocated by the Gang of Four? Naturally criticism should have substantial factual basis and personal attacks and malicious slandering should not be tolerated. This taboo was one of the principles adhered to by our publication, as *Exploration*'s introductory statement to our readers demonstrates. If the prosecutor feels that in this respect I did not do enough, I am willing to accept the criticism put forward by him or anyone else.

That concludes my defense address.

VERDICT AND SENTENCE

JUDGE: Wei Jingsheng betrayed his motherland by supplying a foreigner with state military information. He violated the Constitution by his writing of reactionary articles and, by his propagating counterrevolutionary propaganda and agitation, he endangered the basic national and popular interests. All of this constitutes a serious counterrevolutionary crime of a most heinous nature.

In order to safeguard the socialist system and consolidate the dictatorship of the proletariat, to guarantee the smooth progress of the buildup of our socialist modernization, and to suppress destructive counterrevolutionary activity in accordance with stipulations in Article 2, Article 6 paragraph 1, Article 10 paragraphs 2 and 3, and Articles 16 and 17 of the Act of the People's Republic of China for the Punishment of Counterrevolution, we sentence Wei Jingsheng to fifteen years' imprisonment, with the deprivation of all political rights for a period of three years on completion of his prison sentence.

The prisoner may appeal to the Beijing Municipal Higher People's Court within ten days of the second day of receiving this sentence.

Appendix III

from maoist

fanatic to

political

dissident:

an

autobiographical

essay

(1979)

In early 1979, Wei Jingsheng wrote this autobiographical essay to explore the roots of his dissent and activism in his experiences as a Red Guard during the Cultural Revolution. Left unpublished upon his arrest in March 1979, it was subsequently smuggled out of China and appeared in overseas Chinese newspapers as well as The New York Times Magazine.

I was sixteen and about to graduate from junior high school when the Cultural Revolution broke out in 1966. I would have gone on to high school that year, but the Cultural Revolution disrupted everything, including the education system. Even today, however, I still feel that whatever the turmoil may have cost my generation in formal schooling, we made up for in mental experience. Those chaotic years forced people to abandon the superstitions and prejudices that had dominated their minds for so long and made them begin to scrutinize their own attitudes and beliefs. People started looking at the world objectively—something that had been impossible under ordinary circumstances.

As a student, I loved literature and often lost myself in novels, frequently devouring entire books in a single sitting. Sometimes I even composed poems or stories and showed them to my friends.

I grew interested in philosophy during junior high school. I was in an extremely unruly class that held endless debate sessions every evening after school. The opposing sides would stand on desks, gesturing with pointers and pencil boxes as we shouted at one another. No teacher dared to stop us; that would be asking for trouble. Sometimes we had interminable debates on obscure, even absurd topics, neither side yielding until we had exhausted every line of argument. We soon felt the need to study more theoretical texts in order to increase our reasoning skills, so our little debate group read virtually every important work by Marx, Engels, Lenin, Stalin, and Mao. This is when I began seriously pursuing philosophy.

As a low-ranking bureaucrat in the Communist Party, my father was naturally devoted to his Marxist and Maoist ideas and did his utmost to instill "Marxist–Leninist–Mao Zedong Thought" into the minds of his children. He encouraged us to read political works such as *The Plain Truth*, Liu Shaoqi's *How to Be a Good Communist*, and Stalin's *Dialectical and Historical Materialism*. Although I couldn't fully understand these books at the time, this training turned me into a staunch believer in Marxist–Leninist–Mao Zedong Thought. Indeed, right up until my illusions were later shattered by the reality I witnessed, you could say I was a fanatic Maoist.

My mother, however, had another way of indoctrinating us. Like my father, she frowned on the way I encouraged my younger brother and sisters to read novels, yet she herself often purchased romantic novels and memoirs like *Flowers of a Bitter Plant, Three-Household Lane*, or *Flower Toward the Sun* about the Communist Party's early revolutionary struggles and would strongly recommend them to us. During a disagreement my parents once had, I overheard my mother arguing that they must teach us to understand the difference between love and hate, for only then could we side emotionally with the people and truly grasp the ideas of Marxism and Maoism. If young people didn't understand the people's suffering, she reasoned, then they would never understand the need for revolution. The emotional education my mother gave me was to have a decisive influence on the development of my later thinking. Had it not been for her effort to cultivate my revolutionary devotion by imbuing me with a sense of "sacrifice for those who are suffering," I might have ended up like the children of other cadres, shrugging off the reality of the living conditions of Chinese workers and peasants and glibly dismissing it as the "dark side of socialism." I might have resembled other "city slickers" and children of "good backgrounds," scolding "all those lazy good-for-nothings" whenever I saw a filthy, foul-smelling beggar. But thanks to my mother's education, despite having grown up a cadre's son in the city, I was still able to sympathize with the suffering of workers and peasants. What a priceless gift it would be to the progress of mankind if all mothers were to teach their children fairness and compassion like this.

∙   ∙   ∙

"Cultural Revolution" was an appropriate name for the chaos that broke out in 1966 because its beginnings were basically psychological in nature: It was the result of an explosion of the pent-up rage that had been accumulating for many years due to the ever-widening gap that existed between official policy and actual reality. Wherever struggles broke out during the Cultural Revolution—from the central government down to the rural production brigades—they were nearly always waged by the masses against the leaders who had oppressed them. Even those few who had never been oppressed fought under the banner of victim versus victimizer.

Clearly, the Cultural Revolution was not initiated by the "Great Helmsman" Mao Zedong alone, but was actually the result of years of Communist despotism. Yet somehow this explosion of rage took on the form of tyrant worship, even to the point where struggles and sacrifices were made in the name of despotism. This reveals both the blindness of the mass struggle and the extent to which the people's minds remained shackled by feudalistic ideas, finally resulting in an absurd situation whereby the people rose up to oppose the government only to end up protecting it. They opposed the system of hierarchy and servitude, while waving the banner of the very founder of that system. They demanded democratic rights while treating democracy with contempt and attempting to acquire these rights by following the ideas and instructions of a dictator.

The result was that the people, regardless of what perspective they viewed the situation from, came to the same conclusion: The Cultural Revolution was an utter disaster! Sooner or later the people began to realize that their belief system was deeply flawed and in need of a serious revision.

Thus, the frenzied and foolish masses who in 1966 demonstrated in Tiananmen Square in support of a man who had deprived them of their freedom were to become the confident and courageous people who demonstrated against that same man on Tiananmen Square in April 1976.

The painful experiences of the Cultural Revolution shaped an entire generation of people in China. When many of my friends and

I joined the Red Guards in early 1966, the Red Guards were fanatically Maoist, but more importantly, they were deeply dissatisfied with the status quo. If they'd been simply Maoist organizations, I doubt there would have been much need for them to take on their rebellious attitude. Like me, most of the people who joined the Red Guards were fed up with the lack of social equality in China, and their willingness to sacrifice themselves for this cause turned the Red Guards into a strong fighting force that was nearly invincible.

So why, then, did this force ultimately fail to destroy the unequal social system? Because it was itself armed with the ideology of despotism. Take me, for example. I was an ardent Maoist at the time and felt that the utopian vision described in the works of Mao, Marx, and Lenin had yet to be achieved in reality. I was quite upset that the leaders of our school appeared to have no intention to bring this reality about, so when I heard Mao Zedong say that class struggle still existed in the socialist stage of society, and that class enemies were hiding in the leadership ranks, I figured that all of this inequality and unhappiness had been brought about by those class enemies who had wormed their way into the Communist Party. Therefore, I threw myself completely into the movement aimed at ferreting out such bad persons, picturing them all to resemble the actor who played Bukharin in the movie *Lenin and the October Revolution*.

For a variety of reasons, the Red Guard movement grew rapidly and expanded to every part of China. Red Guards like myself traveled about the country following Mao's orders to "exchange revolutionary experiences" and "light revolutionary fires." Upon arriving at a new place, we would contact people we knew at all levels of society. These tended to be cadres of various ranks, who would fill us in on the other local cadres and "power holders" in particular. Then we would go into all the schools, factories, and mines to stir up rebellion.

But once our initial enthusiasm had worn off a bit, we began to have doubts: If the people who held the power and were the objects of these rebellions were all bad, then, we reasoned, the entire nation and Party must have gone bad! Such ideas were very different from what we had felt at the beginning of the movement. Yet, if they were not universally bad, how was it that the masses at practically every place we visited were able to come up with irrefutable reasons for opposing their leaders? From these reasons we deduced that the power holders were indeed all bad.

After our return to Beijing from the provinces, we grew even more confused as we learned that many of the old cadres whom we ourselves knew well had been branded "capitalist roaders." We had never felt that they were anti-Party or anti-socialist, or plotters of the Bukharin type. Besides, they were all from poor family backgrounds and had joined the revolution in their youth. None of this was easy for a sixteen-year-old kid like myself to figure out. In the midst of all this confusion, the Red Guards began to split up. Of the original four hundred Red Guards at my school, for example, more than a hundred quit to join other organizations, while those remaining split into five or six factions.

At the time, I felt that the only way to accurately interpret this complex and contradictory situation was to gain more practical information, so I led several of my closest classmates on a "field investigation." Never did I imagine that this investigation would continue for so many years.

My friends and I boarded a train heading toward the Northwest—a direction that we hadn't traveled in before. The train was extremely crowded with all sorts of people; many of them were out sightseeing under the pretext of "exchanging revolutionary experiences." Most of them were just dumb country bumpkins who knew little of anything and didn't seem to care whether they did or not. Their minds had been numbed long ago and now they had only one goal in life: pleasure. Such people really disgusted me. There was a middle-aged man of the sort sitting directly opposite me. He claimed to be on an official business trip, but I noticed that he was traveling on an "exchanging experience" ticket. When he saw how many of us there were and that we were Red Guards, he tried hard to strike up a conversation with us, but I pretty much ignored him.

In the stations west of Xi'an there was an extraordinary number of beggars. Whenever I saw beggars, I automatically handed over some of my food to them. Finally the guy sitting across from me said, "Don't give them any more food. They're probably bad class elements, former landlords or rich peasants. Anyway, they're lazy scroungers and we should let them starve." He spoke quite persuasively, so even though I wasn't completely convinced, I took his advice. Still, whenever I saw small children, I couldn't help but give them food out of pity.

Leaving behind the city of Lanzhou, the train approached the famous region known as the "Corridor West of the Yellow River," and we came to a sudden stop at a small station. I call this station small without fear of exaggeration, for it didn't even have a platform, probably because trains rarely stopped to let people get on or off there. The moment our express train came to a halt, a horde of beggars swarmed around nearly every car. In a crowd of youngsters begging below my window, I noticed a young woman, her face smeared with soot and her long hair covering her upper torso, who moved me to pity. I felt that children were innocent, and even if this girl was from a landlord or rich peasant family, she herself certainly wasn't rich or a landlord. I rationalized that therefore giving her a bit of food wouldn't count as having an "unclear class sense." I took out some of the cakes I had bought at the Lanzhou station and reached through the window, but the train was rather high and as the beggars were standing at the bottom of an embankment, our hands were still half a meter apart. So I began to lean out the window in order to put the cakes into their hands.

No sooner had I stuck my head out, however, than a sudden reflex made me pull it back in quickly, my arm still dangling in midair. In that brief instant, I had seen something that I could never have imagined or believed before: Other than the long hair spread over her upper torso, that young woman of about seventeen or eighteen years of age had absolutely nothing covering her body. From a distance, the soot and mud smeared all over her had looked like clothing, and among all the young unclothed boys who were begging, she had not been conspicuous.

I had never been one to blink at reality, and I certainly knew that what I had seen was real, but there was simply no way I could take this in. The girl and the other beggars didn't understand why I had withdrawn so suddenly and begged even more loudly. I immediately realized that to them their hunger was the most pressing matter, so I quickly threw the cakes in my hand out and a great clamor arose by the rails as they fought over them.

The man sitting opposite me chuckled and said knowingly, "Never seen that before? There's a lot of it in this area. Every little station has girls like that and some of them are quite pretty. Just give them something to eat, you don't even need to spend any money, and you can—" I glared at him, glad that he had given me the chance to express the hatred and disgust I felt. I think my look must have been quite frightening, for he stopped immediately and, flustered, changed his tone. "If you took the trains around here more often, you wouldn't find this surprising. But, of course, when you think of how one runs into this at every station, it is indeed pitiful." Not wanting to reveal my emotions in front of a person like this, I turned back toward the window. Again I saw that young woman, now on tiptoe, her hands outstretched, fixing her piteous eyes on me through her disheveled and filthy hair as she pleaded urgently in a local dialect I could barely understand. I knew exactly what she wanted. Perhaps she hadn't snatched up one of the cakes just now, or maybe she had given it to a younger brother or sister, but no matter what, she would go hungry if I didn't give her more. My initial shock and embarrassment had passed, and I took all the leftover bread from my satchel and leaned far out the window to give it to those who hadn't gotten any before.

There was not enough bread in my hand to satisfy the horde of beggars and now those who had been begging at other carriage windows crowded around mine. As I reluctantly began pulling my body back into the car, I heard a voice behind me say, "Here, I have some leftovers." I turned, half disbelieving, to the man opposite me. Looking embarrassed, he added "I can't eat them all anyway," and handed me several packages of biscuits. As I distributed them into the outstretched hands, I noticed that passengers at other windows were now briskly passing out all kinds of food to the beggars as well. Perhaps they were influenced by the Red Guard armband visible on my outstretched arm. Who knows? As the train pulled out, I caught glimpses of the naked girl and the other youngsters around her through the windows—most of them had already lowered their hungry eyes from the train windows to the food in their hands.

• • •

For the remaining two days of the trip, I could not put the scene at that nameless little station out of my mind. Was this the "fruit" of socialism? Or was it the evil doings of a few bad local leaders? If the leader in that town was one of my father's "old comrades," I wanted to know what type of person he was, for at least then I could confirm my feeling that even death would be too good a punishment for him. At the same time, it dawned on me that in order to discern the true face of this society, it was not enough to understand the conditions existing in the cities and among the upper classes; one had to probe the situation at the lowest levels as well.

With this goal in mind, one of my very best friends and I set out to visit the lower echelons of a production and construction corps in Xinjiang, a remote border region of western China. What attracted our attention was not the goods produced or the amount of grain harvested there, but the living conditions of the various people who lived there and their outlook on life. As soon as we arrived in a place, we would try to meet as many people as possible. Our warm, honest approach helped us to make many friends among the former city students, demobilized soldiers, and exiled old rightists who had settled there. We discovered that, despite their divergent aspirations, experiences, and circumstances, they all shared one common attitude toward the present situation: dissatisfaction. The former city students and army veterans all felt that they had been deceived.

One old rightist told us bluntly that when she joined the Communist Party, she never thought that one day it would be controlled by an inhuman bunch of scoundrels. Such views were extremely difficult for us to swallow at first, so much so that we felt that a woman like this truly deserved to be labeled a rightist. But my friend and I were in the habit of listening patiently to all points of view, and the details this woman used to explain her thinking, including episodes from her own life, were hard to refute. She was extremely happy for the chance to speak openly and I was quite moved by her story, so we quickly became good friends. She had been a correspondent for the New China News Agency before being branded a rightist and exiled to Xinjiang. Due to the lack of trained professionals in Xinjiang, however, she was permitted to

work as an editor and reporter for the newspaper at the Second Farm Division of Ku'erle County.

She took us to see many poverty-stricken people in the area, including the chairman of a Poor Peasants' Association, who was of Uighur nationality. When we left this man's home, I felt as though the clock had been turned back twenty years and I had just seen a poor peasant's home from pre-Liberation days of the type described in novels. The only difference was that the poor peasant constantly used words like "revolution" and "revisionism," as if to remind everyone that this was 1966, not 1946.

This reporter also took us to visit a horse stable in an extremely remote and isolated spot. At a fish processing plant near the stable we met more than twenty former students from Shanghai, who immediately asked us if we would take their photographs. They mounted our horses in frightened glee, holding on to the reins tightly. Thinking it somewhat strange, I asked, "Don't you usually ride horses?" A young man wearing glasses, replied with a laugh, "We don't have any horses here." They asked us to send the pictures, each one taken on horseback with the beautiful local scenery in the background, to their families.

As we rode back to the regimental headquarters that evening, I asked the reporter why the students hadn't used the dilapidated thatched huts where they lived as a background for their photographs. In a weary voice, she simply replied, "After not sending home a picture in over ten years, can you imagine how their parents would feel if they were to know their children were living in such broken-down huts?" I couldn't help but express my shock that they hadn't sent pictures home for a decade, and the reporter seemed glad for the chance to explain their situation to me.

"Life is very hard there. Didn't you notice that they lived and ate just the same as the Reform Through Labor inmates?"

"There were *laogai* inmates there? How come I didn't see any?" I asked.

"You're not very observant. That row of huts in front of their living quarters—didn't you see the *laogai* prisoners there?"

I suddenly remembered seeing people watching us silently through the windows of the front huts, but I never would have

guessed that *laogai* prisoners would be living as "freely" as students sent down from the cities.

"They say that none of them is allowed to leave the site of the plant for production reasons, but it's really to deter them from running away. Naturally there's no way for them to have a photograph taken. And didn't you notice that there wasn't a single horse there?" She continued.

Amazingly, it had also never occurred to me that former city students would be living with the same kind of "freedoms" as *laogai* prisoners.

"But can't they just escape?" I persisted.

"Look at how fast this river runs."

Only then did I notice the swift current of the river we were fording as it rushed on toward Bositeng Lake. We had already crossed three such rivers on our way here.

"It's impossible to cross these rivers without a horse," she said, as we looked down at the endlessly swirling current. "And during the spring thaw, even a horse won't do. You can only cross by camel. An unloaded horse would be carried away by the current."

To keep our shoes dry, we tucked our feet back on the horses' buttocks, and I turned my head to look back at those thatched huts, now about ten kilometers away. A few unfortunate souls, who would probably spend the rest of their lives there, still stood watching us disappear over the horizon.

From then on, whenever I read glowing praise in the newspapers for the "superiority of socialism" or heard people brag about how socialism was better than capitalism, I would swear silently, "Bullshit!" Of course I'd read that capitalism wasn't great either, but I didn't think it could be much worse than what I had witnessed. Although I went on believing that all the problems I witnessed were due to policies that ran counter to Chairman Mao's directives, I started to wonder why Chairman Mao had put his trust in those who went against his orders. The case of the woman rightist puzzled me even further: Why were good people always beaten down, while bad people ended up victorious? The woman herself was quite embarrassed about having been labeled a rightist, but from the moment I met her I felt that she was a good person who

could never do anything to harm the interests of the people. It was clear that she had been wrongfully denounced as a rightist, and it was completely wrong that a person of worth and ability should be exiled to such a barren place. I especially admired her for not bearing a grudge against her former husband, who had divorced her and remarried. She had explained it saying, "I was a 'rightist' and I didn't want to implicate him or my children. And, of course, he couldn't go through life alone and the children would always need someone to take care of them. When you visit my home, it would be best not to let anybody know you came from here, in order to avoid giving them any trouble."

Later, when we managed to find her husband and quietly pay him a visit, bearing the gift of pears from distant Ku'erle that she had asked us to bring him, he refused to open the door or admit that he had any relationship to the mother of his children. He would only allow his daughter to take the pears from us in the corridor. My intense disgust and anger soon turned to anguish as I realized that it was probably his heartlessness and lack of conscience that had saved him from being tainted by his rightist wife. Why was it that people like this managed to turn bad luck into fortune and come out on top? Being accustomed to always coming up with solutions to problems, I decided it must be because the theoretical level of the cadres in the entire Party and country was so low that without a true understanding of Marxist–Leninist–Mao Zedong Thought, they had allowed the residue of the old feudal bureaucracy to take over. I believed that Marxist–Leninist–Mao Zedong Thought was the only effective weapon against these "revisionist elements," so I vowed to step up my intense study of these ideas. I learned that there were many others from the earliest group of Red Guards who had similar feelings and were seeking a deeper understanding of society. I heard that some had gone so far as to put on tattered clothing and go begging at Beijing Railway Station in order to learn about life.

But I didn't think that this was a very productive way to "learn about life." Listening to workers and peasants speak their minds was a lot more effective than begging. In order to understand society, one had to understand the different classes and microsocieties within it. I had also adopted a new bias: Unless there was solid evidence to convince me otherwise, I would regard all power holders as ruthless people lacking in conscience who had built their success on others' misfortunes. My thinking coincided with the current anti–Jiang Qing trend among "old Red Guards," and I soon became an active participant in the movement. I found out that this bias against those in power was quite popular among my old comrades. Whatever had anything to do with the government, whether person or theory, we would categorically deny its justification. Of course, there wasn't much real theoretical study going on. All sorts of other activities—from sitting in jail, to holding "smash the Three Commands" (the pro–Jiang Qing factions in the universities at the time) meetings, to raiding the Public Security Bureau, and the like—took up most of our time and energy.

There were even some people at the time calling for a "rechecking of Mao Zedong Thought against Marxism," or declaring that "Chairman Mao was a great man before 1957, but has made mistakes since." Few people today would dare to openly make statements like these, so you can imagine how earth-shattering it was for ordinary people to hear such words back then. But these words were like a beacon of light showing the way for people like me. Chairman Mao had already ordered Jiang Qing to turn against us "rebel babies" and arrest us without mercy. The towering image of the old man that I had held in my mind for so long began to shake when I learned of this and heard other things people were saying. I immediately started wondering if perhaps even the thoughts of Chairman Mao might be "problematic."

In 1967, the "Beijing Red Guard United Action Committee," or United Action, for short, was outlawed for opposing Jiang Qing, and old Red Guards like myself were left without an organization. Our ideas didn't jibe well with any of the other groups around, and besides, they were all afraid to have anything to do with us, so everyone felt an urgent need for an organization of our own. Just then, certain Red Guard leaders in the West District of Beijing formed a chorus, mainly performing songs like "The Long March" and "The Poems of Chairman Mao." Very quickly, many old Red Guards began congregating around this chorus. This chorus was significant in that it voiced the grievances of old cadres—not surprisingly, since its members were mostly children of such cadres. But there was one other characteristic of the chorus that can't be overlooked: It was anti–Jiang Qing and most of those who participated in this organization were members or sympathizers of the now-banned United Action. They opposed Jiang Qing primarily because it was clear that she had manipulated naive young people to bolster her own power and help attack people she personally disliked. She had repeatedly trampled over the students, maligning them whenever she fancied. In addition, the chorus members had heard their parents say many unflattering things about Jiang Qing's moral background; having persecuted so many old cadres, she had also incurred the hatred of their children.

Before long, this organization had grown to more than a hundred choral singers, seventy or eighty musicians, a drama corps, and the nucleus of a film crew. It had even put out a strongly anti–Jiang Qing magazine called *Preparation*. Most of the organization's funds was obtained from a raid led by one of the important leaders, Yang Xiaoyang, on the vault of the Number Thirteen Middle School. In order to form the chorus, he had picked open the vault's lock and removed account books and over two hundred thousand yuan in cash, carrying it home in a burlap sack. All of the group's future activities were funded with this money. As Yang Xiaoyang was my neighbor and the ideological position of the chorus was similar to my own, I decided to join.

At first I handled just general assignments for the chorus, but later I was sent to Canton to set up some performances and make contacts with other like-minded groups. At the time, the anti–Jiang Qing viewpoint of the chorus was in trouble. Gradually many of the more timid members had dropped out and small pro–Jiang Qing organizations had openly taken action against the chorus. The possibility of a new round of arrests like those that had destroyed United Action was near at hand. But even worse was the discord inside the chorus itself. There were few people left who had any real ideas, but there were a great number of people who loved to make trouble just for the sake of it. The core members of the chorus held a meeting and decided to go to Canton to lay low for a time. Yang Xiaoyang and I were sent there in advance to make all the arrangements and then bring the entire chorus to Canton.

When Yang Xiaoyang and I returned from Canton a little more than a week later, the situation had already changed completely and Yang was arrested the moment he walked into his home. An emergency meeting of the core members was held and it was decided that I would take charge of the group and we would proceed to Canton. We felt that going to Canton was our last hope.

At the train station, however, our group of several hundred chorus members encountered a blockade of an equal number of army troops from the Beijing Garrison Command. When I discovered several huge truckloads of deployed soldiers on the square outside the station, I knew that the situation was bad. Several days earlier I had heard the son of a Garrison Command cadre saying that the central authorities were already spreading a rumor that the entire chorus was planning a mass escape to Hong Kong. Realizing the seriousness of the situation, I quickly told everyone I could find to notify those inside the station to come out and asked the central members to order a full pullout. I continued to feel uneasy even after this was done. As our people rushed out, I took about a dozen "bodyguards" and made a quick tour of the station to see if anyone had been detained. Sure enough, I found my sister, who had been ordered to go back in to find a girlfriend of hers, and now both were being guarded by a soldier. Other soldiers were coming into the station to look for people, so we grouped together and rushed the soldiers. Before they could react, we made a great clamor, grabbing the girls and rushing out of the station all at once. We jumped on bicycles, scattered in all directions, and returned home. When I went back to look later, soldiers were still pouring out of the station. Too bad—they were one step too late.

The core members of the chorus met continuously for a few days, and after endless arguments it was determined that my rushed decision to order a pullout was right and everyone agreed that my assessment of the situation at the time had also been correct. The final meeting was held at my home and we debated all day about whether the chorus should be disbanded or not. That evening, with majority approval, I formally announced the dissolution of the chorus. We had little other choice at the time; all meeting halls were strictly controlled, so there was no place for us to perform, and there was no longer any possibility of leaving Beijing. Furthermore, it was rumored that the government was about to take immediate action directed specifically against our organization. Facing possible arrest and unable to do anything, I felt that it was better to dissolve the chorus in order to protect as many people as possible by avoiding arrests similar to those that followed the government crackdown on United Action. But the other reason, which I didn't state openly at the time, was that I felt many of the people involved were simply voicing their own personal grievances or those of their friends or parents; very few were really speaking for the people. Still others were just blind zealots without any clear goal in mind. If we continued this way, we would accomplish nothing more than our own destruction.

During the months following the breakup of the chorus, I was frantically busy, yet I also felt a sense of disillusionment about the future. There didn't seem to be anybody in the current socialist society on whom I could rely or place my hopes. The workers and peasants foolishly believed those new bureaucrats who oppressed and exploited them, and the soldiers, without exception, followed anyone in power. As for the intellectuals, some had been bought out by the Lin Biao–Jiang Qing clique, while the others went on barely making a sound, living with the hope that someday they too might gain favor. I saw no force capable of changing this ignoble situation and I felt extremely pained and depressed.

With wave after wave of mass arrests sweeping through Beijing, I had nowhere to hide. I spent July and August 1968 in Tianjin, completely desperate. After managing to evade yet another police raid by hiding on the roof of a building, my friends emptied the last coins from their pockets to help me escape. Still we didn't have enough money to get me to any of the places I had in mind. Finally I decided that I would go to the home of a friend's girlfriend. I'd only met her once, but luckily I had her address in my pocket and just enough money to get a ticket to Changzhou, where she lived. "What if she doesn't help? What then?" my friends asked. "Well, I have enough food to get me to Shanghai," I replied. "They haven't started arresting people there yet." And so it was decided.

After buying my train ticket, I had less than one yuan left in my pocket. When I got off the train, I didn't know the way and had to take a taxi cart to the girl's home, where she paid the fare. I was very embarrassed to tell her that my real motive for visiting her was to borrow money to get to Wuhan or Canton to take refuge or, failing that, to Shanghai, where I could pull together a bit of money from friends.

When she first told me that she didn't have any money either, I thought she was lying and I grew cold as I thought of the humiliation of having to beg my way along the road. As I stood up to go, she quickly asked me to stay on a few more days in Changzhou so that she could write some letters and ask her friends in Beijing to come up with the money for my ticket to Wuhan. She also informed me that mass arrests had in fact already begun in Shanghai. Later I learned that she did have enough cash to buy me a boat ticket to Wuhan, but she feared that if I went there, it would have been about as safe as walking directly into a Public Security Bureau, since roundups had begun simultaneously in every major city across the country.

After more than a week, I finally received money from friends in Beijing along with a letter from my younger sister giving me the address of our ancestral home in Anhui province. She confirmed what was happening in all the big cities and warned me that the countryside was the only safe place.

I was grateful to my friend's girlfriend. Her grandmother's home in Changzhou had really become a temporary safe haven and allowed me to safely arrange my next move. During my stay in Changzhou, she had taken me to the park or marketplace every day to relax and clear my mind.

Her grandmother had been one of the largest property owners in Changzhou, but after the Communist revolution, with the help of a daughter who had participated in the revolution, she had turned all her property over to the new government and was designated an "enlightened gentry." When I was in Changzhou in 1968, she had already grown senile and was bedridden, but she was still forced to hang a sign on her door stating that she was one of the "Five Black Elements." I thought to myself that although she certainly may have exploited others before the revolution, the conditions of society at the time had necessitated it. Even Marx himself had said that "all human relations are between exploiter and exploited." That aside, a person's having been born on the side of the exploiters shouldn't be the sole criteria for judging that person's goodness or badness. After all, the fact that she had handed over all of her personal property to the public after 1949 should be enough to show that it was not her natural disposition to exploit others. And why when she was about to die did they still need to hang a sign on her door to humiliate her? It was even the people who lived in what was once her house who had hung the sign, although I failed to see what real benefit they got out of it. If it was in their personal interest to do so, that would be easy to under-stand, but the fact that they had little to gain by meddling in someone else's affairs indicated to me that there was someone else directing them and provoking them to do such things. I remember painfully struggling over this question, relating it to everything I had seen and heard since the start of the Cultural Revolution. Finally, I felt only that neither the people who had their homes searched and placards hung on their doors nor those who carried these things out were at fault. The fault lay in their flawed thinking and outlook and the fact that they had all been tricked. At the time, I figured that this was due to force of habit and selfish desperation, but I was never quite satisfied with this explanation.

I reached my father's ancestral village just as the personality cult of Mao Zedong and movements like "cleansing the class ranks" were going strong. In the wake of the expanding class struggle, many who had once stood firmly on the side of Mao Zedong and the Communist Party also fell victim to class struggle and purges. I began to wonder whether class struggle was really supposed to be taken so seriously. Of course I still agreed that former landlords and rich peasants should not hold any special place in the economy after the revolution. But I also felt that ordinary workers and peasants had no special right or need to oppress them either. According to Marxism, "class is a function of economic status," so doesn't that mean that former rich peasants and ordinary workers and peasants were now all members of the same class? As for the cadres, who held real power and economic and political positions far superior to those of the workers and peasants, shouldn't they also be considered a class unto themselves? These two classes were commonly perceived to be as incompatible as fire and water. I was always aware of this, but was only able to clarify it for myself after using methods of Marxist class analysis to think about it on a theoretical level.

I felt as if I had suddenly awakened from a long dream, but everyone around me was still plunged in darkness. I began to feel that all my previous views and political notions were no longer reliable and needed to be completely rethought and reexamined. I made use of the quiet of the village to immerse myself in the classic texts of Marx, Engels, Lenin, and Stalin. Marx and Engels inspired the most trust in me, for I felt that their work was far more scientific than that of the others. I liked only one of Lenin's works, however—*The State and Revolution*, particularly the part on proletarian democracy.

During my stay in the village, the aftermath of the Great Leap Forward and the Communist Wind left a deep impression on me. From the moment I arrived, I frequently heard the peasants discussing the Great Leap Forward in terms of a "doomsday" period and noticed that they could barely hide their feeling of being lucky to have survived. I soon developed a great interest in this topic and would often question them for more details. Gradually I began to realize that there was nothing at all "natural" about the period known as the "three years of natural disaster," for it was actually caused by misguided policies. The peasants recalled how, during the Communist Wind from 1959 to 1960, rice was left to rot in the fields because the peasants were too weak from hunger to harvest it. Many starved to death watching the ripe rice grains blow in the fields, as not a single person was able to go out to harvest in some fields. Once, on the way to a neighboring village with a relative, we passed a deserted village with houses that were no more than roofless mud walls. I figured this village had been merged with another during the Great Leap Forward and asked my relative why the walls hadn't been knocked down to make room for fields. He replied, "These are people's homes. How could they be torn down without their consent?" I had seen clearly that there were no roofs on these houses and didn't believe that anyone was living in them. My relative went on, "Of course there isn't anyone living in them now; the entire village starved to death during the Communist Wind. No one has returned since, so their fields were divided up among the neighboring production teams. People used to think that somebody might return, so they didn't tear down their homes. But it's been years now. I doubt anybody is ever coming back."

Just as the two of us passed by the village, the bright sunlight shone on the green weeds growing through the cracks in the mud walls, making a chilling contrast with the neat rice paddies surrounding it. Later, at a gathering in a friend's home, I heard stories of how villagers had exchanged babies as food. I felt like I could practically see, hovering up from the weeds in the cracks of those mud walls, the pained expressions of parents chewing the flesh of children they had exchanged with their own babies. Were the children happily catching butterflies in the fields nearby reincarnations of those children who had been eaten? I felt sorry for them, and even sorrier for their parents. Who had made them do this? Who had made them swallow, along with the tears and misery of other parents, the human flesh that they had never imagined tasting?

By now I could make out the face of the executioner quite clearly. He was a man of the kind that appears, as the saying goes, only "once every few centuries worldwide, and once in several millennia in China"; he was Mao Zedong. It was Mao and his followers who had used their most evil systems and policies to force those parents, starved beyond reason, to give up their own flesh and blood to feed others in exchange for flesh to feed themselves. It was Mao Zedong, who in order to make up for his crime of smothering democracy and carrying out the Great Leap Forward, had driven millions of dazed peasants to take up their hoes to strike down their neighbors and eat the flesh of people just like themselves to save their own lives. They were not the executioners; Mao Zedong and his followers were. Only then did I understand where Peng Dehuai had found the strength to attack the Mao-led Party Central Committee. Only then did I understand why the peasants so bitterly hated "communism" and why they couldn't comprehend why Liu Shaoqi's policy of calling for more private plots and enterprises and fixed output quotas had been overturned. It was because never again did they want to be forced to give up their own flesh and blood for others to devour or to lose all reason and kill their neighbors for food; it was because they wanted to go on living. This was a much stronger reason than any "ism."

It might seem that to call Mao Zedong an executioner was, under the circumstances, a crazy or at best foolhardy act. But I came to this conclusion very naturally and unpressured because all that I had witnessed with my own eyes had shown me that this was the case. There was no other explanation. What I couldn't understand, however, was how people went on enthusiastically hailing this executioner, even pledging their lives to protect him. After all, weren't the soldiers and police ranks filled with the sons and brothers of peasants, workers, and others?

During the more than a year I spent in the countryside, I saw for myself how Mao's theory of "class struggle" was actually played out in real life; and when I went on to do a stint in the army, I saw once again how the theory of class struggle had seeped into every corner of life. Mao Zedong had used class struggle to divide the people into *imaginary* interest groups, rendering them incapable of distinguishing their true interests and inciting them to murder one another for goals that, in fact, were detrimental to their own interests. It was precisely through this technique that he manipulated the millions he had oppressed and fooled into supporting him. It was precisely for this reason that an executioner was able to masquerade as the leader of the people.

Wei Jingsheng's Lifelong Battle for Democracy

Sophia Woodman

Wei Jingsheng's letters trace the twists and turns of China's recent history; as he repeatedly reminds his silent interlocutors, he cannot be indifferent to the fate of his nation because it is his life. Wei has spent over a third of his forty-seven years in prison or in detention, mostly in solitary confinement, and is now serving his second long prison term. Yet he has faced this ordeal, which has severely damaged his health, without bitterness. Wei's daily life is a microcosm of the struggle for democracy in China: one man upholding his integrity against the unfettered power of the state.

YOUTH: 1950–78

The first child of a couple committed to the Chinese Communist Party (CCP), Wei was born on May 20, 1950, in the flush of optimism after the "Liberation" of China in 1949. His given name Jingsheng means "born in the capital," expressing a triumphant pride in the Party's victory. His father, Wei Zilin, had joined the revolution in the 1930s, first working for the Party underground, later joining the Red Army. His mother, Du Peijun, became a supporter of the Communists as a student in the 1940s. At the time of Wei's birth, both his parents were already members of the Party elite: Wei Zilin was a cadre in the Civil Aviation Administration, while Du Peijun worked in the Ministry of Textiles. During the

1950s, Wei Jingsheng was followed by a sister, Wei Ling, a brother, Wei Xiaotao, and finally another sister, Wei Shanshan.

As he describes in his autobiography, Wei Jingsheng grew up a committed Communist. The Weis lived in a compound with many of the families of the nation's leadership and their children attended the best schools in the country along with other children of high-ranking cadres. Although Wei senior came under a political cloud as a "right deviationist" in Mao Zedong's 1957 attack against his critics, the Anti-Rightist Campaign, and was transferred to a less prestigious job, by 1961 his "problem" had been resolved. Wei Jingsheng had just graduated from the prestigious junior high school attached to People's University when the Cultural Revolution (1966–76) broke out.

Chairman Mao was virtually deified by the fanatical Red Guards he enlisted to fight against imagined "capitalist roaders" in the Party; in the *Little Red Book*, Mao's words became a form of holy writ. Like many in his generation, Wei became a Red Guard out of devotion to Chairman Mao but ended up doubting everything about Chinese socialism. From 1966 on, formal schooling ended as Wei and his fellow rebels across China devoted themselves to transforming society. Traveling around the country to spread the Cultural Revolution, Wei was shocked by the contrast between the deprivation he saw and the workers' paradise of official propaganda. Under the slogans of ceaseless "class struggle" and "permanent revolution," millions were persecuted and the economy stagnated.

In 1969, through family connections, Wei joined the army. This was the only alternative to being "sent down" to the countryside, the fate of many young people after the Red Guards were disbanded. They found that "learning from the workers and peasants" usually consisted of little more than backbreaking labor in sometimes severe conditions, and were rarely permitted to return to their city homes. In the army, Wei became a squad commander and served in the poverty-stricken Northwest, where he had to defend public granaries from hungry mobs. After completing his military service in 1973, Wei went home and was assigned to work as an electrician at the Beijing Zoo.

In the early 1970s, Wei became engaged to a young Tibetan

woman, Ping Ni. Her father, Phuntsog Wanggyal, once head of the Tibetan Communist Party, had been removed from his position in Tibet in 1958 and arrested in 1960. He subsequently spent eighteen years in Qincheng Prison. Ping Ni's mother, Zalina, a Tibetan Muslim, slit her wrists after she came under attack in 1968.

Repelled by the official prejudice against Tibetans reflected in his parents' threat to break off relations with him if he married Ping Ni, Wei became fascinated by the tragic history of his girlfriend and her homeland. After 1949, Tibet's spiritual leader, the Dalai Lama, had reached an accommodation with Beijing under which his country would continue a relationship with China combining autonomy and association. But within a decade the CCP insisted on imposing "socialist" policies in Tibet. After an uprising, the Dalai Lama fled to India and even staunch Communists like Phuntsog Wanggyal lost faith. Wei gained an understanding—unusual even among the dissidents of today—of the brutality of Chinese rule in Tibet. When the universities reopened in 1977, he applied to study Tibetan history, but failed to win a place.

Wei's own family had not remained immune from the savagery of the Cultural Revolution. His father, like many other officials, was sent off to "reform his thinking" through hard labor in the countryside, while his mother was demoted to a post as a party cadre in a shoe and hat factory. The workers treated her harshly, forcing her to write endless self-criticisms. She dared not ask for treatment when she became ill, and the cancer from which she was suffering went undiagnosed until it was quite advanced. She died in 1976.

On April 5, 1976—Grave-Sweeping Day, a traditional day of remembrance—the streets of Beijing were flooded with people mourning the January death of Premier Zhou Enlai. Wei joined the throngs in Tiananmen Square, the symbolic heart of the Chinese nation, where activists were posting commemorative poems about Zhou that suggested if Zhou, not Mao Zedong, had been in charge, the tragedies of the Cultural Revolution might not have occurred. This spontaneous outpouring of public discontent eventually became known as the April Fifth Incident. While Wei's disillusionment with the Party was already complete and he understood the importance of these actions, he did not actively contribute; he considered Zhou as culpable as any for the Party's disastrous policies.

DEMOCRACY WALL: 1978–79

Wei finally revealed his unique talent as a writer and activist during the Democracy Wall Movement. In the two years after the April Fifth demonstrations, young worker-intellectuals like Wei seized the chance to initiate discussion of previously taboo subjects, putting up "big-character" wall posters containing daring political essays and experimental literary works at locations around the city. The activists came from a variety of backgrounds and, like Wei, had been pushed into independent thinking by the devastation of the Cultural Revolution. Some of the most cogent political arguments appeared on a long, low gray brick wall around a bus yard on Beijing's main artery, Chang'an Boulevard, which hundreds of thousands of Beijingers passed by every day. For a few months in the winter of 1978–79, this space became the focus of the movement and an unprecedented independent forum.

In 1978, by the beginning of what was to be an extremely cold winter, Beijing's political atmosphere was positively springlike. At an unusual Party meeting, members of the Central Committee severely criticized leaders identified with Cultural Revolution policies and formalized the return of Deng Xiaoping from the "cow sheds" of the Cultural Revolution. Deng was restored to his pre-1966 position as vice premier and regained his Political Bureau seat; but more importantly his faction won a definitive victory against those identified with Mao's legacy. This was the culmination of a process that had begun with the arrest of the Gang of Four, a group of Party leaders centered around Jiang Qing, soon after Mao's death in September 1976. Hope for change had focused on Deng, one of the Cultural Revolution's principal victims and a pragmatist whose most famous dictum is: "Whether the cat is black or white, as long as it catches mice, it's a good cat."

Deng's rejection of Mao's insistence on class struggle in favor of harnessing people's energies to revive the ailing economy meant the rehabilitation of many former political enemies. On November 15 the newspaper of China's intellectuals, *Guangming Daily*, announced that a hundred thousand people who had been sent to perform hard labor in the Anti-Rightist Campaign had been rehabilitated, and that the April Fifth Movement had been declared "completely revolutionary" in a ringing endorsement of independent political activism.

As he describes in a letter to Deng, Wei did not actually go to Democracy Wall until several weeks after the Beijing poster writers had launched their efforts. His first visit filled him with inspiration: In a single night he wrote "The Fifth Modernization: Democracy." With virtually no revisions, it was posted on Democracy Wall by a friend the following night, at two in the morning on December 5, 1978.

"The Fifth Modernization" argued that Deng's economic reform program—known as the "Four Modernizations" of agriculture, industry, science and technology, and defense—would not result in a real transformation of society without a fifth, democracy. What made Wei's poster a clarion call was that hardly any other activists had dared challenge the notion of "democracy," in which, as the "vanguard of the proletariat," the Party claimed to represent the people's interests for them. "Our history books tell us that the people are the masters and creators of everything, but in reality they are more like faithful servants standing at attention and waiting to be 'led' by leaders who swell like yeasted bread dough," he wrote.

The distinctive style of Wei's wall poster, pungent and full of irreverence, brought him immediate notoriety. When his youngest sister, Wei Shanshan, then studying at the Central College of Fine Arts and Crafts, went home for a visit, she told her brother the campus was abuzz with admiration for the brave author of "The Fifth Modernization." But when Wei told her he had written it, she was horrified. "You absolutely must not write that sort of thing!" she cried. Throughout his involvement in Democracy Wall, Wei's family was constantly remonstrating with him, appealing to him to think more about his safety.

Foreigners also noticed something different and direct about Wei's poster. "We were all so amazed," said Marie Holzman, a French sinologist and journalist for Agence France Presse. Eager to break out of their long isolation and to ensure that news of

Democracy Wall spread abroad, Wei and his fellows made friends among the foreign community of Beijing in defiance of unwritten prohibitions against such associations. Holzman met Wei toward the end of December 1978 and became a close friend, helping to translate his articles and introducing him to other foreign journalists. "All the others were still using the Marxist jargon, but Wei just said exactly what he thought," she said.

"The Fifth Modernization" launched Wei into a fever of activity. He hardly went to his job at the zoo anymore, and spent all the money he had on materials to propagate his ideas. As the movement developed, he and other activists realized that more people could be reached through publications than by single posters, and began to set up independent journals. The statement of purpose of *Exploration*, which Wei founded in January 1979 with a small group of like-minded activists, described the journal's guiding principles as "freedom of speech, publication, and association as provided by the Constitution."

Fully willing to enter forbidden zones, *Exploration* published the results of one of China's first human rights investigations: Wei's exposé of Qincheng, the principal prison for high-ranking political prisoners. As recently as 1993, Chinese officials denied that this jail even existed. Much material for the essay, "A Twentieth Century Bastille," came from Phuntsog Wanggyal, who had just been released from the prison. Wei described the daily regimen, the poor food, the torture, and the use of psychiatric drugs to control uncooperative prisoners, as well as the stories of some leaders imprisoned there during the Cultural Revolution.

FACING DANGER: SPRING 1979

From the very beginning, the police kept the Democracy Wall activists under surveillance, although Deng appeared to have personally endorsed their movement in November, when he remarked that it was "very good." The Party organ, *People's Daily*, had published comments approving greater freedom of speech, while avoiding reporting on the extent of the protests or on specific demands. Members of the movement had supported Deng directly or approved of his pragmatic policies; but after the movement had served his purposes in returning him to power, Deng began to reconsider this tactical alliance. More conservative leaders in the Party had long been calling for the suppression of the movement, which by the beginning of 1979 had spread to cities around the country.

In response to rumors of an impending crackdown, editors of Democracy Wall journals, including *Exploration*, argued that their activities represented a legitimate exercise of free speech in accordance with China's Constitution. By February, Deng returned from a triumphal trip to the United States, where he had been embraced by human rights champion President Jimmy Carter; now seen as de facto leader of China, Deng was determined to suppress the Democracy Wall Movement. On March 16, in a secret speech that quickly spread on Beijing's grapevine, Deng endorsed a crackdown.

Wei Jingsheng argued with other activists, including Liu Qing, an editor of *April Fifth Forum* and head of the liaison group representing the various Democracy Wall publications, over the turn events were taking. Wei insisted that Deng's plan for a crackdown should be exposed and denounced, while Liu and others felt this might bring down the Party's wrath on the movement. Two days after Wei had insisted that *Exploration* would act alone if necessary, on March 25, a biting essay—"Do We Want Democracy or New Autocracy?"—was pasted on Democracy Wall.

Most believe this article was the principal reason for Wei's arrest, which came four days after the piece appeared in a special edition of *Exploration*, and a day after regulations banning "slogans, posters, books, magazines, photographs, and other materials that oppose socialism, the dictatorship of the proletariat, the leadership of the Communist Party, and Marxism-Leninism and Mao Zedong Thought." The people must be vigilant, Wei warned, lest Deng become a dictator like Mao before him. "Does Deng Xiaoping want democracy? No, he does not. He says that the spontaneous struggle for democratic rights is just an excuse to make trouble, that it destroys the normal order and must be suppressed. Especially in politics, only if different kinds of ideas exist can the situation be called normal."

In criticizing Deng by name, Wei crossed a crucial boundary. It was not just a clear case of lèse-majesté—he was questioning the Party's fundamental commitment to reform. He realized that the Party's new line—ending Mao's focus on class struggle and instituting more pragmatic economic policies—did not necessarily involve real political change. Deng was attempting to save the CCP, not to transform it. It would be another ten years before a substantial group of top intellectuals, including most of the luminaries of the current Chinese democracy movement in exile, would reach this same conclusion.

ON TRIAL: OCTOBER 1979

Wei knew his arrest was inevitable, yet still could not quite believe that it would come. According to Liu Qing, Wei thought he would be treated leniently, but with Holzman he even discussed the possibility that he could be executed. This was not idle talk; executions of obscure political prisoners had continued even after the fall of the Gang of Four. But he was adamant that his fellow *Exploration* editors allow him to assume full responsibility for their activities, and insisted they should even testify against him if this would bring them lighter punishment.

On March 29, 1979, in the middle of the night, some twenty police officers arrived at Wei's home to take him away. Some people tried to stop them, and Wei almost escaped in the scuffle. His family knew he had been detained, but were given no information about him until he went on trial; his arrest was not reported in the media, but word soon spread among Democracy Wall activists. He disappeared into the notorious Banbuqiao, the main Beijing detention center, where for about six months he was held without trial in a solitary cell on death row. His arrest began a sweep against the movement's most outspoken activists and the closure of the hundreds of Democracy Wall publications. The total number of Democracy Wall activists arrested is not known, but around a hundred likely ended up in prisons in a nationwide crackdown that continued for two years after Wei's arrest.

Wei's October 16, 1979, trial was strictly in the tradition of communist political theater. The verdict was aimed as much at the

Chinese public as at Wei himself, and was reported in government-controlled newspapers and on TV. Democracy activists discussed the trial details widely. Politically, Wei's prosecution was considered "killing the chicken to frighten the monkey": a way for Deng to send others a clear sign that he had no intention of allowing pluralism to accompany his liberalization of the economy. Wei appeared in court wearing the prison uniform and with his head shaved, a glaring indication that he was presumed guilty. The trial was also designed as a showcase for the "socialist legality" Deng was proposing as an alternative to the mob rule of the Cultural Revolution.

Neither Liu Qing, whom Wei had asked to speak in his defense, nor Wei's family were officially informed that the trial was about to begin. The family had managed to find a young lawyer at Beijing University to defend him, but she was never given the indictment or informed of the trial date. No one from Wei's side—friends, family, or lawyers—was permitted to attend the proceedings.

Wei mounted his own outspoken defense against the state's charges that he had divulged military secrets to a foreigner and conducted "counterrevolutionary propaganda and incitement" aimed at overthrowing the socialist system. "Rule by socialist law is the embodiment of the will of the proletariat and the numerous laboring people. If we allow freedom for such a tiny minority as [Wei Jingsheng's] to spread unchecked, the larger number of the population run the risk of losing their own freedoms," the prosecution argued.

The prosecution called him "a lackey of Vietnam"—with which China was then at war—for allegedly passing "situation reports" about China's "defensive counterattack" to a foreign journalist. The charge was based on a taped conversation on February 20, in which Wei told a Reuters Beijing correspondent about China's first moves in the war, including which generals were leading the Chinese offensive, how many troops were being mobilized, and casualty figures. This information had been known to many Beijing residents, including most of the Democracy Wall activists. "Never once in the period that followed the outbreak of the Sino-Vietnamese War did I come into contact with anything whatsoever marked as a classified secret," Wei said. "Thus, there is no question of my furnishing anyone with anything that can be described as secret in the terms of the legal definition."

The main thrust of Wei's defense focused on his writings and the publishing of *Exploration*, which the prosecution had labeled "counterrevolutionary." He rejected this description. Candid discussion of problems and new ideas was vital if China's polity was to develop, he argued. "Criticism may not always be pretty or pleasant to hear, nor can it always be completely accurate," he continued. "If one insists on hearing pleasant criticism only and demands its absolute accuracy on pain of punishment, this is as good as forbidding criticism and banning reforms altogether." All his activities had been a legitimate exercise of his constitutional right to freedom of expression, Wei argued, and he had no intention of overthrowing the government, the Party, or socialism. "We never once joined up with any conspiratorial organization, nor did we ever take part in the activities of any violent organization," he said.

Since Wei had refused to plead guilty, the prosecution had called for a severe sentence for him. But the fifteen-year term came as a shock, even to the handpicked trial audience, according to Liu Qing, who saw them emerging, somber-faced, from the courtroom.

Protests against the sentence were heard around the world. Soviet dissident Andrei Sakharov appealed for Wei in a telegram addressed "with deep respect" to then Premier Hua Guofeng: "I ask you to use your influence to review the sentence of Wei Jingsheng," he wrote. Democracy Wall activists spoke out vigorously and within days were circulating the transcript of his trial made from a tape handed over by a sympathetic Chinese journalist. *April Fifth Forum* had the temerity to publish it in full, which led to the arrest of several people, including Liu Qing. The Chinese press, however, generally applauded the verdict, and most of the just-rehabilitated older critics were silent. Deng is widely thought to have decided Wei's arrest, sentence, and conditions of imprisonment personally; Wei certainly believes that this was the case.

During his years of imprisonment, Wei suffered deprivations that, he believed, were expressly intended to make him die of "natural causes." In these early years in Banbuqiao, he was beaten by trusties—prisoners trusted by the guards and assigned to watch him. Apart from an appeal against his sentence, he was generally not permitted to write, and there are no letters from the first two years. For much of the time his only reading material was the *People's Daily*. "I can't believe that because I have become a criminal, even the books I read are implicated and become counterrevolutionary," he complained.

In the summer of 1981 Wei was transferred to a solitary cell in the "strict-regime brigade"—the punishment section—of Beijing No. 1 Prison. He was permitted his first family visit soon after the transfer, and from then on his sisters and brother (Wei addresses them in his letters as Lingling, Taotao, and Shanshan) were able to see him every two or three months. By mutual agreement—but with much sadness on Wei's part—he and Ping Ni ended their engagement, and she did not visit or correspond with him.

Wei had to learn to deal with the crushing isolation. Even the guards were forbidden to speak to him. "The loneliness, the impression that no one was concerned about me anymore weighed on me terribly," he later told Marie Holzman. "In 1984, it was difficult for me to speak, since my vocal cords had lost the habit of functioning." He was not allowed to leave his tiny cell for almost two years. The light was left on all night, disrupting his sleep, and the already inadequate food became increasingly meager. "When I asked to buy fruit with the money my brother and sisters sent me," Wei said, "they just laughed in my face." Normally, if prisoners had money, they could ask the guards to purchase food.

His health declined precipitously. His teeth began to fall out as a result of severe gum disease, and he could barely chew the coarse grains that were his main food. The poor diet also caused serious digestive problems. He developed high blood pressure and rheumatoid arthritis. After suffering chest pain and weakness for some time, he was finally taken to the Beijing Public Security

Hospital in mid-1983, where doctors diagnosed him with heart disease and apparently said that the conditions under which he was imprisoned were "life-threatening."

In these desperate times, Wei wrote long letters to his siblings reminiscing about the past and exploring ideas on art, history, literature, politics, and the general hostility in Chinese culture to creative people with unusual points of view. Although he spoke of his own living conditions only obliquely, few of these letters were approved to be sent. Much to the chagrin of his guards, Wei also subverted the Party's thought reform technique of requiring prisoners to express their "reflections" by commenting on an official document. For example, prisoners were undoubtedly supposed to praise the revised Constitution as the apotheosis of Deng's efforts to establish a legal system, but Wei preferred to explain how, by prescribing a particular political line, the Constitution had guaranteed its own obsolescence. Those in charge of "educating" Wei sometimes complained that his intransigence endangered them!

He was usually permitted to write only one letter a month to his family, and those letters were often not mailed but kept in a prison file instead. However, his jailers told him he could write to the "higher authorities" as much as he liked. Consequently, he filled hundreds of pages with questions and comments, on such subjects as the history and future of Tibet, his own health, the treatment of political prisoners, the development of China's economy, and human rights. There is no indication whether the intended recipients ever read these missives, but Wei speaks to them as if they were engaged in an ongoing dialogue. "I've written to you so many times now that I'm probably beginning to get on your nerves," began a 1989 letter to Deng.

Apart from reporting his illnesses, asking for release on medical parole, or proper medical attention at the very least, one of Wei's most frequent requests to the leaders was that he be allowed to contribute to the construction of the nation and to have access to books so he could study. He had begun to turn his mind to the practical science that had fascinated him as a youth, drawing up plans for inventions like an energy-saving pressure cooker and a wind-resistant lighter, as well as a scheme to solve water shortages by towing icebergs from the Arctic to China's coast. He tried to send his plans and sketches to his siblings but was prevented from doing so, with the only explanation being that it was "against the regulations."

In April 1984, Wei wrote to Party leaders asking to be exiled to the remote region of northwestern China, where he hoped he might at least be able to do some useful work to reclaim the arid, uninhabitable lands there. That fall Wei was transferred to a *laogai* (a prison similar to the Russian "gulag," the term literally means "reform through labor") camp at Tanggemu Farm, in Qinghai province. The three-thousand-meter altitude of the desert plateau exacerbated his headaches, but his health initially appeared to have improved somewhat, although the severe cold of the winters affected him badly, and his teeth continued to fall out. Wei was not allowed to carry out the desert reclamation work he had hoped to do, but he was able to go outside on occasion and for a period of time was allowed to raise rabbits in a nearby cell. Although he was still held in solitary confinement, Wei had some contact with the three other prisoners in the tiny "politicals" wing. Ironically, two were former enemies, the most notorious Red Guard leaders in the pro–Jiang Qing faction during the Cultural Revolution.

During this time, Wei saw his brother and sisters only once, or at most twice, a year. His siblings all suffered varying degrees of discrimination because of his status and were pressured to "participate in educating Wei" before they went to see him. Every encounter was recorded. "If we asked anything about his situation, about the conditions in the prison or how he was treated, the guards would immediately say, 'It is not permitted to talk about such things,'" recalled Wei Shanshan. But they continued to appeal for him to receive medical treatment and attempted to have his case reopened.

In all his years in prison, Wei Jingsheng never knew of the campaigns being waged for his release. He certainly would not have heard that, at the beginning of 1989, astrophysicist and democracy advocate Fang Lizhi sent an open letter to Deng calling for Wei and other political prisoners to be released to mark the fortieth anniversary of the People's Republic of China. An amnesty, Fang said, would show the Party's commitment to the political reform Deng had promised a decade before. Other intellectuals within

China and Chinese students abroad issued similar open letters, contributing to the ferment that culminated in the 1989 pro-democracy demonstrations on Tiananmen Square in Beijing. Wei had become living proof of the Party's bad faith.

Political reform was the initial focus of demonstrations launched by Beijing students in April 1989, following the death of former CCP General Secretary Hu Yaobang, who had been considered a proponent of political liberalization. The protests were spurred by a series of significant anniversaries, including that of the 1919 May Fourth Movement, a seminal event marking the birth of Chinese nationalism in which students mobilized the country in opposition to the granting of Chinese territory to Japan in the treaty concluding World War I. In 1989, students with an equally strong sense of mission occupied Tiananmen Square for weeks and engaged in an emotive hunger strike to press their demands for dialogue with the government. Gradually demonstrations spread to cities around the country and drew in people from all walks of life. By the middle of May, over a million marchers crammed the streets of Beijing.

Attempts at compromise culminated in a dramatic televised meeting between a stern Premier Li Peng and hunger-striking students in pajamas, but failed, as Li and Deng pronounced the movement "turmoil" and declared martial law in Beijing on May 20. Party General Secretary Zhao Ziyang was forced to resign after opposing this move. A tense standoff ensued until the night of June 3, when the People's Liberation Army stormed the city with tanks and machine guns, killing and wounding hundreds, perhaps even thousands, of unarmed civilians. What the official media described as the "suppression of the counterrevolutionary rebellion" was the start of a nationwide crackdown in which thousands of protestors, young and old, were sent to labor camps.

The usual censorship of media broke down for some days as journalists joined and reported on the demonstrations, and thus Wei Jingsheng, locked away in remote Qinghai, learned of the protests and their bloody conclusion. "You've already set a precedent of using the military to decide political questions, so once you are dead, what Communist Party official will rely solely on his mouth and pen, and swear off the use of tanks, machine guns, and large artillery?" Wei asked Deng. "How will you deal with the hoodlums who make up the so-called 'people's army,' but who eat the people's food and use guns purchased by the people to kill the people?"

In late summer 1989, Wei was again transferred, this time to the Nanpu New Life Salt Works, a massive labor camp on the Bohai Gulf near the city of Tangshan. He was told this was for his health, as he and his family had long been requesting a transfer. But although the weather was less harsh in the new location, Wei found the human climate much worse. He was not able to bathe for months at a time, was not permitted to have a heater in his damp cell, had less access to reading materials, and was allowed no contact with fellow prisoners. The prison doctors refused to diagnose the illnesses from which he had long suffered or to treat his worsening condition. "They are police doctors worthy of the name," Wei wrote. By the end of the year, he was requesting transfer back to Tanggemu. Wei protested numerous times for improvements in living conditions for himself and other political prisoners and for a reexamination of his case. He staged a number of hunger strikes; during one, lasting close to a hundred days, he consumed only a teaspoon of sugar dissolved in water per day.

RELEASE: *1993*

International concern about the situation of China's political prisoners reached a high point after the suppression of the 1989 democracy movement, and governments and human rights organizations around the globe called for Wei's release. In May 1992, the first picture of Wei seen abroad since his trial was published in a pro-Beijing magazine in Hong Kong. The picture showed a doctor looking into Wei's mouth and was said to disprove reports that he had been tortured and lost his teeth.

As the final year of his term began, questions began to be raised about whether Wei would be allowed out the following year. Early in 1993, a Ministry of Justice official replied to inquiries about Wei from U.S. human rights activist and businessman John Kamm: "Frankly, his reform is going too slowly. He persists in his strong anti-government attitude. And his attitude is not cooperative. He likes to rise late and then stay up late watching TV. He always likes to argue with and try to refute the guards."

Just before the 1993 anniversary of his arrest, the government released to the foreign press a videotape of Wei made around the New Year, showing him being taken on a trip to a museum and a store in Tangshan before eating a large meal and visiting the dentist. The tape, which was not shown in China, was a first salvo in an aggressive Chinese government campaign to win Beijing the 2000 Olympic Games. Wei had also been taken on a visit to Beijing in the hope that, seeing the bustling commerce, new highways, and towering hotels of the capital, he would say he had been wrong about China's need for a "fifth modernization." But when Kamm asked what impact the visits had had on Wei's views, the official admitted "None whatsoever," a conclusion confirmed by the final letter in this collection. The official insisted that unless Wei's behavior and attitude changed, he would not be considered for early release.

But suddenly, on September 14, 1993, nine days before the International Olympic Committee's vote on Beijing's bid, the authorities put out pictures and videotape of Wei signing papers for his release on probation. Wei had exacted concessions of his own: He refused to leave prison without the hundreds of pages of letters and comments he had written over the years. He "voluntarily" stayed in a guest house outside Beijing for a week before returning home. Just before the decision on Beijing's Olympic bid, Wei told *The New York Times* that trading political prisoners for the games was "dirty and abnormal." At any rate, his release seemed to boomerang, further focusing the world's attention on China's human rights record. Beijing ended up losing the privilege of hosting the games to Sydney by a very close margin.

Wei had been told he was prohibited from speaking to the media or expressing his opinions, as well as from setting up any kind of organization or even doing business, until his parole ended in March 1994. After that date, according to his original sentence, he was still to be deprived of his political rights for three years. Yet, days after his release, Wei told journalists that he would continue to press for democratization and respect for human rights and would bring a lawsuit challenging his conviction. He fully expected to be jailed again, he said, because he rejected the validity of restrictions on his right to free expression. Wei ignored the authorities' specific injunction against speaking about his time in jail, but he was not particularly interested in reexamining the past. He was looking toward the future, worrying about the potential for conflict created by a government that he believed had cut itself off from the people.

His family and friends begged him to lay low for a while: He was still seriously ill. Wei suspected that the prison authorities had secretly laced his food with steroids to produce the speedy weight gain that had left him looking healthily chubby on his release. He continued to loose teeth—only twelve remained on his release—making a joke of it when one fell out during a meal. Although his doctor had told him that if he spent time resting he could gradually make a full recovery from the heart condition that left him exhausted after walking only a short distance, Wei immediately resumed his activism.

Weeks after his release he sought out Ding Zilin, a People's University professor whose seventeen-year-old son had died when he was shot in the head on the night of June 3, 1989. Since then, Ding has devoted her life to collecting the names of those killed and wounded during the military crackdown, channeling assistance from overseas groups to the bereaved families and the injured and helping such people to support each other in the face of government harassment and discrimination. Wei was ready to give Ding all the money from various prizes he had been awarded. She dissuaded him, reminding him that he would need money for his own life, but he did contribute significant resources to her work.

Living first in his father's house and later in an apartment belonging to his brother, Wei met with many of his old friends and gave freely of his time to dissidents and journalists alike, talking for hours wreathed in the smoke of endless cigarettes. He set up an office staffed by a young secretary and interpreter, Tong Yi, a veteran of the 1989 student movement, and went around Beijing with a wallet stuffed full of bills. At the homes of needy friends, he would quietly slip several hundred yuan into a book on the table or stuff banknotes into their pockets.

In moments between the constant stream of visitors, Wei tried to write, but his hand would quickly tire and he would be left exhausted. However, he did manage to write two opinion pieces for *The New York Times*, and a number of columns and articles for Hong Kong papers. In his first piece, a November 18 editorial in *The New York Times* published on the eve of a Sino-U.S. summit in Seattle between President Jiang Zemin and President Bill Clinton, Wei bravely argued for the United States to increase pressure on China to improve human rights, a position the Chinese leadership considered virtually tantamount to treason.

"If there wasn't international pressure," Wei told a reporter around this time, "a lot of political prisoners wouldn't have been set free, including me. According to the standards of the CCP, many of us, including me, would have been executed." Pressure had also contributed to a growing sense of rights among ordinary people. "Many Communist Party cadres at least now have the concept of human rights and of the violation of human rights," he said. But Wei pointed out that the major force for change had to come from within China. Democratization would not happen merely through a change of leadership, he said, but could only be built through a slow, painful process starting at the grassroots. He had hope, since he believed that this had already begun and was gathering strength.

DISAPPEARED: APRIL 1994

Wei was under constant, often obtrusive, surveillance. The Public Security Bureau repeatedly threatened him with rearrest, warning him that as a "criminal" released on parole he was not permitted to grant interviews or publish his own writings. But his courage and continued outspokenness gave new impetus to the dissident movement in a China otherwise preoccupied with commerce. Although he was not personally involved in any of the various dissident initiatives launched in 1993 and 1994—he thought his name would merely jeopardize them—he provided inspiration and counsel for many activists as they increasingly focused their efforts on practical means for addressing human rights problems, such as filing lawsuits to seek redress for abuses and raising money for victims of repression.

This new wave of activism coincided with increased pressure on the Chinese government by the United States. In May 1993, President Clinton declared that he would not renew China's Most Favored Nation trading status the following year unless clear progress was made on human rights, and the deadline for a decision was fast approaching. When John Shattuck, U.S. assistant secretary of state for human rights and humanitarian affairs, was sent to Beijing, he met Wei for dinner on the evening of February 27, 1994. In their conversation, Wei insisted that the United States should extend Most Favored Nation status—sanctions would only hurt ordinary people, not officials, he argued—while continuing its pressure on China to improve human rights.

This meeting outraged the Chinese authorities: It was the first time a dissident in China had met with a high-ranking visiting U.S. diplomat. Even before he left China, officials were accusing Shattuck of having "broken Chinese law." Wei was detained for "questioning" for twenty-four hours. Then, on March 5, 1994, he was sent on a "tour" in the company of a high-ranking officer in the political section of the Beijing Public Security Bureau. For the next three weeks, he was moved to locations including Tianjin and Hebei province, but was able to telephone his father every day.

By the end of the month, Wei insisted on returning to Beijing. According to Tong Yi, who went to bring him home, she and Wei were in a car on April 1 driving back to Beijing from Tianjin when about seven police cars pulled them over. While Wei was taken away, Tong Yi returned to Beijing and reported his detention to the foreign press. On April 5, she was present during a search of Wei's apartment during which manuscripts, bank books, and cash were confiscated. That same day Tong Yi too was detained. On December 22, 1994, she was sentenced to a two-and-a-half-year term of Reeducation Through Labor, an administrative penalty that requires no trial, for "disturbing social order." In the labor camp near her hometown of Wuhan, she was savagely beaten by other prisoners and forced to work extremely long hours.

A few days after Wei's detention, a Foreign Ministry spokesman told reporters Wei had "broken the law and must be prosecuted." He described Wei and other dissidents as "outsiders cut off from the Chinese reality." But in classic double-speak, for almost two years the authorities responded to queries about Wei's whereabouts by denying that he was in detention. He had disappeared into a legal limbo, held under "residential surveillance," theoretically a form of house arrest. His family was told only that he was in a "hotel" in the Beijing suburbs and requests to send him clothing, books, or other personal items were refused.

In May 1995, a year after Wei's disappearance, Wei Shanshan returned from Germany, where she had lived since 1990, to find out what had happened to her brother. She spent several weeks visiting government departments, and often officials admitted to her that Wei's detention appeared to violate legal procedures. But, they said, there was nothing they could do, because they were "carrying out orders from above."

SECOND TRIAL: DECEMBER 1995

There had always been some hope that Wei's long incommunicado detention meant that the Chinese authorities felt constrained by possible international reaction from taking further action against him. Rumors that Wei was to be tried on treason charges had appeared periodically in the foreign media but had been denied. Finally, almost twenty months after Wei's disappearance, the authorities announced his formal arrest on November 21, 1995, and that he would stand trial. This was the culmination of a concerted campaign against the resurgent dissident movement of 1993–94, in which virtually all the leading campaigners for democracy and human rights had been detained.

The news of Wei's formal arrest brought condemnation from around the world, and even in China a number of dissidents braved the frigid political atmosphere to issue statements about the prosecution of Wei. Ding Zilin wrote of Wei's selfless support for her work with victims of the Beijing Massacre; a group of dissidents in Zhejiang province appealed for Wei's release and were promptly detained themselves.

While the prosecution had had over twenty months to develop

its case, Wei's family was given just ten days. On December 3, Wei Ling was told she should find a lawyer for her brother, as he had been given the indictment on December 1, but she was not given a copy. She and Wei Xiaotao engaged Zhang Sizhi, who had defended a number of prominent dissidents, and another lawyer to act for Wei. They were informed of the trial date on December 8, less than a week before it was to begin. The lawyers were only able to meet with Wei Jingsheng two or three days before the trial opened on December 13, and had less than twenty-four hours to review a 1,996-page case dossier.

Although Wei Ling and Wei Xiaotao were able to attend the trial and the two defense lawyers were allowed to challenge the prosecution's arguments on both legal and substantive grounds, the proceedings were actually little different from Wei's first trial. In fact, the Beijing Intermediate People's Court spent less time hearing Wei's case than it had in 1979. A few days before, an official spokesman had said that Wei would have an "open trial." But as usual the "public" was represented by a handpicked audience while hundreds of police kept reporters, foreign diplomats, and a handful of Wei's friends and supporters far away from the courthouse.

Again the prosecution based its charges primarily on Wei's writings, including the prison letters on human rights and Tibet— which appear in this collection—that had been published in the fall of 1993 in the overseas Chinese press. The publication of these writings and Wei's efforts to promote human rights and democracy were labeled "illegal activities under the cloak of legality." The actions cited by the prosecution included encouraging the United States to pressure China to improve human rights, buying shares in a credit union, planning an art exhibition, discussing the "struggle" with friends inside and outside China, and collecting names of "political victims" and their families who needed financial assistance in order to arrange for overseas groups to help them.

The trial was riddled with procedural errors: Wei's lawyers had not been shown all the evidence, and at one point a shoving match broke out as a prosecutor tried to stop Zhang Sizhi from looking at a key document; none of the witnesses the defense had asked to be called gave evidence.

Wei presented a forceful defense statement, despite his poor health—he had to stop to rest and take medicine in the middle of his speech while the court recessed for twenty minutes. Little had changed politically since the Cultural Revolution, he said, if the kind of economic, labor, humanitarian, and cultural activities he had discussed and engaged in were still considered illegal. "We resort to no illegal means in our democracy movement. We have limited ourselves to mass political activities of a general nature as well as cultural and art activities. Nothing could be further from any 'conspiracy,' " he argued.

On the question of his writings, Wei denounced the prosecution's attempt to twist his reasoned disquisition on Tibet policy and history—aimed at rectifying errors that were destroying the possibility of a real unity between Tibet and China—into an intention to "split the motherland." He defended his right to speak and write freely. "Actions to promote human rights and democracy and to expose and fight against the enemies of democracy and human rights do not constitute a crime," Wei concluded.

His eloquent words fell on deaf ears. After a break for lunch, the court issued a typewritten verdict that repeated the indictment's conclusions almost verbatim, finding Wei guilty and sentencing him to fourteen years' imprisonment and three years' deprivation of political rights. On December 28, Wei's appeal was dismissed with even greater alacrity, and he was sent back to his old cell at the Nanpu New Life Salt Works.

Wei's sentence was condemned around the globe—parliaments held hearings, there were appeals to the Chinese government to reconsider—to no avail. There has been a worldwide campaign to nominate Wei for the Nobel Peace Prize. He has won numerous awards including in 1995 the Olof Palme Award, and in 1996 the European Parliament's Sakharov Prize for Freedom of Thought. The Chinese authorities have reacted angrily to the Nobel nomination, protesting that as a "criminal" Wei is not qualified for the prize. The many parliamentarians, university professors, and former Peace Prize winners who have nominated him—in 1996, these included 81 members of the U.S. Congress, 12 members of Hong Kong's Legislative Council, 110 British MPs, and the Dalai Lama—clearly do not agree.

Since Wei's twenty months in incommunicado detention were not counted toward his sentence, he is not due for release until 2009. Friends and family wonder if he will survive that long. Following their visit to Wei after his trial, his siblings reported that he was calm and smiling but could hardly walk because his joints were so swollen. His heart condition has recently worsened. The small concessions he had won during his last stay at Nanpu, such as a heater, have now been withdrawn, and in the spring of 1996, five criminal prisoners were moved into his cell to keep watch over him.

Although Wei has had little opportunity to work with fellow dissidents or develop a career, his unswerving commitment to universal principles has made him the paramount symbol of the fight for democracy and human rights in China. Despite the fact that he has remained behind bars for most of the past two decades and his writings have never been published officially inside the country, he has inspired several generations of Chinese activists. Wei himself is sustained in his lonely struggle by the knowledge that history is on his side, as the experience of fellow dissidents such as Nelson Mandela, Václav Havel, and Andrei Sakharov shows. Supporters of democracy and reform, he pointed out at his 1995 trial, are "in harmony with the historical trend," while it is the "autocratic conservatives" who stand in the way of human progress.

Glossary

AH Q—Fictional character in Lu Xun's famous 1921 satire, *The True Story of Ah Q*, in which Ah Q foolishly rationalizes all his defeats into victories, leading ultimately to his own execution; Lu Xun considered "Ah Q-ism" a flaw in the Chinese national character.

AMBAN—Civil official appointed to Lhasa as the representative of the Chinese emperor to the Tibetan government during the Qing dynasty (1644–1911).

ANTI-RIGHTIST CAMPAIGN—Political movement launched by Mao Zedong in late 1957 aimed at intellectuals who voiced criticisms of Chinese Communist Party (CCP) leadership during the Hundred Flowers Campaign earlier that year; over five hundred thousand intellectuals were labeled "rightists" and sent to labor camps or banished to the countryside.

APRIL FIFTH FORUM—Unofficial Democracy Wall Movement journal edited by Liu Qing and others; named after the spontaneous public demonstrations of April 5, 1976.

APRIL FIFTH INCIDENT—Public demonstrations on Tiananmen Square on April 5, 1976, following the death of Premier Zhou Enlai that came to symbolize the end of the Cultural Revolution.

BANBUQIAO—Main detention center in Beijing where Wei Jingsheng was held from the time of his arrest in 1979 until his transfer to Beijing

Number One Prison in 1991; he often refers to his solitary confinement cell at Banbuqiao as "Cell Forty-four."

BEIJING MASSACRE—Violent government crackdown on unarmed pro-democracy demonstrators in Beijing on June 3–4, 1989; also referred to as the June Fourth or Tiananmen Square Massacre.

BO YIBO (1908–)—High-ranking Party official and economic reformer before he was purged during the Cultural Revolution; rehabilitated following Deng's ascension to power in the late 1970s.

CENTRAL COMMITTEE—Highest ruling body of the Chinese Communist Party; the Political Bureau and Standing Committee are drawn from its members.

CHEN YI (1901–1972)—Early CCP member and military leader; foreign minister and a prominent member of the Central Committee when he came under attack by Mao in 1968 for voicing criticisms of the Cultural Revolution.

CHEN YUN (1905–1995)—Leading CCP economic planner in the 1950s who fell out of favor during the Cultural Revolution but regained high-level Party and government posts in the 1980s as a supporter of economic reform, although he remained a formidable critic of bourgeois liberalization.

CHIANG CHING-KUO (1909–1988)—Son of Chiang Kai-shek, inherited father's position as president of Taiwan from 1978 until his death.

CHIANG KAI-SHEK (1887–1975)—Leader of the Nationalist Party since the 1920s and president of the Nationalist government in Taiwan from 1949 until his death.

CHINESE PEOPLE'S POLITICAL CONSULTATIVE CONFERENCE (CPPCC)—Chinese government institution coordinating formal interaction between Party and state leaders, mass organizations, and other consultative bodies.

CIXI (1835–1908)—"Empress Dowager" and de facto ruler of the late Qing dynasty government as regent to three successive emperors; resisted reform efforts until too late to save the Qing from collapse in 1911 following her death.

"CLEAR OUT THREE TYPES OF PEOPLE"—Political movement called for in the early 1980s aimed at diminishing the influence of those deemed to be sympathetic with the causes of the Gang of Four and the Cultural Revolution.

CULTURAL REVOLUTION—Political movement launched in 1966 by Mao Zedong to regain credibility after the debacle of the Great Leap Forward and reinvigorate political fervor outside of the CCP institutional framework; officially ended with the arrest of the Gang of Four in October 1976.

DALAI LAMA—Institution housing the successive reincarnations of the supreme spiritual and political leader of Tibetan Buddhism and Tibet; the current Dalai Lama has lived in exile in India since fleeing China in 1959.

DEMOCRACY WALL MOVEMENT—Grassroots pro-democracy movement of 1978–79, named for posters displayed on a large wall in the Xidan section of Beijing, during which Wei Jingsheng first came to prominence for his "Fifth Modernization" wall poster.

DENG XIAOPING (1904–1997)—Communist Party member since youth, who rose to high official posts in the 1950s and 1960s only to be purged twice during the Cultural Revolution before establishing self as China's paramount leader after Mao in the late 1970s; architect of reforms in the 1980s as well as responsible for ordering the 1989 Beijing Massacre.

DING LING (1904–1986)—Prominent woman writer and Communist Party member; imprisoned for over twenty years during the anti-rightist campaign and the Cultural Revolution; rehabilitated in the 1970s.

DREAM OF THE RED CHAMBER—Eighteenth-century novel by Cao Xueqin depicting the downfall of a large and powerful family; considered a masterpiece of classical Chinese fiction; its main character, Jia Baoyu, is a romantic boy plagued by his own sentimentalities.

DUAN QIRUI (1865–1936)—Premier of China after the death of Yuan Shikai in 1916 and during the signing of the Versailles Treaty in 1919 that transferred former German territory in China into Japanese hands.

"ELIMINATE SPIRITUAL POLLUTION"—Political movement initiated by Deng Xiaoping and several conservative CCP elders in 1983 aimed at eradicating "decadent" Western influences in Chinese art and culture.

EXPLORATION—Unofficial journal edited by Wei Jingsheng and others for several months in early 1979 during the Democracy Wall Movement.

FAN ZENG (1938–)—Well-known traditional-style Chinese painter.

FANFAN—Wei Jingsheng's niece; his sister Wei Ling's daughter.

FANG LIZHI (1936–)—Astrophysicist and the most outspoken Chinese intellectual on human rights and democracy in the 1980s; sought sanctuary in the U.S. Embassy in Beijing following the 1989 Beijing Massacre, and currently resides in the U.S.

"THE FIFTH MODERNIZATION"—"Democracy" as Wei Jingsheng referred to it in his December 5, 1978, Democracy Wall poster of the same title (see Appendix I).

"THE FIVE BLACK ELEMENTS"—Landlords, rich peasants, counter-revolutionaries, bad elements, and rightists—designations used for members of society regarded as "class enemies" by CCP ideology, particularly during the Cultural Revolution; most such labels were removed after 1979.

FOUR CARDINAL PRINCIPLES—Guiding political principles advocated by Deng Xiaoping in 1979: to uphold the socialist road, the dictatorship of the proletariat, the leadership of the Communist Party, and Marxist–Leninist–Mao Zedong Thought.

FOUR MODERNIZATIONS—Domestic policy goals introduced first by Premier Zhou Enlai in 1975 to spur development in the four areas of agriculture, industry, national defense, and science and technology.

GANG OF FOUR—Refers to Jiang Qing (Mao Zedong's wife), Yao Wenyuan, Zhang Chunqiao, and Wang Hongwen, who were arrested in 1976 and subsequently officially blamed for and convicted of orchestrating the Cultural Revolution as a tool for promoting their own goals.

GREAT LEAP FORWARD—Mass campaign initiated by Mao Zedong in 1958 to dramatically speed up economic productivity through establishing "people's communes" and decentralizing industrial production; resulted in widespread famine.

HAN AIJING—Leading Red Guard in the pro–Jiang Qing faction during the Cultural Revolution who was later imprisoned in the solitary confinement wing of Tanggemu *laogai* in Qinghai with Wei Jingsheng.

HE DONGCHANG (1923–)—Vice-director of the State Education Commission and government spokesperson during the 1989 pro-democracy student demonstrations on Tiananmen Square.

Hᴜ Yᴀᴏʙᴀɴɢ (1915–1989)—CCP general secretary and Deng's protégé until his 1987 dismissal from all official posts for views seen as too liberal by conservative Party elders. His sudden death in April 1989 helped to trigger the student demonstrations on Tiananmen Square that culminated in the Beijing Massacre of June 4, 1989.

Hᴜᴀ Gᴜᴏꜰᴇɴɢ (1921–)—President of China and chairman of the CCP following Mao Zedong's death in 1976, who subsequently lost power to Deng Xiaoping and his followers in 1978.

Jɪᴀɴɢ Qɪɴɢ (1914–1991)—Former film actress who became Mao Zedong's third wife and whose attacks on feudalism and bourgeois ideology during the Cultural Revolution led to her 1976 arrest as leader of the Gang of Four, for which she was tried in 1981 and received a death sentence, later commuted to life under house arrest.

Jɪᴀɴɢ Zᴇᴍɪɴ (1926–)—Current CCP general secretary, president of China, and chairman of the Central Military Commission; former mayor and CCP chief in Shanghai who rose to national power following the 1989 Beijing Massacre.

ᴊɪɴ—Unit of weight slightly heavier than a pound (1 *jin* = 0.5 kilogram).

Kᴜᴀɪ Dᴀꜰᴜ—Leading Red Guard in the pro–Jiang Qing faction during the Cultural Revolution who was later imprisoned in the same labor camp as Wei Jingsheng in Qinghai.

ʟᴀᴏɢᴀɪ—Chinese abbreviation for "reform through labor"; prison camps often likened to the Soviet "gulags" where prisoners are subject to hard labor and political reeducation.

Lᴇɪ Fᴇɴɢ (1940–1962)—A mythical soldier in the People's Liberation Army whose selfless devotion to the people and the Communist Party made him a role model used in propaganda campaigns since the early 1960s.

Lɪ Bᴀɪ (Lɪ Pᴏ, 701–762)—One of the Tang dynasty (618–907) masters of classical Chinese poetry best known for his poems on the joys of wine, nature, and friendship.

Lɪ Dɪɴɢᴍɪɴɢ (1881–1947)—An "enlightened" former landlord who was praised by Mao Zedong in his famous 1944 speech "Serve the People" for offering criticism of Communist Party policy.

LI PENG (1928–)—Premier of China since 1988; dubbed the "Butcher of Beijing" for his role in ordering the military suppression of unarmed pro-democracy demonstrators in 1989.

LI XIANNIAN (1909–1992)—Party elder since the 1950s who held high positions, including president of China from 1983 to 1987.

LIBERATION—Term commonly used to refer to 1949 or, more precisely, October 1, 1949, when Mao Zedong declared the founding of the People's Republic of China.

LIN BIAO (1908–1971)—Leader of the People's Liberation Army and minister of defense from 1958; Mao Zedong's acknowledged successor during the Cultural Revolution who died mysteriously in a plane crash supposedly after a failed coup against Mao.

LINGLING—Family nickname for Wei Ling, Wei Jingsheng's younger sister, a doctor currently living in Beijing.

LITTLE CUI—Painter and friend of Wei Jingsheng's in the mid-1970s.

LITTLE YING—Painter and daughter of art teacher to Wei Shanshan, Wei Jingsheng's sister.

LIU BINYAN (1925–)—Former investigative reporter for the *People's Daily* who was expelled from the Communist Party both in the Anti-Rightist Campaign in the 1950s and in 1987 after writing articles exposing official corruption.

LIU QING (1946–)—Central figure during the Democracy Wall Movement and coeditor of the unofficial journal *April Fifth Forum*; imprisoned for ten years for publishing the transcript of Wei Jingsheng's 1979 trial and smuggling his own writings out from prison.

LIU SHAOQI (1898–1969)—Powerful CCP leader and theoretician until 1966, when he was purged as a "capitalist roader" during the Cultural Revolution, placed under house arrest, and died following a beating by Red Guards.

LU XUN (1881–1936)—China's best-known modern writer and author of *The True Story of Ah Q*; famous for his scathing critiques of China's backward thinking and feudal mentality.

LU YOU (1125–1210)—Prolific Song dynasty (960–1279) poet well known for his romanticism, individualism, and patriotism.

MAO ZEDONG (1893–1976)—Founding leader of the People's Republic of China in 1949 and supreme leader of the Communist Party and the country until his death.

NANPU NEW LIFE SALT WORKS—*Laogai* prison camp in Tangshan, Hebei province, where Wei Jingsheng was imprisoned from late summer 1989 until his release in 1993, and where he is currently serving a fourteen-year term.

NATIONAL PEOPLE'S CONGRESS (NPC)—Constitutionally, the sovereign organ of the Chinese government; its delegates are elected on the provincial level and meet every year to pass legislation, amend the constitution, and elect government officials including officers of the Supreme People's Court and Procuratorate; has little real authority to generate legislation independently of its Standing Committee or the CCP Central Committee.

NATIONALIST PARTY (GUOMINDANG, KMT)—Ruling party in China from 1927 on and the current dominant party on Taiwan.

PENG DEHUAI (1898–1974)—Early member of the CCP and venerated general who was purged from his position as minister of defense after criticizing Mao Zedong's Great Leap Forward policies in 1959.

PENG ZHEN (1902–)—Mayor of Beijing during the 1950s and early 1960s who was purged in the Cultural Revolution and regained prominent position in the CCP Central Committee and as chairman of the Standing Committee of the National People's Congress during the 1980s.

PHUNTSOG WANGGYAL (1921–)—Former leader of the Tibetan Communist Party imprisoned from 1960 to 1978 for his "nationalist tendencies"; father of Wei Jingsheng's former fiancée, Ping Ni.

PING NI—Wei Jingsheng's former fiancée, daughter of former head of the Tibetan Communist Party, Phuntsog Wanggyal.

QIN SHIHUANG (221–206 B.C.)—Known as the "First Emperor," the founder of the Qin dynasty whose ruthless purges of cultural figures are as legendary as the opulence of the tombs filled with clay soldiers he left behind in the present-day city of Xi'an.

RED GUARDS—Bands of university and secondary school students formed under the direction of Mao Zedong during the early Cultural Revolution who led attacks on "reactionary" social elements. As a member of an anti–Jiang Qing faction of the Red Guards, Wei Jingsheng participated in the violent factional clashes before the Red Guards were disbanded in the 1968.

REFORM THROUGH LABOR—*See LAOGAI.*

SECRETARIAT—CCP body that carries out day-to-day administration of the CCP under the leadership of the general secretary and the direction of the Standing Committee.

SHANSHAN—Wei Shanshan, Wei Jingsheng's youngest sister, an artist who presently lives in Hamburg, Germany.

SONG RENQIONG—Party elder who was purged during the Cultural Revolution and regained leadership roles in the 1980s, including acting chairman of the Central Advisory Commission in 1987.

STRICT-REGIME BRIGADE (YANGUANDUI)—Section of prison where offenders who are unwilling to admit their crimes are kept for severe punishment; Wei Jingsheng was in the strict-regime brigade for most of his imprisonment.

"STRIKE HARD"—Periodic crackdown campaigns on crime and corruption initiated by Deng Xiaoping and CCP elders beginning in 1983.

SU SHI (SU TUNG-P'O, 1037–1101)—Poet, essayist, and calligrapher of the Song dynasty (960–1279); the poem Wei quotes, known by the title "Prelude to Water Music," is based on an earlier drinking poem by Li Bai.

SUNZI (SUN-TZU)—Believed to be the author of *The Art of War*, the classic Chinese military treatise dating from the Spring and Autumn period (722–481 B.C.).

TANGGEMU FARM—*Laogai* prison camp in Qinghai province where Wei Jingsheng was held from late fall 1984 to the summer of 1989.

TANGSHAN—City close to Nanpu New Life Salt Works about two hundred miles east of Beijing.

TAOTAO—Family nickname for Wei Xiaotao, Wei Jingsheng's younger brother, an engineer currently living in Beijing.

THIRD PLENUM—Third Plenum of the Eleventh Central Committee meeting convened in December 1978, which marked the ascension of

Deng Xiaoping to power and the formulation of the ideological basis for economic reform.

THE THREE KINGDOMS—Sixteenth-century classical Chinese novel about rivalries fought among three third-century kingdoms; Yuan Shao, the character Wei likens to Deng Xiaoping, is considered ambitious and fierce, but indecisive and lacking in courage and talent, and is eventually defeated.

"THREE RED BANNERS"—Mass movement launched by the CCP in 1958 championing the Great Leap Forward, the People's Communes, and the Party line.

TONG YI (1968–)—Student activist in the pro-democracy demonstrations on Tiananmen Square and assistant to Wei Jingsheng from September 1993 until detained in April 1994 and sentenced to a three-year "reeducation through labor" term.

TRUSTIES—Prisoners trusted by prison guards and given duties inside the prison; in China this practice often involves criminal offense prisoners who are assigned to monitor political prisoners and in many cases carry out beatings and other forms of physical punishment.

UNITED ACTION—Anti–Jiang Qing Red Guard faction during the Cultural Revolution of which Wei Jingsheng was a member until it was disbanded in 1967.

WANG GUANGMEI (1922–)—Wife of former Communist Party leader Liu Shaoqi who was denounced and imprisoned during the Cultural Revolution.

WANG HONGWEN (1934–1992)—Former vice chairman of the Central Committee and member of the Gang of Four who was tried and convicted for his role in the Cultural Revolution.

WEINA—Wei Jingsheng's former sister-in-law, Wang Weina; his brother Wei Xiaotao's first wife.

WEIWEI—Wei Jingsheng's niece, his brother Wei Xiaotao's daughter.

XIAMEN—Southern coastal city in Fujian province where Wei's brother, Wei Xiaotao, once worked.

XIANG YU—Rebellious Qin dynasty (221–206 B.C.) general famous for his gallant defeat in battle.

XIAOYI—Wei Jingsheng's former brother-in-law, Huang Xiaoyi; his sister Wei Shanshan's first husband.

XINING—Capital city of Qinghai province where Wei was imprisoned at Tanggemu Reform Through Labor Farm.

XU BEIHONG (1895–1953)—Painter who trained in Paris in the 1920s before returning to China to become one of the major figures in modern Chinese art.

YA HANZHANG (1916–1989)—Former director of the Minority Studies Institute at the Chinese Academy of Social Sciences and author of a biography of the Dalai Lama; sent to labor camp during the Cultural Revolution.

YAN'AN—Mountainous region in Shaanxi province and base of Communist Party guerrilla activities from 1936 to 1947.

YANG GUANG—Wei Jingsheng's fellow editor of *Exploration* who was arrested on May 22, 1979, and testified against Wei at his trial.

YUAN—Unit of Chinese currency (current equivalent approximately 8 to 1 U.S. dollar).

YUAN MU (1928–)—Government spokesperson during the 1989 pro-democracy demonstrations on Tiananmen Square.

YUAN SHIKAI (1859–1916)—Powerful military leader who helped orchestrate the end of the Qing dynasty in 1911–12 and was subsequently made the president of the republic. He died shortly after proclaiming himself emperor in 1915.

ZHANG XIANLIANG (1936–)—Contemporary writer whose 1985 novel *Half of Man Is Woman* stirred up great controversy for its depiction of a political prisoner in a labor camp.

ZHAO ZIYANG (1919–)—Deng protégé who became premier of the State Council in 1980, succeeding Hu Yaobang as CCP general secretary in 1987 until his dismissal from all posts for sympathizing with the 1989 pro-democracy student demonstrations on Tiananmen Square.

ZHOU ENLAI (1899–1976)—Veteran member of the CCP and one of its most powerful and admired leaders, who served as premier of China from 1954. His death inspired memorial demonstrations in Beijing known as the April Fifth Incident.

ZHOU YANG (1908–1989)—Longtime CCP cultural affairs officer and director of Propaganda Department until 1982.

STEFAN ZWEIG (1881–1942)—Austrian-born writer whose 1942 work *The Story of Chess* (also translated into English as *The Royal Game*) Wei Jingsheng refers to because of its haunting depiction of a man who is held in isolation by Nazi Gestapo and forbidden to read or write; he begins going mad until a chess handbook he manages to obtain allows him to play the game in his head and maintain his sanity.

Contributors

LIU QING is the chairman of Human Rights in China, a nonprofit, nongovernmental organization based in New York. A leading pro-democracy activist since the Democracy Wall Movement of 1978–79, Liu was imprisoned in China for ten years after publishing the transcript of his friend Wei Jingsheng's 1979 trial and subsequently smuggling his own manuscript on the horrors of incarceration in China out of prison in the early 1980s; he arrived in the United States in 1992.

ANDREW J. NATHAN is a professor of political science at Columbia University and the chairman of the advisory committee of Human Rights Watch/Asia. He is author of *Chinese Democracy* (1985), *China's Crisis* (1990), and, with Robert S. Ross, *The Great Wall and the Empty City: China's Search for Security* (1997).

KRISTINA M. TORGESON holds degrees in Chinese from Wesleyan University and Columbia University, and is a Ph.D. candidate in modern Chinese literature at Columbia. She was a Fulbright fellow at Beijing University in 1992–93 and has taught at Duke University. She is the editor and translator, with Amy D. Dooling, of *Writing Women in Modern China: An Anthology of Women's Literature from the Early 20th Century* (1998).

SOPHIA WOODMAN has worked at Human Rights in China since 1991 and is currently the organization's representative in Hong Kong. She is executive editor of HRIC's quarterly journal, *China Rights Forum*, and director of the Economic and Social Rights Research Project. She has master's degrees in Chinese politics from the School of Oriental and African Studies in London and in journalism from the Columbia Graduate School of Journalism.

For more information about the human rights situation in China and Tibet, to find out what you can do to aid Wei Jingsheng and the other victims of human rights abuses, and to support the ongoing struggle for democracy in China and Tibet, please contact any of the following organizations:

Human Rights in China
485 Fifth Avenue, 3rd Floor
New York, NY 10017
e-mail address:
  hrichina@igc.org
http://www.igc.org/hric

International Campaign for
  Tibet
1825 K Street NW, Suite 520
Washington, DC 20006
e-mail address:
  ict@peacenet.org
http://www.peacenet.org/ict

Human Rights Watch/Asia
485 Fifth Avenue, 3rd Floor
New York, NY 10017
e-mail address: hrwnyc@igc.org
http://www.hrw.org

Amnesty International
International Secretariat
1 Easton Street
London WC1X 8DJ
United Kingdom
e-mail address:
  amnesty@amnesty.org
http://www.amnestyis.org

Included in this book is a pre-addressed postcard which you can send to President Clinton, calling for the United States government to do everything in its power to gain the immediate and unconditional release of Wei Jingsheng and other political prisoners in China. If the card is not still in this copy, here is the suggested text:

Dear President Clinton,

I am deeply concerned about the fate of Wei Jingsheng and other political prisoners in the People's Republic of China. I believe that people like Mr. Wei, who peacefully advocate for human rights and democratization in China, are in prison for exercising their internationally recognized right to freedom of expression. I urge you and the United States government to do everything in your power to gain the immediate and unconditional release of Wei Jingsheng and other political prisoners in China. As Mr. Wei himself has courageously observed, economic progress means little to any nation when the values of freedom and democracy are not respected.

Sincerely,

You can also write letters to your own members of Congress to tell them that you are concerned about the human rights situation in China, and you can write directly to President Jiang Zemin of China expressing your concerns about those people who are in prison for exercising their internationally recognized right to freedom of expression. His address is:

President Jiang Zemin
Zhongguo gongchandang
Zhongyang weiyuanhui
Beijing, 1007001
People's Republic of China

If you want to let Wei Jingsheng himself know that you are aware of his plight, send him a card or letter at the following address:

Wei Jingsheng
Jidong No. 2 Prison
Nanpu kaifaqu
Tangshan, Hebei province, 063305
People's Republic of China